GROUPS

Process & Practice

GROUPS
Process & Practice

GERALD COREY
California State University at Fullerton

MARIANNE SCHNEIDER COREY
Private Practice

BROOKS/COLE PUBLISHING COMPANY
MONTEREY, CALIFORNIA

A Division of Wadsworth Publishing Company, Inc.

Printed in the United States of America

10   9   8   7   6   5   4   3

Library of Congress Cataloging in Publication Data

Corey, Gerald F
    Groups.

        Includes index.
        1. Group psychotherapy.   I. Corey,
Marianne Schneider, 1942–   joint author.
II. Title.
RC488.C59   616.8'915   77-8324
ISBN 0-8185-0235-5

Production Editor: *Valerie Faraday Daigen*
Interior Design: *Laurie Cook*
Cover Design: *Sharon Marie Bird*

To Karola and Heinrich Schneider
and Josephine and Joseph Corey
our parents
our leaders
our friends
And to Heidi and Cindy Corey
our children
our group
our friends

PREFACE

Although there are many books that deal with the theory of group counseling, with group dynamics, and with group membership, there are few books that both outline the basic issues and key concepts of group process and show how group leaders can apply these concepts to their work with a wide range of types of groups. This is the purpose of our book.

In Part 1, we deal with the basic issues and concepts of group process, outlining: the advantages and limitations of therapeutic groups; eight theories of group process; some guidelines for the behavior of group members; what makes a good group leader; basic issues in group leadership; the developmental stages of a group, from screening of participants to termination and follow-up; methods of evaluating the outcomes of groups; ethical and professional issues in group work; and the supervision and training of group leaders.

In Part 2, we show how the ideas we explored in Part 1 can be applied to specific types of therapeutic groups. We offer guidelines for group leaders who want to design groups specifically for children, adolescents, college students, couples, and the elderly and who would like to lead residential personal-growth groups. These guidelines are based on our actual experiences in designing and leading each of these types of groups. In addition to suggesting ways of structuring these groups, we describe techniques when we think they are called for and emphasize how attitudes of group leaders may be crucial to the success of groups. Although we do describe methods and techniques, we discourage the reader from using any technique without first developing a sound rationale for doing so in a particular situation. Our emphasis is on the goals of groups, the hazards a leader should watch out for, the qualities of the members that leaders need to consider, the basic attitudes and values of the effective group leader, and the special issues involved in the leading of each of the various types of groups. In many ways, this is a "how to" book, but it is also a book about the "why" of group leadership.

Whom is this book for? It is for graduate and undergraduate students majoring in psychology, sociology, education, or human services who are taking courses in group counseling, group dynamics, or group process. It is also for practitioners who are involved in leading groups and for counselors who are training to lead various types of groups. Others who may find this book useful in their work are teachers, ministers, social workers, correctional counselors, and marriage and family counselors. Increasingly, the mental-health professional and paraprofessional are expected to possess the skills necessary for group counseling. We have found that students in counseling and clinical-psychology programs often must complete an internship involving work with a variety of types of people. A student may find himself or herself working with the aged one semester, with alcoholics or drug addicts the next semester, with children or adolescents the next, and with outpatients in a community clinic the last semester. This is our reason for writing about a range of types of therapeutic groups. We hope to get readers thinking realistically about the problems they will face as they begin or continue to work with groups.

We want to express our appreciation to three special people who have been very influential in helping us form our views of group process: Patrick Callanan, J. Michael Russell, and Jean Marie Lyon. They have been leading residential workshop groups with us for four years, they reviewed our manuscript, and their influence on our style of group leadership is reflected in the pages of this book.

We also wish to express our appreciation to several others who read the manuscript and made helpful suggestions. The people are: Karen Palmer, who reviewed and edited the original manuscript and who had many ideas for making the book more interesting to the reader; Merri Chalenor, who reviewed and typed the manuscript; and Marge Maes, who provided the information for the chart that appears in Chapter 10.

Other students who reviewed the book and gave valuable suggestions from the viewpoint of our intended audience were Randy Corliss, Jim Morelock, Paul Jacobson, Dennis Harris, and Richard Kühlenschmidt. The photography for the book was done by Richard Kühlenschmidt.

We would also like to thank the following people for reviewing our manuscript: Richard L. Bednar of the University of Kentucky; Irene Burnside; William H. Culp of Indiana University; Peter Ebersole of California State University at Fullerton; José George Iglesias of Pima Community College; William H. Lyon of Chapman College; Paul Obler of California State University at Fullerton; and Donald L. Thompson of the University of Connecticut.

We especially appreciate the excellent job of editing done by our production editor at Brooks/Cole, Val Daigen; her suggestions allowed us to increase the readability of this book. Finally, we would like to thank Terry Hendrix, Claire Verduin, and Todd Lueders, three editors on the Brooks/Cole staff, for their support and encouragement.

Gerald Corey
Marianne Schneider Corey

CONTENTS

GROUPS
Process & Practice

Part 1

GROUP PROCESS:
Basic Issues and
Key Concepts

1. INTRODUCTION

1. What are the advantages of the group as an intervention strategy?

2. What are some limitations of the group approach? What are its risks?

3. If you were to address yourself to the issue of misconceptions about groups, what kinds of things would you say?

4. As you begin this course, you might reflect on your own perceptions about groups. What are some of your ideas about the group movement? Do you have any reservations about participating in groups as a member?

5. What are some of your reactions when you think about yourself as a potential group leader? Do you have any fears? Concerns? Expectations? Hopes?

ABOUT THE AUTHORS

Because we feel that students reading a textbook have a right to know what the perspectives of the authors are, we would like to open this book with brief descriptions of our backgrounds.

Marianne Schneider Corey

My perspective, in coauthoring this book, was based largely on my group work as an intern for my master's degree in marriage, family, and child counseling. Thus, I was primarily oriented toward the beginning student of group counseling and, in my writing, was especially sensitive to the needs and struggles of those who are just beginning to lead groups. In particular, I kept in mind the institutional obstacles that inexperienced group leaders may encounter in designing and implementing their groups.

For the past six years, I've been leading groups for various types of clientele in conjunction with various types of institutions—college groups at a college counseling center, adolescent groups at several high schools, groups of elderly people in a state institution, groups of elementary-school children, professional workshops with teachers and counselors, groups for couples, and groups for outpatients at a day-treatment center. Additionally, I have been co-leading week-long residential workshops, which are described in this book, couples groups, and groups for beginning group leaders. I have a private practice as a counselor of both individuals and groups and am presently leading some groups for women. I've also been a client in both individual and group psychotherapy. I feel strongly that my personal therapy has contributed not only to my personal growth but to my skills as a counselor as well. I've come to believe very strongly in the group process as a means of reaching a wide variety of people. Even so, I do have concerns about the potential for misuse of group approaches. Throughout the book, my attempt was to stress ways of minimizing hazards and to indicate guidelines for sound professional practice.

Jerry Corey

Since I received my doctorate in counseling psychology, one of my primary professional interests has been in group practice, particularly with college students, human-service workers, teachers, and counselors. In addition to doing this work on a university campus, I've been in private practice as a licensed psychologist, both providing individual therapy and leading therapeutic groups. I've also worked as a consultant with representatives of elementary-school districts, high schools, and a junior college, offering recommendations on how to incorporate group approaches into the classroom and how to run human-relations workshops for the teaching staff.

At California State University at Fullerton, where I'm a professor in the Human Services program, I teach courses in counseling theory and practice, and I train and supervise group leaders. I've also been involved in counselor-education and teacher-education programs for close to ten years. I've taught a variety of psychology courses on the college and university level, and I taught in high school for four years. For several years, I've worked in the counseling centers of two universities as a counseling psychologist, usually on a part-time basis, with a special interest in ongoing weekly counseling groups with students. A common denominator in my professional experience at all levels has been my interest in the development of group approaches.

Finally, I've experienced individual and group psychotherapy as a client, too, and doing so has had a profound impact on me, both personally and professionally.

Like Marianne, I have a belief in the value of groups and, at the same time, many reservations concerning the abuses of the group movement. I hope that, throughout this book, I both convey my enthusiasm about the potentials of groups and communicate the need for safeguards.

As we were writing the various chapters, particularly the ones dealing with the group leader's personhood and skills, we came to fully realize how very difficult it is to become a good leader. A concern that we both had at times was that we were writing in a way that would make the reader think that there is such an entity as "the perfect leader." We do not believe that we're perfect. We do believe that we have something to offer our groups and our readers.

SOME SUGGESTIONS FOR READING AND USING THIS BOOK

One of our hopes is that as you read you will formulate your own guidelines for group practice. We encourage you to read critically and with an eye for material that may be particularly useful to you. The exercises at the ends of the chapters in Part 1 are intended for use in class. We're convinced that one way to learn how to lead groups is to experience group as a participant. Ideally, a group-counseling course can be taught in such a manner that the didactic and experiential components are integrated. The exercises are designed to help you deal with the issues presented in Part 1 in a personal way rather than merely as abstractions to be studied. The focus questions at the beginning of each chapter in Part 1 should be read before reading the chapter and again after reading the chapter. These questions are designed to assist you in clarifying your own position on basic issues in group process.

You are also asked to develop your own exercises, or at least to adapt the ones presented here to your unique situation. If your course becomes a group in which you can experience some group activities, you will be able to more fully understand group practice. Rather than merely talk about group process, you can directly experience the process of your group in action and discuss significant issues as they arise.

There are some problems inherent in combining a group experience with an academic course. A course requires certain procedures that are not part of a group. We aren't suggesting that a group course be converted into a personal-growth group; we've found that it's difficult to do justice to either the group or the class when this is done. Instead, we're suggesting that the class primarily focus on the issues and concepts involved in designing groups but that it also include experiential activities.

We also suggest that you not limit your reading to this book but rather take a look at some of the suggested books listed after Part 1 and after each of the chapters in Part 2. Select a reading program that is meaningful for you, and, as you read, attempt to clarify your own position concerning the questions we raise in the chapters and concerning your own questions.

AN OVERVIEW OF THE VARIOUS TYPES OF GROUPS

Throughout this book, the phrase *therapeutic group* is used as a general term to indicate any of the various types of groups. By *therapeutic,* we don't mean having to do with treatment of emotional and behavioral disorders but rather having as its broad purpose increasing people's knowledge of themselves and others, assisting people to clarify the changes they most want to make in their lives, and giving people some of the tools necessary to make these desired changes. By interacting with others in a trusting and permissive environment, participants are given the opportunity to experiment with novel behavior and to receive honest feedback from others concerning the effects of their behavior. As a result, the participants learn how they appear to others. When we use the phrase *therapeutic group,* we refer to group counseling, group therapy, T-groups, encounter groups, awareness groups, consciousness-raising groups, self-help and leaderless groups, sensitivity-training groups, and personal-growth groups, among others. Such groups may include only members of, and deal exclusively with the problems of, a certain group—children, adolescents, adults, college students, the elderly, and so forth. In the second part of this book, some of these special types of groups will be described in detail. For now it is sufficient to note that these groups do differ with respect to goals, techniques used, the role of the leader, and the kind of people involved in the group. The following brief descriptions will give you some idea of the diversity of these groups.

The Encounter Group

Encounter groups, or personal-growth groups, offer an intense group experience designed to assist relatively healthy or normal people to gain closer contact with themselves and others. The activities of these groups are designed both to teach participants about growth and development and to help them achieve these goals.

Most people join a personal-growth group with the intention of being intimate with others and exploring aspects of themselves that block the realization of their full potential. Such groups are designed to encourage intimacy and sharing, openness, honesty, and intense interpersonal relating. The emphasis is on expressing one's feelings, on spontaneity, on engaging in risk-taking behavior, and on living in the present. Nonverbal techniques, such as touching, sensory-awakening exercises, and other structured encounter exercises are used to foster interaction.

Encounter and personal-growth groups are usually time-limited, and they frequently meet for several days in a residential setting. During this time, the participants are encouraged to become increasingly aware of their feelings and to risk experimenting with behavior that they might have felt was not appropriate to their role—to let themselves "be."

The rationale for these groups is that people in a materialistic and technological society are alienated from themselves, from others, and even from nature. The encounter group, as a reaction to what its proponents consider an overemphasis on rationality and thinking, tends to emphasize feelings and direct experiencing.

There are several different types of encounter groups, ranging from those that are characterized by an open structure, with the participants shaping the direction of the group, to those that are characterized by specific exercises and other activities that are initiated by the group leader. What all of these groups have in common is their focus on personal growth.

T-Groups, or Laboratory-Training Groups

T-groups (or training groups, or laboratory-training groups) tend to emphasize the human-relations skills required for successful functioning in a business organization. In laboratory groups, the emphasis is on education through experience in an environment in which experimentation can occur, data can be analyzed, new ideas are encouraged, and decisions can be made or problems solved. Frequently, these groups are task oriented, and the focus is on specific organizational problems, such as: How can leadership become a more shared function? By what vehicle can employees creatively express themselves?

The focus of T-groups is on the group process rather than on personal growth. (*Group process* refers to the stages of development of a group and the interactions that characterize each stage.) Members are taught how to observe their own processes, and they are also taught how to develop a leadership role so that they can continue these groups on their own.

Group Therapy

Group therapy originated in response to a shortage, which developed during World War II, of personnel trained to provide individual therapy. At first the group therapist assumed a traditional, therapeutic role, frequently working with a small number of clients with a common problem. However, leaders gradually began to experiment with different roles. Many of them discovered that the group setting offered unique therapeutic possibilities, and they began to take advantage of these possibilities. The dynamics of a group offered support, caring, confrontation, and other qualities not found in the framework of individual therapy. Within the group context, members could practice new social skills and apply some of their new knowledge.

While encounter groups usually involve a relatively well-functioning population seeking growth and self-actualization, group therapy generally attracts a different population. Many people participate in group therapy to try to alleviate specific symptoms or problems, such as depression, sexual problems, anxiety, and psychosomatic disorders. Group therapy may be of longer duration than encounter groups or group counseling. In group therapy, attention is given to unconscious factors and one's past.

Some therapy groups are organized for the purpose of correcting a specific emotional or behavioral disorder that impedes people's functioning. The group goal may be a minor or a major transformation of members' personality structure, depending on the theoretical orientation of the group leader. However, it is important to make clear that, in many private-practice therapy groups, the population is made up of sophisticated clients who are not any more neurotic than those who attend encounter groups. Many emotionally healthy people are finding group therapy personally valuable. In a group of such people, the primary emphasis is on providing a climate in which relatively healthy clients can become healthier.

The training requirements for group therapists are more stringent than for the leaders, or *facilitators,* of personal-growth groups. Group therapists are generally expected to have an advanced degree in psychology, psychiatry, or social work; sometimes they must also have experienced individual and group therapy as clients.

Group Counseling

Group counseling often focuses on a particular type of problem—educational, vocational, social, or personal—and is often carried out in institutional settings, such as schools, community mental-health clinics, and other human-service agencies. The counseling group generally differs from the therapy group in that it deals with conscious problems, is not aimed at major personality changes, is frequently oriented toward the resolution of specific and short-term issues, and is not concerned with treatment of neurotic or psychotic disorders.

The group counselor may use a variety of techniques, such as reflection (mirroring the verbal and nonverbal messages of a group member), clarification (helping the member understand more clearly what he or she is saying or feeling), and role-playing. The group counselor's job is to structure the activities of the group, to see that a climate favorable to productive work is maintained, and to facilitate member interaction.

THE PROS AND CONS OF GROUPS

The Advantages of Groups

Therapeutic groups have certain distinct advantages over other intervention strategies. A few of the values of group work are:

1. Participants are able to explore their style of relating to others and to learn more effective social skills.

2. The group setting offers support for new behavior and encourages experimentation. Members can try out new behaviors and decide whether they want to incorporate them into their outside life.

3. There is a re-creation of the everyday world in some groups, particularly if the membership is diverse with respect to age, interest, background, socioeconomic status, and type of problem. When this occurs, a member has the unique advantage of contacting a wide range of personalities, and the feedback received can be richer and more diverse than that available in a one-to-one setting.

4. Certain factors that facilitate personal growth are more likely to exist in groups. For instance, in groups, members have the opportunity to learn about themselves through the experience of others, to experience emotional closeness and caring that encourage meaningful disclosure of self, and to identify with the struggles of other members.

The Limitations of Groups

While there are some distinct advantages to group methods in helping people reach their potential, there are some limitations to the effectiveness of therapeutic groups.

1. Groups are not "cure-alls." Unfortunately, some practitioners and participants view groups as the exclusive means of changing people's behavior. Worse yet, some hope that a brief and intense group experience can remake people's lives. Counseling and therapy are difficult forms of work, and we believe that shortcuts are not necessarily fruitful.

2. There is often a subtle pressure to conform to group norms and expectations. Group participants sometimes unquestioningly substitute group norms for norms they had unquestioningly acquired in the first place.

3. Some people become hooked on groups and make the group experience an end in itself. Instead of using their group as a laboratory for human learning and as a place where they can learn behavior that will facilitate their day-to-day living, they stop short, savoring the delights of the group for their own sake.

4. Not all people are suited for groups. The idea that groups are for everybody has done serious harm to the reputation of the group movement. Some people are too suspicious, or too hostile, or too fragile to benefit from a group experience. Some individuals are psychologically damaged by attending certain groups. Before a person is accepted into a group, the factors need to be carefully weighed by both the counselor and the client to increase the chances that the person will benefit from such an experience. The issue of who should be included in and who excluded from groups will be explored in more detail in Chapter 5.

5. Some people have made group a place to ventilate their miseries and be rewarded for "baring their soul." Unfortunately, some use groups as a vehicle for expressing their woes, in the hope that they will be understood and totally accepted, and make no attempt to do what is necessary to effect substantial change in their lives.

The Risks of Participating in Groups

Related to the issue of limitations of group counseling is the issue of possible psychological hazards. If group treatment is powerful as a change agent and if people can be convinced of the necessity to face themselves honestly and even create a new life for themselves, then these groups are also risky. At this point, we wish to indicate some of these possible risks; later in the book, we'll expand our treatment of the issue by developing guidelines for making the participants aware of these risks and for preparing the members in a way that will reduce the chances of their having a negative experience.

1. There is a danger that people, in opening themselves up to themselves and others during a group, will become very vulnerable. Individuals' insecurities need to

be explored in some depth, and conflicts need to be worked through. It is important that the participants have some resources available to them when they leave a group, for the difficult part of their personal change will occur when they have to face the significant people in their lives. The risk is that such resources may not be available.

2. Self-disclosure is sometimes misused by group members. This issue will be dealt with at greater length in a later chapter, but we do want to mention that action needs to follow self-disclosure. The group ethic has been misunderstood to be: the more disclosure the better. Privacy can be violated by indiscriminate sharing of one's personal life. Self-disclosure is an essential aspect of any working group, but this disclosure is a means to the end of fuller self-understanding and should not be glorified in its own right, at the expense of follow-through.

3. Some of the disclosures made during a session may not remain in the group. Confidentiality is an issue that needs continual emphasis in any group, but, even when this has been done, the possibility that members will talk about what they've heard in the group remains.

4. Scapegoating may occur in a group, particularly if a group leader does not intervene when he or she sees members "ganging up on" one particular group member. When confrontation occurs, we find it useful to ask the person doing the confronting to state what reactions he or she is having to the person being confronted. This usually stops the person from merely throwing judgmental labels at another. At times, we've seen several other members join a confronter in an unjustified attack that leaves the victim feeling ravaged.

5. It appears that interest in groups is increasing. The danger of inadequate leadership is a by-product of the growth of the group movement. Some people attend a few weekend workshops as participants and then decide, with very little additional experience, to lead groups of their own. Because they experienced a "high," they decide that groups are the answer for any seeker of self-fulfillment. Lacking adequate training or experience, they hastily gather a group together, without bothering to screen members or even prepare members for the particular group. These kinds of leaders can do extensive damage and, in the process, cause participants to close themselves off from the possibility of seeking any type of therapy or counseling in the future.

6. Another risk of group participation is the possibility of experiencing a major disruption in one's life—changes in life-style and values and a loss of security. Before participating in a group, a person may tolerate a mediocre marriage, ask for very little for himself or herself, value security over growth, and settle for a predictable existence devoid of any challenges. As a result of group experiences, the same person may begin an intense and painful process of searching and questioning, and this increased self-consciousness may lead to drastic changes in his or her values and behavior. Of course, these changes may be constructive and lead to revitalization of the individual's personal life, but the process may involve crisis and turmoil. Members of groups should be advised before they enter a group that their life-style may become disorganized—at least temporarily—as a result of their participating in the group.

Misconceptions about Groups

Some myths about groups need to be critically appraised, for these misconceptions regarding the purpose and functioning of groups can lead people to conclude that the disadvantages far outweigh the advantages. What follows are some key myths and the facts to debunk them.

1. "The group is a place to get emotionally high." If people leave a group feeling high, then this might be considered frosting on the cake, but we don't see this as the main reason for participating in them. Participants need to be aware that a "high" may change to a "low" when they encounter difficulty being the way they were in the group in their real life. In the group, they may have received positive feedback and support for daring to change. When they return home, they may well meet with resistance and antagonism when they deviate from old and familiar ways. Others may have an investment in keeping them as they were, because that way they're more predictable and more easily controlled. The depression that so often follows the feeling of being able to conquer the world is a reality that participants need to examine.

2. "The goal of a group is to leave feeling close and loving toward everyone in the group." The genuine closeness that can be achieved in an intensive group can be the result of shared struggles, and the worth of this emotional bond is not to be discounted. However, the basic purpose of a group is not to create a loving bond among all the members. Rather, intimacy should be considered a by-product of meaningful work in a group.

3. "Groups are places where people tear you down and then don't rebuild you." So frequently we hear people express the fear that they will leave the group defenseless and that they will not have the resources to rebuild what they fear was destroyed. This belief relates to the issues of confrontation and scapegoating. Our hope is that people can learn that rigid defenses are not always necessary and that they can safely remove unnecessary walls that separate them from others. When people become more authentic, even though they may become vulnerable, they discover a core of strength within themselves. We certainly don't support the type of attack group that aims ruthlessly at stripping away all defenses.

4. "Groups make people more miserable and unhappy because their problems surface." To some extent this is true. When people face the truth about their life, pain and conflict may be the result, although we don't think that people must remain fixated in this unhappy condition. Once people recognize those aspects of themselves or their environment that are contributing to this misery, they can take some decisive steps to change. Continued group counseling or individual therapy can be useful in assisting people to work through the personal conflicts that surface in the group.

5. "Groups practice a form of brainwashing." Instead of merely accepting the dictates or suggestions of others, successful group members acquire an increased ability to look within themselves for their own answers to the present and future problems life poses. Groups are neither places to dispense cheap advice nor means of

indoctrinating people into agreement with a particular philosophy of life. Hopefully, the leaders and members can challenge a person to reexamine his or her own philosophy without imposing their beliefs on that person.

6. "Only people who are sick seek groups." There is a misconception that therapy or counseling, either individual or group, is designed to cure people of mental and emotional illness. It is true that some groups are aimed at helping the disturbed population discover some relief; on the other hand, there are many groups for developmental purposes—groups designed to help people recognize their potentials and remove blocks to personal growth. Healthy people can use the group experience as an aid in viewing themselves more honestly and critically and seeing themselves as others see them. There are a wide variety of groups that focus on a well population, and these groups contend that therapy can be used for preventive as well as remedial purposes.

7. "Groups are artificial and unreal." Some attack groups on the grounds that what goes on in them goes on in an unreal context. We believe that a group setting can be more real than so-called "real life," in the sense that, in an effective group, people shed many of the pretenses that characterize their everyday interactions. Certain aspects of this experience may seem artificial, but, if the participants can discover ways of putting into practice what was learned in a group, the real value of the experience is undeniable. That some groups never transcend an artificial level does not necessarily mean that what is experienced in all groups is artificial.

EXERCISES

Form subgroups within your class and discuss the following statements.

1. In groups there is often a subtle pressure to conform to group norms and expectations.
2. Groups practice a subtle form of indoctrination.
3. A desirable result of a group experience is for everyone to feel close, intimate, loving, and united with others.
4. Groups are places where people tear you down and then don't rebuild you.
5. Groups have the potential to make people miserable by making their problems apparent.
6. Support in a group means that people should avoid expressing negative feelings toward one another and should instead try to make one another feel good.
7. Groups are basically artificial and unreal.
8. Groups are designed mainly for sick people who are in need of treatment.
9. Not everyone is suited for group participation.
10. Groups are places where people can experiment with new behavior.
11. One limitation of groups is that participants often make them a way of life.
12. Groups should be designed to assist people to make the changes they want outside, as well as inside, the group.

13. Groups are frequently places where people ventilate their feelings but do very little to actually change their behavior.
14. Participants should be cautioned of certain psychological risks before they are admitted to a given group.
15. There is always a certain degree of psychological risk associated with group participation, even if the group is well run.

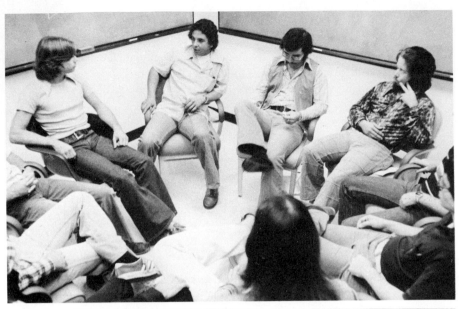

2. GROUP PROCESS:
An Overview

1. What is your concept of a therapeutic group? Consider factors such as purpose and procedures.

2. Contracts are frequently used to help group people achieve their goals in a group setting. What value do you see in contracts in groups? You might formulate your own learning contract as it relates to this course and your participation in it.

3. What would you propose as essential guidelines for group functioning? Think of as many as you can.

4. Think of as many therapeutic factors of groups as you can. Then select the three factors you deem most significant and think about why you judged these factors to be crucial.

5. What group theory or model appeals to you the most at this point in your studies? What value do you see in acquiring a theoretical background? What features do you think you will borrow from the various models and incorporate into your own personalized theory of group work?

THE CONCEPT OF THE THERAPEUTIC GROUP

Groups are designed for a broader purpose than the curing of emotional ills. Through a group experience—a therapeutic and not a toxic one—the participants can learn about themselves and about their relationships with others.

Essentially, the group can be a microcosm of society. It can offer a behavior sample of reality, for the struggles and conflicts people experience there are no different from those they experience in the world. In this sample of how they relate to others, people can also get feedback on how others experience and react to them. From the feedback, members obtain a picture of how they are viewed by others. They can then decide for themselves, on the basis of experimentation with alternative behaviors, what kinds of changes they wish to make. Members compare their self-perceptions with how they are perceived by others, they open themselves to risks, including the risk of behaving differently, they confront others and are confronted by others, and they give and receive support for the expression of their deepest feelings and thoughts. Using these methods, members are able to bring more clearly into focus the kind of person they would like to become and to see what is preventing them from becoming that person.

Some Goals for Group Members

We view the group as an invitation to self-exploration that can lead to reassessment of one's values and behaviors. It is an invitation—never a command —to examine seriously a segment of one's personhood or behavior. It is up to the group member to decide what, how much, and when he or she wishes to explore and to change. Whereas group members must decide for themselves the specific goals of a group experience, we think that there are some broad goals that are common to most therapeutic groups. While it is difficult to enumerate goals that are appropriate for members of all types of groups, we think that the following are universal goals:

- to become more open and honest with selected others,
- to decrease game-playing and manipulation, which prevent intimacy,
- to learn how to trust oneself and others,
- to move toward authenticity and genuineness,
- to become freer and less bound by external "shoulds," "oughts," and "musts,"
- to grow in self-acceptance and learn not to demand perfection of oneself,
- to recognize and accept certain polarities within oneself,
- to lessen one's fears of intimacy and to learn to reach out to those one would like to be closer to,
- to move away from merely meeting others' expectations and decide for oneself the standards that will guide one,
- to learn how to confront others with care, concern, honesty, and directness,
- to learn how to ask directly for what one wants,
- to increase self-awareness and thereby increase the possibilities for choice and action,
- to learn the distinction between having feelings and acting on them,
- to free oneself from the inappropriate early decisions that keep one less than the person one could or would like to be,
- to recognize that others struggle too,
- to clarify the values one has and to decide whether and how to modify them,
- to be able to tolerate more ambiguity—to learn to make choices in a world where nothing is guaranteed,
- to find ways of resolving personal problems,
- to explore hidden potentials and creativity,

- to increase one's capacity to care for others,
- to learn how to give to others, and
- to become more sensitive to the needs and feelings of others.

THE ROLE OF CONTRACTS

We believe that the contract is a very useful device for helping people to achieve their personal goals in a group. Basically, a contract is a statement by the group member concerning what he or she is willing to do during a group session or outside of the group meeting. In our view, contracts can be used in most of the types of groups discussed in this book. The purpose of the contract is to specify what kinds of problems the member wants to explore and what kinds of behaviors he or she is willing to change. It is a way of causing the member to think about the group and about his or her role in it. In the contract method, the group member assumes an active and responsible stance. Of course, contracts can be open-ended; that is, they can be modified or replaced as appropriate.

Contracts and homework assignments can be combined fruitfully. For example, consider a woman in an assertive-training group who decides that she would like to spend more time on activities that interest her. She might make a contract that calls for her to do more of the things she would like to do for herself, and she might assign herself certain activities as experiments to be carried out during the week. At the next group session, she would report the emotional results. Partly on the basis of these results, she could decide how much and in what ways she really wants to change. Then she could do further work in the group toward her chosen ends.

SOME GENERAL GUIDELINES FOR GROUPS

The following is a list of guidelines that, if followed, will increase the chances that the group will be productive. Some of these issues will be explored in more depth in later chapters.

1. It is important to teach group process to the members. This need not involve giving a lecture; rather, issues can be discussed as they arise in the course of a group.

2. The issue of confidentiality should be emphasized in the group. The dangers of inappropriate sharing of what occurs during a session need to be highlighted, and members need to have an opportunity to express their fears or reservations concerning the respect of the rest of the group for the disclosures that are made.

3. Instead of talking about a group member, the leader and other members should speak directly to the person in question.

4. Each member is free to decide for himself or herself what issues to work on in the group, and each person may decide how far to explore a problem. A person's right to say "I pass" should be respected. It is the member who is responsible for the decision to disclose or not to disclose.

5. Confrontation is an essential ingredient in most groups, but members must learn how to confront others in a responsible manner. Essentially, confrontation is a challenge from another to look at some aspect of one's behavior, or to look at the discrepancy between what one says and what one does, or to examine the degree to which one is being honest.

6. Questioning is more often a distraction than a help in group process, and members should be warned of this. Generally, questions of a probing nature have the effect of pulling the questioned participant away from the experience of feeling. Asking questions can generate a never-ending series of "whys" and "becauses." It is an impersonal way of relating that keeps the interrogator at a safe distance.

7. If members are to engage in any personal work, it is imperative that a climate of trust and support be established. If people feel they can be themselves and be respected for what they feel, they are far more inclined to take the risk of sharing intimate aspects of themselves than if they expect to be harshly judged.

8. Groups should emphasize the importance of integrating the thinking and feeling functions. Unfortunately, too many groups emphasize experiencing and expressing feelings and don't place much value on the thinking and deciding that we believe should take place after certain feelings have been expressed.

9. Members need to learn how to listen without thinking of a quick rebuttal and without becoming overly defensive. We don't encourage people to accept everything they hear, but we do ask them to really hear what others say to them and to seriously consider these messages—particularly those messages that are repeated consistently.

10. The issue of how what is learned in a group can be translated into out-of-group behavior should be given priority. Contracts and homework assignments can help members carry the new behaviors they develop in a group over into their daily lives.

THERAPEUTIC FACTORS THAT OPERATE IN GROUPS

In this section, attention is on the special forces within counseling groups that produce constructive changes. We came up with the therapeutic factors listed below by reflecting on our experiences in leading a variety of groups and by reading the reports of hundreds of people who have participated in our groups. We've always had the participants in our groups write follow-up reaction papers telling what factors they think were related to their changes in attitudes and behavior. We've come to believe that there are a variety of forces within groups that can be termed *curative*, *healing*, or *therapeutic* and that these forces are interrelated. We consider the following the most significant therapeutic factors operating in groups.

1. *Hope*. This is a belief that change is possible—that one is not a victim of the past and that new decisions can be made. Hope is therapeutic in itself, for it gives members confidence that they have the power to choose to be different.

2. *Commitment to change*. A resolve to change is also therapeutic in itself.

If one is motivated to the point of becoming an active group participant, the chances are good that change will occur. This commitment to change involves a willingness to specify what changes are desired and to make use of the tools offered by group process to explore ways of modifying one's behavior.

3. *Willingness to risk and trust.* Risking involves opening one's self to others, being vulnerable, and actively doing in a group that which is necessary for change. This willingness to reveal one's self is largely a function of how much one trusts the other group members and the leader. Trust is therapeutic, for it allows persons to show the many facets of themselves, encourages experimental behavior, and allows persons to look at themselves in new ways.

4. *Care.* Caring is demonstrated by the listening and involvement of others. It can be expressed by tenderness, compassion, support, and even confrontation. If members sense a lack of caring from either group members or group leaders, their willingness to drop their masks will be reduced. Clients are able to risk being vulnerable if they sense that their concerns are important to others and that they are valued as persons.

5. *Acceptance.* This involves a genuine support from others that says, in effect, ''We will accept all of your feelings. You do count here. It's OK to be yourself—you don't have to strive to please everyone.'' Acceptance involves affirming a person's right to have his or her own feelings and values and to express them.

6. *Empathy.* A true sense of empathy involves a deep understanding of another's struggles. In groups, commonalities emerge that unite the members. The realization that certain problems—such as loneliness, need for acceptance, fear of rejection, fear of intimacy, and hurt over past experiences—are universal lessens the feeling that one is alone. And, through identification with others, one is able to see oneself more clearly.

7. *Intimacy.* People are able to experience closeness in a group, and from this intimacy develops a new sense of trust in others. Participants may become aware, after experiencing this feeling of closeness to others, that there are barriers in their outside lives that prevent intimacy.

8. *Power.* This feeling emerges from the recognition that one has untapped reserves of spontaneity, creativity, courage, and strength within. In groups, personal power may be experienced in ways that were formerly denied, and persons can discover ways in which they block their strengths. This power is not a power over others; rather, it is the sense that one has the internal resources necessary to direct the course of one's life.

9. *Freedom to experiment.* The group situation provides a safe place for experimentation with new behavior. After trying new behavior, persons can gauge how much they want to change their existing behavior.

10. *Feedback.* Members determine the effects of their behavior on others from the feedback they receive. If feedback is given honestly and with care, members are able to understand more clearly the impact they have on others. Then it is up to them to decide what to do with this feedback.

11. *Catharsis*. The expression of pent-up feelings can be therapeutic in that energy can be released that has been tied up in withholding certain threatening feelings. Catharsis may allow a person to realize that negative and positive feelings toward another may coexist. A woman may be suppressing a great deal of resentment toward her mother and, by releasing it, may discover a need for her mother's affection and a feeling of love for her mother.

12. *The cognitive component*. Catharsis is even more useful if a person attempts to find words to explain the feelings expressed. Some conceptualization of the meaning of the intense feelings associated with certain experiences can give one the tools to make significant changes.

13. *Learning interpersonal skills*. Participants in groups can discover ways of enhancing their interpersonal relationships. Thus, a woman who feels isolated from others may come to understand concrete things she does to lead to these feelings and may then learn to lessen this isolation by asking others for what she needs.

14. *Humor*. Laughing at oneself can be extremely therapeutic. This requires seeing one's problems in some perspective. Thus, a man who sees himself as stupid may eventually be able to laugh at the stupidity of continually convincing himself that he's stupid. People who are able to laugh at themselves are better able to cope with seeing themselves clearly.

15. *Group cohesion*. A group is characterized by a high degree of "togetherness" at times, providing a climate in which participants feel free to share problems, try new behaviors, and in other ways reveal the many dimensions of themselves. Group cohesion is influenced by many variables, a few of which are the attraction of the group for the members, the enthusiasm of the leaders, the trust level of the group, and the extent to which the members identify with one another.

Another way of conceptualizing the therapeutic forces within a group is in terms of what group participants say that they've learned from a group experience. Recently, at the closing session of a therapeutic group, we asked the members to say what they had learned about themselves and other people from participation in the group. They responded that they had learned that

- others will care for me if I allow them to,
- I'm not alone in my pain,
- I'm not helpless, as I had convinced myself I was,
- I don't need to be liked by everyone,
- it's not too late to change if I want to,
- the choice is mine if I want more from others,
- experiencing intense feelings will not make me crazy,
- there are others close to me, and I need not be isolated,
- I alone am responsible for my misery,
- I can trust people, and this trust can be freeing,
- I do have options,
- whether I change or not depends on my decisions,

- being spontaneous is fun,
- I'm a lot more attractive than I gave myself credit for before,
- I'll never be truly accepted unless I'm willing to risk rejection,
- I get from a group about what I put into it,
- my greatest fears did not come true when I revealed myself,
- I'm more lovable than I thought I was,
- I need to ask others for what I want and need,
- I'm hopeful about the future, even though it may involve struggle,
- some degree of risk and uncertainty is necessary—there are no guarantees,
- I'm able to identify with the emotions of others; regardless of age, there is a common bond linking humans,
- intimacy is frightening, but it's worth it,
- decisions about my behavior must come from within and not from the group members or leaders,
- making changes takes sustained effort,
- people can be beautiful and creative when they shed their masks, and
- it takes a great effort to maintain a facade.

GROUP-PROCESS CONCEPTS

When we speak of group process, we are speaking of stages groups tend to go through. These stages are characterized by certain feelings and behaviors. Initially, as the members get to know one another, there is a feeling of anxiety. Each waits for someone else to begin the work. Tension, hostility, and even boredom build up. Someone may attack the leader or another member. Then, if things go well, the members learn to trust one another and the leader and begin to express openly feelings, thoughts, and reactions. These are the types of elements that constitute the group process. Included under the rubric *group process* are activities such as establishing norms and group cohesion, learning to work cooperatively, establishing ways of solving problems, and learning to express conflict openly. We'll now discuss in depth a couple of these group-process concepts.

Group Cohesion

Cohesiveness is necessary for the success of a group. Some indicators of the level of cohesiveness in a group are: the extent of cooperation among group members, the degree of initiative shown by participants, attendance rates, punctuality, the level of trust shown, and the degree of support, encouragement, and caring that members demonstrate in their interactions. Group cohesion can be developed, maintained, and increased in a number of ways. The following are some of these ways.

1. Trust must be developed during the early stages of a group. One of the best

ways of building trust is to create a group climate characterized by respect for the opinions and feelings of the members. It is essential that members openly express their feelings concerning the degree of trust they experience in their group. An opportunity can be provided at the outset for members to share their reservations, and this open sharing of concerns will pave the way for productive work.

2. If group members share meaningful aspects of themselves, they both learn to take risks and increase group cohesiveness. By modeling—for instance, by sharing their own reactions to what is occurring within the group—group leaders can encourage risk-taking behavior. When group members do take risks, they can be reinforced with sincere recognition and support, which will increase their sense of closeness to the others.

3. Group goals and individual goals can be jointly determined by the group members and the leader. If a group is without clearly stated goals, animosity can build up that will tend to lead to the fragmentation of the group.

4. Group norms and procedures that will help the group attain its goals can be developed during the early stages of a group and clearly stated. If the norms are fuzzy, then not only will valuable time be lost but also tensions will arise over the uncertainty about what is appropriate and what is inappropriate.

5. Cohesion can be increased by inviting (but not forcing) all members to become active participants. Members who appear to be passive or withdrawn can be invited to express their feelings toward the group. These members may be silent observers for a number of reasons, and these reasons ought to be examined openly in the group.

6. Cohesion can be both established and increased by the sharing of the leadership role by all members of the group. In autocratic groups, all the decisions are made by the leader. A cooperative type of group is more likely to develop when members are encouraged to initiate discussion of issues they want to explore. Also, instead of fostering a leader-to-member style of interaction, group leaders can foster member-to-member interactions. This can be done by inviting the members to respond to one another, by encouraging feedback and sharing, and by searching for ways to involve as many members as possible in group interactions.

7. Conflict is inevitable in groups. It is desirable for group members to recognize sources of conflict and to openly deal with conflict when it arises. A group can be strengthened by acceptance of conflict and by the honest working-through of differences.

8. Attraction and group cohesion are related; it is generally accepted that, the greater the degree of attractiveness of a group to its members, the greater the level of cohesion. Thus, ways of increasing the attractiveness of the group are important. If the group deals with matters that interest the members, if the members feel that they are respected, and if the atmosphere is supportive, the chances are good that the group will be perceived as attractive.

9. Members can be encouraged to disclose their ideas, feelings, and reactions to what occurs within their group. The expression of both positive and negative

reactions should be encouraged. If this is done, an honest exchange can take place, which is essential if a sense of group belongingness is to develop.

Group Norms

As you just saw, the establishment of certain norms is necessary if group cohesion is to be created. By *norms,* we mean rules about what behavior is appropriate in the group. These rules can be formal or informal, explicit or implied. If the norms are to influence participants' behavior, then the participants need to be both aware of and willing to accept them. Members are most likely to accept and internalize standards that they see the reason for and ones that they've had a part in formulating; it is wise for the leader to avoid imposing rules about group behavior autocratically, without discussion.

The following are three group norms that might be instituted in various groups.

1. Group members should attend regularly and show up on time. When members attend sessions only sporadically, the entire group suffers. Members who regularly attend may resent the lack of commitment on the part of those who miss sessions.

2. Members should be personal and share meaningful aspects of themselves. They should talk about themselves, communicate directly with others in the group, and in general become active participants.

3. Members should give feedback to one another. Members can evaluate the effects of their behavior on others only if others are willing to state how they are affected. It is important for members not to withhold their perceptions and reactions but rather to let others know what they perceive.

These are merely a few examples of norms. The important point is that norms be discussed in the group as the group unfolds and develops. Many groups become bogged down because members are unsure of what is expected of them. For instance, a member may want to intervene and share her perceptions while a leader is working with an individual in the group. However, she might be inhibited because she is not sure whether she should interrupt the group leader at work. Another member might feel an inclination to support a fellow group member at the time when that member is experiencing some pain or sadness but might refrain from giving verbal or nonverbal support because he is uncertain of the impact this will have on the person experiencing pain. Will it detract from the other's experience? Another example is the member who is bored session after session. She might keep this feeling to herself because she is not sure of the appropriateness of revealing it. Perhaps if she were told that it is permissible to experience and valuable to express boredom, she might be more open with her group and, consequently, less bored.

In summary, if group norms are clearly presented and if the members see the value of them and cooperatively decide on some of them, then these norms will be potent forces in the shaping of the group.

AN OVERVIEW OF EIGHT MODELS OF
GROUP PROCESS

A detailed discussion of the various group models is beyond the scope of this book. Group leaders do need a theory of group process, however, on which to base their techniques and procedures. Each theoretical model has something unique to offer group leaders, and we believe that effective leaders are continually defining, describing, and refining a personalized group theory that allows them to make sense of what occurs in groups.

The various models emphasize different concepts, view the role of the group leader differently, see the members' roles differently, and involve different techniques and procedures. The group leader who operates from a behavioral orientation will conduct a group differently from a leader with an existential orientation (or a client-centered or Gestalt one). Unique processes will emerge in each type of group. The group may be viewed as a place to experiment with new behavior, a place to challenge irrational beliefs, a place to develop highly personal relationships, a place to work through feelings toward a person not in the group, and so forth. The following are brief descriptions of various ways of understanding group process. We encourage you to do further reading about each of these theories. A more detailed treatment of these therapeutic approaches is offered in *Theory and Practice of Counseling and Psychotherapy,* by Gerald Corey.

The Psychoanalytic Model

Key concepts. With this model, the emphasis is on childhood experiences; healthy personality development is believed to be based on the successful resolution of each of the psychosexual stages of development. The group represents the family and offers the members the opportunity to work through significant experiences and conflicts. The goal of the group process is to make unconscious conflicts conscious and to allow the members to reexperience, and thereby resolve, these conflicts.

The role of the leader. The leader draws attention to the manifestations of transference (reenactment of a past conflict in a present relationship) and resistance (avoidance of facing unconscious material), interprets at appropriate times, aids insight through verbalization, and helps members recall early childhood experiences.

Group techniques. Five procedures are used:
1. *Free association.* Group members are encouraged to say whatever comes to their minds and to express feelings and thoughts without censorship.
2. *Interpretation.* Both the group leader and the members explain the meaning of certain behaviors manifested in group. Interpretations are thought to lead to an unblocking of unconscious material.

3. *Dream work*. Since dreaming is a shorthand way of making unconscious material conscious, dreams are interpreted in the group.

4. *Analysis and interpretation of resistance*. Resistance is whatever the participant does to avoid producing unconscious material. Attention is called to the resistances observable in the interactions of the members.

5. *Analysis and interpretation of transference*. Transference involves reliving past conflicts by acting them out in interactions with other members and the group leader.

The Existential-Humanistic Model

Key concepts. According to this group model, the human condition should be viewed in terms of purpose, choice, freedom, and responsibility; its proponents hold that humans define themselves by their choices and actions. The basic assumption is that humans have the capacity to expand their self-awareness; self-awareness leads to increased freedom and responsibility but also to existential anxiety. In this model, the following dimensions are stressed: individual freedom, anxiety as a function of recognizing choices, the search for meaning and values, dealing with the fact that, ultimately, one is alone, and the importance of death in giving significance to living. This approach stresses the uniqueness of the individual and focuses on the present, the person-to-person relationship, the tendency toward self-actualization, and the understanding of one's subjective world.

The role of the leader. The function of the group leader is to encourage the members to grasp one another's subjective worlds and to establish authentic encounters—that is, encounters without pretenses. The group leader does this by modeling authentic behavior. The leader keeps the focus on the present—what existential-humanistic theorists call the "here-and-now"—as the members interact with one another and helps the members discover their own capacity to make choices.

Group techniques. The main goal of this approach is to create a climate in which growth, awareness, and spontaneity will be maximized. To attain this goal, practitioners using this approach stress understanding first and technique second. The approach is basically an attitude toward people, and thus few clearly defined techniques are associated with it. Confrontation is frequently used, and members are encouraged to clarify what their alternatives are for action. The selves of the leader and the members are seen as the key instruments.

Group process. The existential group focuses on inauthentic ways members relate to one another—hence its attention to the present. The existential-humanistic model has generated many variations in the group movement, and many encounter groups use its concepts.

The Client-Centered Model

Key concepts. This model is based on the assumption that humans have an innate urge to become "fully functioning." If the leader recognizes and accepts the potential of the members to resolve their own problems, proponents argue, the members are able to freely explore aspects of themselves that were formerly denied to awareness. Thus, the group climate is characterized by openness and honesty, permission to express all feelings, respect and caring, what theorists call "unconditional positive regard," and genuineness on the leader's part.

The role of the leader. In this model, the leader is viewed as a facilitator with the main job of creating and maintaining a threat-free and accepting group climate. The facilitator points out blocks to effective communication and helps members to communicate directly and honestly with one another. The leader listens actively (that is, with full attention and without judging), mirrors members' behavior for them to see, and clarifies what members say.

Group process. The client-centered viewpoint is based on the assumption that the group can find its own direction if there is an absence of manipulation on the part of the group facilitator. According to the client-centered view, the intensive group evolves in a predictable way. First, there is a period of getting acquainted. Resistance to expressing personal material and to being seen without social fronts can be seen, and members describe past feelings and experiences. Then members begin to express negative feelings toward the other group members and toward the facilitator, taking the risks of expressing material that is personally meaningful and dealing more with the present. The group members begin to take a genuine interest in one another, exhibiting caring and understanding, and this has a therapeutic effect; members begin to accept aspects of themselves that they had denied, and the beginning of significant personal change occurs. Masks are gradually given up, and in that sense the level of interaction becomes real. Members engage in new behavior and are given feedback, and members are confronted when there is an incongruity between what they say and what they do. Genuine encounter takes place between persons who allow themselves to become vulnerable. Positive feelings are expressed, and, as trust is built up, there is an increase in closeness. Toward the end of a group, behavior change is observable within the group.

The Gestalt Model

Key concepts. This group model is designed to assist persons to more fully experience the present moment and to gain insight into their behavior. Emphasis is on acceptance of personal responsibility for what one feels and does. Members are encouraged to take care of unfinished business from the past by reliving it, as opposed to merely talking about it. Body language is thought to offer clues to underlying conflicts and messages. The goal of this approach is to cause the members to pay close attention to moment-to-moment experiencing, so that they may recognize, and ultimately reintegrate, disowned parts of the self.

The role of the leader. The group leader, according to this model, suggests techniques that will help the participants intensify their experience and alert them to the messages conveyed by their body language. The leader's job is not to interpret the clients' behavior but rather to assist the clients in identifying the unfinished business that interferes with their present functioning. The leader focuses on how the members behave—in particular, whether they tend to avoid contact with others and with their own feelings. Members make their own interpretations.

Group techniques. The Gestalt techniques are designed to intensify direct experiencing and to allow people to integrate conflicting feelings. Stress is placed on confronting conflicts and assuming responsibility for one's feelings. A few of the techniques that are used are: (1) the empty-chair procedure, in which members imagine that a person they're in conflict with is in a chair before them and talk to the person as though he or she were there now, (2) playing the projection, in which members are encouraged to apply to themselves the things they say to others in the group, and (3) the go-around technique, in which members face each of the other members in turn and say a sentence, usually one that they feel uncomfortable saying. All the Gestalt exercises are designed to intensify the level of awareness of participants so that they can recognize what they're doing at a particular moment. Members can then make a decision to change based on this self-awareness.

The Transactional-Analysis Model

Key concepts. Transactional Analysis (TA) is an interactional and contractual therapeutic approach that is particularly suited for use in groups. The basic assumption is that what we once decided can be redecided. The therapeutic goal is to give members a degree of awareness that will enable them to make new decisions regarding the direction of their lives. To develop this awareness, clients examine their early programming, early parental injunctions, and early decisions about their worth and their life position. In TA, participants learn how to identify the games they play to avoid intimacy, and they gain awareness of which ego state—parent, adult, or child—they typically function in. In these ways they gain control of their lives.

The role of the leader. TA is designed to give members insight into both the intellectual and the emotional sides of themselves, although the emphasis tends to be on the rational component of behavior. Thus, the role of the group leader is partly didactic. As a teacher, the group leader explains key concepts in TA and helps clients discover the disadvantageous conditions under which they made early decisions, adopted life plans, and developed strategies for dealing with people. With this knowledge, the clients may reconsider these early decisions.

Group techniques. Contracts are considered essential by proponents of this model. The treatment contract contains a statement of concrete objectives that the client will attain and the criteria by which it can be determined that these goals have been met. Transactions that are not related to the contract are avoided; the leader does not go on unauthorized fishing expeditions with members. To implement the goals specified in the contracts, assignments are developed by the client and the leader; these "homework assignments" are ways of putting the responsibility for change on the client. Thus, the clients are expected to act on their new self-awareness.

The Behavior-Therapy Model

Key concepts. There is no single model of behavior therapy in groups; rather, there are many types of behavior therapy. A common assumption underlying these therapies is that all behavior is learned through reinforcement and that learning principles can be applied to problem-solving. The focus is on present, overt behavior. Treatment goals and the treatment plan are concrete, and the evaluation of outcomes is objective. The goal of this approach is the elimination of maladaptive behaviors and the learning of effective behavior patterns. Although the goals are defined by the client, the leader helps make them concrete.

The role of the leader. The group leader must be active and directive, often functioning as a teacher or trainer. The client must be willing to experiment with new behaviors. Frequently, group leaders impart information or teach new coping skills, and they also have the job of organizing the proceedings of the group. The group interaction is characterized by comments from the leader to a member or to the group. With this approach, there is generally less member-to-member interaction than in some of the other group approaches, and the leader is generally more intent on keeping the proceedings of the group in line with a predetermined set of activities.

Group techniques. Behavior-therapy groups use techniques, based on learning principles, that are geared to behavior change. There are several types of behavior-therapy groups, each designed to deal with a particular type of problem.

One type of behavior-therapy group that is gaining popularity is *assertiveness training*. This approach is designed for people who feel that it is inappropriate for them to assert themselves and for those who cannot express anger, are overly polite, allow others to take advantage of them, find it difficult to express affection and other positive responses—in general, for people who need practice in asserting their rights in a nonaggressive manner. Behavioral rehearsal and other techniques, such as coaching and modeling, are used in this kind of group.

Another type of behavior-therapy group is concerned with the alleviation of a specific behavior, such as drinking, overeating, or smoking. In still another type of group—the *systematic-desensitization* group—members are taught how to relax, and the response of anxiety to particular events is replaced with the response of relaxation. Often, the members of a particular group are chosen on the basis of their fear of a certain type of event. For instance, all of the members of a group may become very anxious when faced with a test at school.

The Rational-Emotive-Therapy Model *Cognitur / didache)*

Key concepts. Rational-Emotive Therapy (RET) is a highly didactic, cognitive, behavior-oriented approach. Its proponents believe that one must take action to combat one's belief in irrational ideas—ideas that result from self-indoctrination. Thinking, evaluating, analyzing, questioning, doing, practicing, and redeciding are the bases of behavior change. Thus, proponents of this model see therapy as a process of reeducation. In childhood, people begin telling themselves irrational and illogical things, and they continue this process of self-indoctrination as they grow older. Emotional problems are the results of these belief systems, and challenging these systems is necessary for the recovery of emotional health. The scientific method of logical and rational thought is applied to irrational beliefs. Some common irrational ideas are: that it is a dire necessity to be loved by all and approved by all, that one should be perfect, that one has little control over one's personal problems, and that one should be blamed and punished for one's inadequacies.

The role of the leader. The activities of RET are carried out with one central purpose—that of assisting the client to become free of illogical ideas and to replace them with logical ideas. The aim is to help members internalize a rational philosophy of life. The leader's task is to help group members gain awareness of their present condition—to bring them to face and act on the fact that some of their behavior is self-defeating because it is based on irrational beliefs. To accomplish this, the group leader uses a didactic approach, explaining to clients how to understand themselves and how to change. RET leaders direct and persuade in a rapid-fire manner that requires members to use, above all, their cognitive skills.

Group techniques. RET is very suitable for group work, for the members are taught to apply RET principles to one another. In addition, "homework" is assigned. In the group setting, members experience assertiveness training, take part in role-playing, practice developing new social skills, and get feedback from one another. Many behavior-therapy techniques are used by leaders working with this model.

The Reality-Therapy Model

Key concepts. Reality Therapy is a system that focuses on present behavior; it is a form of behavior modification. The model involves a didactic approach stressing problem-solving and coping with the demands of reality in society. As such, it focuses on the present and on the person's strengths that will allow the learning of more realistic behavior. It rejects the medical model of mental illness. Case histories are not stressed, nor is the role of the unconscious. Clients are encouraged to examine their behavior and to make a value judgment about it. Insight and attitude change are not deemed crucial, as the focus is solely on behavior change. Mental health is equated with acceptance of personal responsibility. The core concept of this model is that people are responsible for their behavior and that, in order to achieve a "success identity," they must accept this responsibility.

The role of the leader. The job of the group leader is to get involved with the clients and to encourage them to face reality and make choices that will allow them to fulfill their needs in a socially acceptable way. The group members must judge whether their behavior meets their needs. If they feel that it doesn't, they must decide on specific changes, formulate plans for change, carry out the change, and evaluate the results. The group leader helps by establishing a personal relationship with the group members and by not accepting excuses for irresponsible behavior. Often, clients make contracts and then report back on their successes and failures at carrying them out. Group leaders, according to this model, need to be demanding but sensitive; they need to be personal, not aloof. By fulfilling their own needs in reality and by being open about their own values and struggles, they provide a model for the group members. They demonstrate courage by continually confronting clients who are not living realistically.

Group techniques. In many ways, the techniques used in reality-therapy groups are techniques of behavior modification. The focus is on the person's strengths and potentials in such procedures as role-playing and confrontation. Other group activities involve forming specific plans for action, setting limits, and discussing values.

Concluding Comments

We encourage you to think about the various theoretical models of group and to begin to formulate your own conception of the group process. Your position on issues such as the role of the group leader, the role of the members, the nature of the group process, and the goals of group practice is vitally related to the way you function as a group leader. At this stage, you probably have not developed a theory of group work, and we think it is important that you consider the advantages and disadvantages of each of the various theories. Our hope is that you will begin to develop a personalized approach to group work—an approach that is uniquely suited to you.

EXERCISES

As you review this chapter, think about factors such as group goals, contracts, and guidelines in terms of what you would do if you were running a group. Then think about these issues in terms of their applicability to your class. Are there any features of group experience that you would like to see incorporated into the structure of your class? What are some of the guidelines that you think should govern the activities of your class?

Then, in your class, form small groups and exchange your ideas. The goal of this activity is for you to get actively involved in your learning by making some concrete suggestions concerning its structure and direction. As you do this exercise, consider in particular how your experience in this course might be a therapeutic one (meaning that you learn more about yourself and your way of relating to others), without becoming a therapy group.

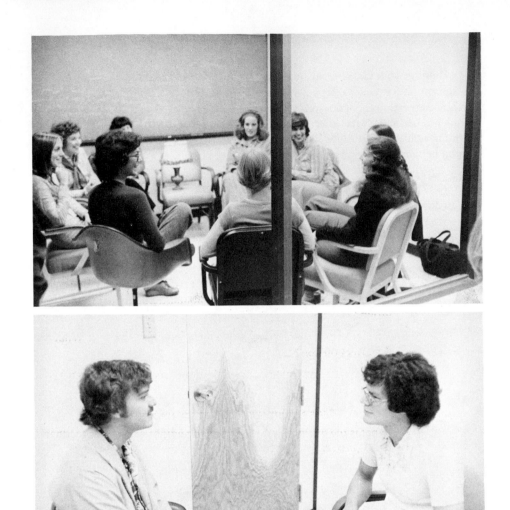

3. THE GROUP MEMBER

1. How do you think group members can derive the maximum benefit from a group experience?

2. What are some reasons you can think of for nonparticipating behavior in groups? Have you been a nonparticipating member in any group?

3. Have you been in a group with people who monopolize? What was the effect on you?

4. What might you say (as a group leader or member) to a person who tells anecdotes about his or her past?

5. What effect does being questioned have on you in a group?

6. What is the distinction between giving advice and giving feedback? Do you think giving advice is ever warranted? If so, when?

7. What distinction is there between smoothing things over and giving genuine support?

8. How might you, as a leader, deal with a member's hostility?

9. What member behavior would you find most difficult to deal with as a leader?

10. Have you been in group before? If so, how did you select the group? How do you think a group should be selected?

This chapter deals primarily with the issue of how group members can get the most from a group experience. We'll present guidelines for productive member behavior and examples of both productive and nonproductive behavior. As you read this chapter, consider how many of these guidelines were followed in the groups you've participated in. Also as you read, keep in mind these questions: What kind of member behaviors help to create a group atmosphere that is conducive to meaningful self-exploration? What specific behaviors are counterproductive to the development of a cohesive working group? How might you deal with disruptive behavior, both as a group member and as a group leader?

HOW TO GET THE MOST FROM A GROUP EXPERIENCE: SOME GUIDELINES FOR MEMBERS

Some behaviors and attitudes facilitate the establishment of a cohesive and productive group—that is, a group in which meaningful self-exploration takes place and in which honest and appropriate feedback is given and received. In this section, we'll describe some of these behaviors. Our discussion of these guidelines will be supplemented by examples from our own groups.

Realize that the group is a means to an end. Unfortunately, there are those who consider a group experience an end in itself; for them, the main payoffs are the social interaction within the group setting and the temporary excitement and closeness they feel during the sessions. Some use a group as a place to get their batteries charged, a place to get positive strokes and support, or a place to grab for intimacy. While these experiences may be pleasant, the purpose of a group is to enable participants to make decisions about how they will change their outside lives. Groups that are therapeutic encourage persons to look at themselves, to decide whether they like what they see, and to make plans for change.

Example: Marnie came to the group as a frightened, tough, isolated, hurt, and skeptical person. To survive her hurts, she had learned to suppress her need for others, and she prided herself on her independence. During the course of the group, she demonstrated great courage by letting others become important to her. She allowed herself to be needy and to trust people and, finally, made a decision to at least share the pain of her isolation and loneliness. The point is that, after the group, she acted on what she had learned during the group—that some people can be trusted. Marnie allowed herself to be loved by a few people outside of group. She discovered that, although she could still make it alone, life was more fulfilling if she allowed herself to care for others and them to care for her.

Learn to help establish trust. So often participants wait for some other person to take the first risk or to make some gesture of trust. Members can enhance their experience in groups by helping to create a trusting climate. They can do this, paradoxically, by revealing their lack of trust. While certain "trust exercises" can be initiated by group leaders, members can gain from initiating a discussion that will allow genuine trust to develop.

Example: Harold was older than most of the other group members, and he feared they would not be able to empathize with him, that he would be excluded from activities, that he would be viewed as an outsider—a parent figure—and that he would not be able to open up. After he daringly disclosed these things, many members gave Harold honest feedback concerning his courage in revealing his mistrust. His disclosure, and the response to it, stimulated trust in the entire group by making it clear that it was OK to express fear. Instead of being rejected, Harold was accepted and appreciated, for he was willing to make a real part of himself known to the rest of the group.

Decide for yourself how much to disclose. At times, group members are led to believe that, the more self-disclosure, the better. They are asked not to think about the need for privacy. While self-disclosure is an important tool of group process, it is up to each participant to decide what aspects of his or her life to reveal. This principle cannot be stressed too much in groups, for the idea that one will have to tell everything contributes to the resistance of many to becoming participants in group.

The kind of disclosure that is most useful is disclosure that is unrehearsed. It expresses present concern and may entail some risk. As one opens up to a group, there is the fear of how what is being revealed will be received by the members. Self-disclosure that is appropriate can open doors of self-knowledge and can encourage other members to open up.

Example: In a weekend encounter group, Tom chose to disclose and explore his struggles with his work situation. This problem was presently important for him, and he was willing to work on it. Although he was aware that he was having some serious conflicts with his wife, he chose not to open this issue to the group, because he didn't feel ready to do so at the time. This decision should be respected by others and by Tom himself. It is Tom's responsibility—and his right—to decide what areas of his personal life he is willing to reveal and to explore with the group.

Be an active participant, not an observer. Example: When Roger was asked what he wanted from the group, he replied "I haven't really given that much thought. I figured I'd just be spontaneous and wait to see what happens." As the sessions progressed, Roger did learn to let the other members know what he wanted from them. Instead of being a passive observer, without any clear goals, who would be content to wait for things to happen to him, he began to take more initiative. He showed that he wanted to talk about how lonely he felt, how desperate and inadequate he frequently felt, how fearful he was of being weak with women, and how he dreaded facing his world every morning. As Roger learned to focus on his wants, he learned that he could benefit from his weekly sessions.

Expect some disruption of your life. Participants in therapeutic groups should be given the warning that their involvement may complicate their outside lives for a time. As a result of group experiences, members tend to assume that the persons in their lives are both ready and willing to make significant changes. It can be shocking for members to discover that others thought they were "just fine" the way they were, and the friction that results may make it more difficult than ever to modify old, familiar patterns. Therefore, it is important for members to be prepared for the fact that not everyone will like or accept some of the changes they want to make. Perhaps some relationships will be discontinued and some new ones formed.

Example: Ron came away from his group with the awareness that he was frightened of his wife, that he consistently refrained from expressing his wants to her, and that he related to her as he would to a protective mother. He feared that, if he asserted himself with her, she would leave. In the group, not only did he become disgusted with his dependent style, but he also decided that he would treat her as an equal and give up his hope of having her become his mother. Ron's wife did not cooperate with his valiant efforts to change the nature of their relationship. The more assertive Ron became, the more disharmony there was in his home. While he wanted to become independent, his wife struggled to keep their relationship the way it was; she was not willing to change.

Expect setbacks and realize that change may be slow and subtle. *Example:* In her group-therapy sessions, Barbara decided no longer to allow herself to be controlled by her husband and children. She engaged in rehearsing and role-playing, saw that she had become what she thought her husband expected, and eventually made contracts to change those behaviors that resulted in her feeling powerless. Later she reported to her group that she had regressed—that she seemed to be even more susceptible to being controlled. She didn't fulfill her contracts, and she began losing hope that she could really change. It would have been helpful if she had realized that setbacks are a part of the growth process, that changing entrenched habits cannot be done quickly, and that she had in fact made many strides that she was not giving herself full credit for. Her expectations of overnight changes were unrealistic. More important than dramatic life-style changes are directional shifts in attitudes and behavior, for these subtle beginnings may be significant in the redecision and relearning processes.

Don't expect one group alone to renovate your life. Those who seek a therapeutic group sometimes cling to unrealistic expectations. They expect rapid change; they want to be "cured," and they want it immediately. Group leaders need to emphasize that a single therapeutic experience, as potent as it may be in itself as a catalyst for significant change, is not sufficient to sustain many of the members' decisions. We spend many years creating our unique personalities, with our masks, our defenses, and our games, and it takes time to establish constructive alternatives. People do not easily relinquish familiar defenses, for, even though the defenses may entail some pain, they do work. The change process is just that—a process, not a product. Unfortunately, many group members see the group experience as a convenient shortcut to becoming their ideal "finished product."

Example: Betty, a very busy university professor, joined a week-long group and said at the initial session "I really think that I need to clean up some personal problems that are interfering with my research, writing, and teaching. So I've set aside this week to get myself in psychological shape." She seriously thought that, in one week, she could see what her problems were, work through them, and be able to resume her work without the annoying distractions of personal conflicts. The leaders of the group reminded Betty that personal growth can't be made to proceed according to a schedule. They told her they hoped her expectations would change so that she wouldn't wind up disappointed.

Realize that you don't have to be sick to benefit. Some people shy away from involvement in counseling groups because they believe that groups are only for "sickies." Members should be taught that a minor tune-up is possible without a major overhaul. Groups can offer the opportunity to examine how past decisions influence one's present life. The group can provide the challenge and support necessary for evaluating one's direction.

Example: Sharon was hesitant to involve herself fully in her group because she accepted the notion that any kind of therapy is for people with serious emotional and mental disorders. Gradually, she found, through the example of fellow group members, that struggling for change is not sick but, rather, courageous. She then felt freer to use the group as a place to try out new behavior, and she became open to working with internal blocks that were preventing her from forming close ties with those she cared about.

Expect to discover positive aspects of yourself. A common fear about therapy is that one will discover how "rotten," how unlovable, how empty, how hopeless, or how powerless one is. More often than not, though, people in groups begin to realize that they're lovable, that they can control their own destiny, and that they have talents they never knew about. Groups need not be devoted exclusively to the reliving of pain and to intense struggle; they can also be happenings of great joy. For instance, many participants experience an inner strength, or discover a real wit and sense of humor, or create moving poetry or songs, or dare for the first time to show a creative side of themselves that they have kept hidden from others—and from themselves. A group experience, then, can show persons a positive, even ecstatic, dimension of themselves.

Beware of misusing jargon. It is sad that the group movement offers another way of being phony. People can learn an entirely new language and can lose themselves in groups, since language can remove people from their experiencing. Take, for example, phrases such as "I can really relate to you," "I want to get closer to my feelings," "I get good vibes from you," "I'd like to stop playing all these games with myself," "Let me be in the present moment," and "I have to be spontaneous." If terms such as "relate to," "get closer to," and "vibes" aren't clearly defined and reserved for certain circumstances, then the quality of communication will be poor. People who learn to use this vague language may deceive themselves into thinking they're self-actualized. What a refreshing experience it is to talk with a person who has had no prior group experience and who is able to say in plain English what it is he or she wants and why he or she decided to get involved in a group.

You must decide what to do with what you've learned. At its best, a group will provide moments of truth during which clients see who they are and how they present themselves to others. Ultimately, it is up to the members to do something with the glimpses of truth they gain.

Example: Linda became aware that she (not her husband) was primarily responsible for her misery and depression. Prior to her participation in the group, she had blamed other people for her unhappiness. If only they would change, she thought, then I might taste happiness. In the group, she came to accept that, if she waited for others to make her feel worthwhile, she might indeed be condemned to a hopeless existence; by accepting that only she could change things, she opened up options for redecisions. Regardless of what she decided to do, she now knew that she was not helpless. The realization that we do have choices and that we're responsible for how we live and what we experience through our decisions may well be the most valuable outcome of participation in a group.

Listen closely but discriminately. Group members should listen carefully to what the other members say about them, neither accepting it wholesale nor rejecting it outright. Members should listen discriminately, deciding for themselves what does and what doesn't apply to them.

Example: In an adolescent group, Jack received feedback that he was seductive and controlling. Members told him that, when the focus was not on him, he would attempt to draw attention to himself. Jack became defensive and angry and denied that he acted that way. It would have been useful for him to have thought over the feedback before so vigorously rejecting it.

Express persistent feelings. There are times when group members keep their feelings of boredom, or anger, or disappointment a secret from the rest of the group. It is most important that persistent feelings related to the group process be aired.

Example: In a group of adolescents that met once a week for ten weeks, Christine waited until the last session to disclose that she didn't trust either the members or the leader, that she was angry because she felt pressured to participate, that she was scared to express what she felt because she might look foolish, and that she really didn't know what was expected of her as a group member. She had had these feelings since the initial sessions but had withheld them from the group. Had Christine expressed her feelings earlier, they could have been explored and, possibly, resolved. As it was, she left the group feeling that she had accomplished nothing.

Think for yourself. Many people seek therapy because they've lost the ability to find their own way and have become dependent on others to direct their lives and take the responsibility for their decisions. When such people enter a group, they adopt a new standard (that of the group) as their own. While they may shed some of their inhibitions, they are still not deciding on their own direction. They expect the group to decide for them, or they are sensitively tuned to being what the group expects them to be.

Example: Very soon after disclosing her unhappiness with her marriage, Shirley decided to leave her husband. This decision was reached after a one-weekend workshop. Some participants had felt that, since she said she didn't love her husband any more, for her own good she should file for divorce. Ultimately, this may have been Shirley's decision, but she appeared to act in haste and somewhat under the influence of what other members felt.

Pay attention to consistent feedback. A person may get similar feedback from many people in different groups, yet may still dismiss it as invalid. While it is important to listen discriminately, it is also important to realize that a message that has been received from a variety of people is likely to have a degree of validity.

Example: In several groups, Dan heard people tell him that he looked bored, distant, and detached. The other members felt that Dan was present partially—bodily—but that he was psychologically removed from the group. Dan insisted, each time he heard this, that his behavior in group was different from his behavior in outside life—that, on the outside, he felt close to people and was interested and involved. It seems unlikely that someone could be so different in the two areas, however, and he might have done well to pay attention to the fact that so many people were saying the same thing.

Don't categorize yourself. During the initial stages of a group, members often present themselves to the other members in terms of a role—one that they dislike but at the same time appear to cling to. For instance, we've heard people introduce themselves as: "the group mother," "a hard-ass," "the fragile person who can't stand confrontation," and "the one in this group whom nobody will like." There are times when a person who views himself or herself as a "hard-ass" would like to be different. What is important is for people not to fatalistically pin labels on themselves and for the group not to fulfill the expectations and thereby even further convince members that they are what they fear. It may be helpful for group leaders to remind themselves and the group members of how certain participants can be pegged with labels such as "the monopolist," "the storyteller," "the intellectualizer," "the withdrawn one," "the obsessive compulsive," and so on. People may exhibit behaviors that characterize them in one way or another, and it is appropriate to confront them with this during the group, but this can be done without cementing people into rigid molds that become very difficult to shatter.

Example: Roz presented herself to the group as withdrawn and fragile. She made a contract requiring her to speak out and to at least act as though she were strong. In this way, she was able to put on the shelf an old image she had clung to and experiment with behavior associated with other images.

Do work before and after a group. In order to get the maximum benefit from a group, it is vitally important that members prepare themselves before entering a group. How? By reading, by thinking, and by deciding specifically what they want from the experience. The clearer they are concerning what issues they want to examine, the better the chance that they'll leave with what they wanted. Also, after a group, there are things to do that will increase the chances of retaining what was learned. In an ongoing journal, recent members can record how well they're progressing toward their goals. Self-assigned homework can help people extend the effects of their group experience.

PROBLEM BEHAVIORS AND DIFFICULT GROUP MEMBERS

We think it is important to describe specific behaviors that interfere with the establishment of a cohesive and productive group, yet at the same time we want to resist the temptation to characterize any member as "the monopolist," "the group nurse,'' ''the assistant therapist,'' ''the calculator,'' and so on. Certain problems inherent in such labeling have already been discussed. In addition, placing a fixed label on a participant represents a failure to take into account what the person is besides that behavior he or she tends to exhibit. While a man may exhibit overly supportive behavior, he is surely more than a ''group nurse.'' And, even though a woman is prone to intellectualizing and story-telling, she is surely more than just an ''avoider.'' With this caution, we will now describe member behaviors that are counterproductive to group functioning.

Nonparticipating Behavior

Silence and withdrawal are two forms of behavior that most group leaders must eventually learn to deal with. Even though the silent and withdrawn member does not interfere verbally with group functioning, his or her behavior may constitute a problem for both the member and the group. We are convinced that the active members are the ones who derive the most benefit from therapeutic groups.

Some nonparticipating group members may argue that their lack of verbal participation is not an index of their involvement. They may claim that they are learning by listening and by identifying with others' problems. These members may claim that they ''don't feel like talking just to hear themselves talk'' or that when they have something important to contribute they'll do so. Group leaders should encourage these members to discuss their silence in the group. The danger is that quiet or withdrawn members will go unnoticed and that their pattern of silence may indicate a problem. There are many reasons for nonparticipating behavior, and these should be explored within the group. Some of these reasons are

1. the feeling that one doesn't have anything worthwhile to say,
2. the feeling that one shouldn't talk about oneself or that one should be seen and not heard,
3. fear of looking foolish; not knowing the appropriate thing to say or do,
4. fear of certain members in the group or of the authority of the group leader,
5. resistance, particularly if the person doesn't really want to be a member of the group,
6. uncertainty about how the group process works,
7. fear of being rejected or of being accepted, and
8. lack of trust in the group; fear of leaks of confidentiality.

Silent members can be invited to explore what their silence means. For example, is this the way they are outside of the group as well? How does it feel for them to be in this group? Do they want to do anything about becoming verbally active participants? It is important that they not be attacked for their silence but instead invited to participate in the group. Also, group leaders must be careful to avoid consistently calling on the silent person, for in this way the member is relieved of the responsibility of initiating interaction. A game can be made of drawing out the person, and this can lead to resentment on the part of the rest of the group and the member who is being prodded and frustration on the part of the leader who perpetuates the game.

The rest of the group can participate in this discussion, for, generally, group members do have reactions to nonparticipating members. They may feel cheated that they know so little of that person, or they may resent that the person observes them as they risk and reveal themselves. If there are several silent members in a group, the verbally active members may become less revealing because they don't trust those who aren't revealing also.

Silent members can be taught that others will not know of their involvement unless they express it in words. The leader may ask such members to make a contract to speak at every session, sharing with the group at some point how they responded to the session that day. Another way for the leader to handle this behavior is to ask the relatively silent members, at the end of a session, whether they got from the session what they wanted. If they indicate that there were some things they wanted to talk about but that time ran out before they got a chance, then they can make a contract to be the first on the agenda at the next group meeting.

A group technique that can serve as a way of dealing directly with those who feel that they are not active participants is to ask these people to form an inner circle within the group. Those who identify themselves as active participants sit in an outer circle. The members of the inner circle are then instructed to talk among themselves about how they feel in the group, what their fears and concerns are, and in what ways they want to change their behavior. After a time, the members of the outer group can take the inner circle and react to what they've heard. In this way, the entire group is involved in the discussion of the issue of participation/nonparticipation. If certain members remain extremely silent or withdrawn, the group leader can meet with them privately to discuss the reasons for the silent behavior and the advisability of their staying in the group.

Monopolistic Behavior

At the other end of the participation continuum is the person who exhibits a high degree of self-centeredness by monopolizing the activities of the group. This person is continually "identifying with others"—that is, taking others' statements as openings for beginning detailed stories about his or her own life. Through his or her compulsive, self-centered chattering, this person prevents others from getting their share of group time.

During the beginning stages of a group, members may be relieved that someone else is "going first," but they soon tire of hearing the same person over and over. As group meetings continue, the group generally becomes less tolerant of the person who monopolizes, and, unless these feelings of annoyance are dealt with early, they may be bottled up and then released in an explosive way. For this reason, it is essential that the person monopolizing be gently challenged to look at the effects of his or her behavior on the group. Hopefully, members will initiate by letting the person know how they feel about his or her continually stepping into the spotlight. If the group does not take this initiative, the group leader might ask "I wonder why so many of you seem to be willing to let Ralph take up so much group time?"

The person who monopolizes should not be silenced by mandate. Instead, his or her behavior should be examined in the group. The person is sending messages with his or her antics, and these messages can be productively analyzed. For example, Ralph initially seemed very charming. He seemed to reveal personal aspects of himself, he readily made suggestions to others, he could identify with most who spoke, he became an "assistant therapist" by questioning and interpreting, he told juicy stories of his past, and most of his behavior was an expression of the message "Please notice me and like me." The group leader intervened firmly but gently with "You seem desperate to get people's attention, and now you have it, yet I imagine that this is still not what you want. How would it be if we talked about how your behavior in here may be an extension of the way you are outside of group, so you can see whether this behavior is really working for you?"

Story-Telling

Self-disclosure is frequently misunderstood by some group members to mean a lengthy recitation about their lives, past and present. If they are confronted about continually relating their detailed histories, they sometimes express resentment, claiming that they were risking disclosing themselves. In teaching group process, leaders need to differentiate between pseudodisclosure, which is merely a talking about oneself or about others and life situations, and disclosure of what a person is thinking and feeling now. During the beginning stages of a group, the leader may allow some story-telling, for people who are new to group frequently express a need to hear facts about others or to share some of their own past. However, if story-telling behavior becomes a familiar style (either for the whole group or for one member), the leader should recognize this and deal with it. The following stories illustrate how story-telling can be handled.

Richard would, almost predictably, bring the group up to date each week on developments in his marriage. He would focus on details of his wife's behavior during the week, but he would rarely describe his own feelings or behavior. Since Richard was the spouse in group, the leader pointed out, it was Richard whom the group was interested in. As Richard and the group looked more at this behavior, it became obvious to Richard that this was his way of avoiding talking about himself. He thus made a contract to talk about his reactions and not to bring his wife into the group each week.

Sandra typically told every detail of her earlier experiences, but, even though the group knew a lot about the events in her past, they knew very little about how Sandra felt about what she had experienced. Like Richard, she felt that she was open in sharing her private life with the group; but, like Richard's group, her group wanted to know more about how she responded to her life situations. The group leader told Sandra that he was "losing Sandra" in all of the details. He let Sandra know that he was indeed interested in knowing her but that the information she was offering was not helping him do so.

Story-telling can be any form of talking about out-of-group life that leaves the person telling the story unknown. Feedback from the group given directly, without judgment, can assist the person to speak in personal terms and keep the focus on feelings, thoughts, and reactions.

Questioning

A form of behavior that is counterproductive in group is interrogation. Some group members develop a style of relating involving questioning others, and they intervene at inappropriate times, asking for details or reasons why a person feels a certain way. People who habitually ask questions should be helped to see that this may be a way of hiding, of remaining safe and unknown in a group. And they should be taught that the people to whom the questions are addressed typically lose the intensity of any emotion they may have been experiencing; questions tend to direct people to thought and away from emotion.

If questioners can be made to understand that questions not only intrude on others but also keep the questioner's feelings about others disguised, there is a good chance that change will occur. Practice for behavior change might consist of trying to make only direct statements.

Advice-Giving

A problem behavior that is related to questioning is advice-giving. It is one thing to offer a perception or opinion to another member, and it is quite another matter to tell that person what they should feel or what they should or shouldn't do. The advice-giving may be subtle: "You shouldn't feel guilty that your parents divorced, because that was their decision and not something you made them do." While this is true, the point is that the young woman does feel guilty and believes that, if it had not been for her, her parents might still be married. It does not serve the best interest of the woman to advise her not to feel guilty. She has to resolve this feeling for herself. The man who had a need to tell her that she shouldn't feel guilty could profit from examining his own motives for wanting to remove the guilt. What does this mean about him? At this point, the focus might be shifted to the advice-giver, and the meaning of his giving such advice might be explored.

Advice-giving can be less subtle. Pam has been considering not only leaving her husband but also leaving her two teenage daughters with him. Pam is confused, and, while she thinks she wants to live alone, she feels somewhat guilty. Robin intervenes with "Pam, you owe it to yourself to do what you want to do. Why should you be stuck with your kids? Why not let him take them? Pam, if I were you, I'd leave both my kids and my husband, get an apartment, and take that job as an interior decorator." This type of behavior on Robin's part says a lot about her. What are her values and possible unresolved problems? Why does she feel a need to straighten Pam out? Wouldn't it be better for Robin to talk about herself, instead of trying to be helpful by deciding what is best for Pam? The group might now focus on Robin's need to provide others with a pat solution. Robin might learn about what she is getting from giving others advice.

Band-Aiding

Related to the advice-giving style is the style that some adopt of trying to sooth wounds, lessen pains, and keep people cheerful. This is sometimes manifested by a person who complains of how negative the group is and who wants to focus more on the positive side. The following are two examples of Band-Aiding.

Jack is finally able to feel his sadness over the distance between his boys and himself, and he sobs in group as he talks about how much he wants to be a better father. Before Jack can even have a cathartic cry, Randy puts his hands on Jack's shoulders and tries to reassure him that he's not such a bad father, because at least he lives with his kids. Randy may want to make Jack feel better so that he (Randy) will feel more comfortable.

Jan finally reveals her memories of the loneliness, rejection, and fright that she felt when she had an abortion as an adolescent. Jan is reliving the loneliness that she felt earlier. Louise moves across the room and holds Jan and tries as best she can to take Jan's lonely feelings away. What has Jan provoked in Louise? Why does Louise need to protect Jan from the intensity of her pain?

There is a real difference between behavior that is Band-Aiding and behavior that is a genuine expression of care, concern, and empathy. Where there is real caring, the interests of the person who is experiencing the pain are given paramount importance. Sometimes it is in the interest of people to allow them to experience the depths of their pain, for, ultimately, they may be better off for having done so. They can be supported after they've had the chance to intensely experience their pain. Band-Aiding is pseudosupport, designed primarily to aid the one who is supporting. Finding it too difficult to witness another's pain, the supportive one attempts to distract the other. Like questioning and advice-giving, Band-Aiding needs to be examined, at some point, for its meaning to the person who performs it.

Hostile Behavior

Hostility is difficult to deal with in a group because the person who expresses hostility often works indirectly. Hostility can take the form of caustic remarks, jokes, sarcasm, and other hit-and-run tactics. Members can express it by missing group sessions, by coming late, by becoming obviously bored and detached, by leaving the group, by being overly polite, and in a number of other indirect ways. Extremely hostile people are not generally good candidates for group, for they are so defensive that many of them will not acknowledge their fears. In addition, extreme hostility can have a devastating effect on the group climate. People are not going to make themselves vulnerable if there is a good chance that they will be ridiculed or in some other way devalued.

One way to deal with the person who behaves in a hostile way is to request that the person listen without responding while the group members tell how they see that individual. It is important that the members not be allowed to dump their own feelings of hostility, however. Instead, they can describe how they feel in the group with the person and what they would like the person to do differently. Then it should be ascertained what the individual wants from the group. Hostile behavior may be a manifestation of a fear of getting intimate or of a limited capacity for vulnerability. If the fears underneath the hostility can be brought to the surface and dealt with, the hostility may decrease.

One notable manifestation of hostility is passive-aggressive behavior. This behavior characteristically involves the element of surprise; the person confronts and then quickly retreats. The confrontation has a sharp and cutting quality, and the person attacking withdraws, leaving the attacked person stunned. Another form of passive aggression is obvious detachment or boredom.

Dependency

Group members who are excessively dependent pose a problem, for they typically look either to the group leader or to the other members to direct them and take care of them. Dependency is manifested in a variety of behaviors in group, such as exclaiming that one couldn't live without one's wife (or husband, or parents, or children), presenting oneself as stupid so that others will provide one with answers, and playing helpless.

A special variety of the dependency syndrome is the "Yes, but" style of interaction. The person requests help, and the group gives feedback, perhaps pointing out options that the person had not considered. Without even allowing this input to register, the individual replies with a "Yes, but" type of rebuttal. Consider Donald, 25 years old, living with his mother. Donald has been complaining that his mother constantly harasses him, treating him like a child—reminding him to take his vitamins, telling him to do his homework, reminding him that he should not stay out too late, and on and on. The group members soon tire of listening to his litany of complaints, and the following exchanges occur.

"If things are as bad as you say, why do you stay at home? Wouldn't it be a good idea to leave?"

"Yes, but I don't have a job, and I'm broke."

"If you don't like the way your mother treats you, wouldn't it help to let her know?"

"Yes, but my mother would just disintegrate if I were to confront her."

The essential point is that dependent persons are not helped by being allowed to lure others into the trap of giving pity. They can't use advice, because, no matter what is suggested, they can show why it will fail. The starting point for helping dependent people is to refuse to reinforce the helpless position, by refusing to fill the dependency needs. At the same time, it should be pointed out to such people the means they use to keep themselves dependent.

Acting Superior

Sometimes group members take a superior tone. A person may be moralistic or may even send the message "I'm cured, and I'm here to observe the rest of you sickies!" This person can find no personal problems to explore but is very willing to listen to others and even to offer them compassion. This individual may antagonize others with comments such as "I can identify with you because at one time I was where you are." In the member's condescending tone is the message "I really don't need anything for myself, and there are no problems in my life; I'm perfectly content now." A group leader can legitimately counter by asking what the person is doing in the group.

"Superior" behavior tends to have the same effect on a group as hostility. It freezes up participants, for they don't want to expose their weaknesses to someone who's perfect.

Seductive Behavior

Seductive behavior can take many forms, including some of the behaviors already mentioned. The person using seduction is attempting to manipulate others in the group in order to avoid any genuine encounter. Three types of seductive behavior are:

1. *Quiet seduction*. This involves trying to get others to draw one out. The game element consists of the individual's underlying belief that "If people really care about me, then they'll come and reach out to me first."

2. *Active seduction*. This involves trying to get intimacy instantly, to get acceptance without earning it. The person tells others what they want to hear, touches others a lot, suggests all sorts of "touchie-feelie" exercises, and is scared of genuine intimacy.

3. *Playing fragile*. Individuals may pretend that they're so fragile that, if confronted, they'll be devastated.

Intellectualizing

It is a mistake to see groups as places where people are allowed to have only "gut reactions" and where only immediate feelings are valued. The leaders of the encounter movement, reacting to what they feel is a fragmentation of the person resulting from an overemphasis on thinking, do see groups in this way, but they represent an extreme viewpoint.

We, on the other hand, feel that thoughtful analysis is a necessary part of group process but that it should be integrated with feeling. When group members discuss, in a very detached way, as though out of intellectual interest, topics that for most people are emotionally loaded, they can be said to be intellectualizing. Intellectualizing is a defense against feelings. Most people use this defense at times; it is when it comes to characterize a person's behavior that it becomes a problem.

It is important for people who intellectualize to be made aware of what they're doing. Some Gestalt awareness techniques can be useful in helping such people more directly experience the emotions associated with the events they talk about. Individuals can be directed to reexperience events, perhaps via role-playing. Group leaders need to be alert, however, when dealing with intellectualizing as well as with other counterproductive styles, that there is obviously some defensive purpose being served. Leaders ought to ask themselves whether they're competent to deal with what would be revealed should the defenses be stripped away.

Addiction

A real danger posed by groups is that people may become addicted to them. The person who lives from group to group, who makes participation in groups a life-style, is misusing groups. If participation in groups becomes an end in itself, if people depend on groups to give meaning to their lives and to provide them with acceptance, then an important concept has been lost. Groups are for the learning and practicing of behavior for use in the outside environment. Groups are not places to make friends but to learn that making friends is possible. Every group leader should be alert for members who are becoming addicted to the by-products of group interactions and, at the very least, should encourage group discussion of the phenomenon.

THE "GOOD" GROUP MEMBER

Now that we've discussed a variety of problem behaviors, we'd like to describe the combination of traits that makes an effective group member. We encourage you to create your own profile of the ideal group member. As a means of describing our ideal member, we'll give a picture of a person we'll call Sandy.

Sandy wants to participate in a weekly, ongoing counseling group. She wants to take a good look at herself, her marriage, her career goals, and her relationship with her son, and she wants to discover more ways of feeling alive. Sandy seeks group counseling voluntarily. She is motivated to work, as evidenced by her willingness to spend time thinking about what she wants from her group sessions. Sandy eventually forms a contract that guides her work in the group. She is specific about what she wants, and she is willing to explore her problems with the group. Sandy is sometimes scared by her feelings, and she expresses these fears. For example, she sometimes doubts that she wants to stay with her husband, and she's willing to face this issue squarely. She has never told anyone of her need to control in her sexual relationship, yet in her group she deals with this need and considers relinquishing the control. Sandy says what she feels, not what others in her group (including the therapist) might expect of her. She confronts both leader and members when she feels that something needs to be challenged, and she does so by bringing her own reactions into the confrontation. She avoids labeling or judging and instead speaks of how she is affected by what others are doing in the group. Sandy gives feedback when she has something to offer and gives support or affection when she genuinely feels this toward another. She resists participating in activities that don't seem right for her, and she is not pressured into doing or saying something to please anyone but herself. During the group sessions, she listens undefensively to what others tell her, and, when she is given feedback, she doesn't try to rationalize her behavior. Instead, she considers the feedback seriously. Then she decides for herself how accurate others' perceptions of her are and what she will do with this information. She devotes time between sessions to reflecting on her involvement in the group, and she eventually makes decisions to change her behavior. Sandy not only tries out new behavior in her group, but she also risks applying what she's learned in the group to her daily affairs. In between sessions, she reads books dealing with areas of struggle for her and keeps a daily journal. She brings into therapy any insights she has about herself or about the group. Sandy commits herself to doing things actively outside her group, yet at times she doesn't live up to these contracts. If she feels that she's backsliding, she mentions this in her sessions. At this point, she evaluates her contracts and determines how realistic her expectations are. Sandy realizes that she's not perfect, yet she accepts herself.

HOW TO SELECT A GROUP: SOME GUIDELINES FOR CONSUMERS

Potential group members often ask how they can make an informed decision regarding joining a particular group. While there are no assurances that the group one picks will be the right one, we think that, by following the suggestions below, a consumer can make a wise choice in selecting a group.

1. Do not join a group just because someone you know thinks you should. Decide for yourself whether you want to be a member of a particular kind of group.

2. Check with others who know the group leader before you make your decision. While some reports may be biased (either positively or negatively), feedback from people who have participated in a group conducted by that particular leader can be valuable.

3. Before you join a group, interview the group leader. Many group leaders will want a private session with a prospective group client to determine the person's readiness for a group. By the same token, it is reasonable for the prospective client to want to know about the personal and professional qualifications of the person who leads the group. If the therapist is indignant over such a request, you should probably avoid this person's group. If you do speak to the leader, try to decide whether he or she inspires your trust.

4. Questions such as the following can be asked of a group leader:

- What is the purpose of your group?
- What are the responsibilities of the leader and of the members?
- What do you see as the risks of participation, and what safeguards do you take to minimize the risks?
- What kinds of results do you see in your groups?
- What kinds of techniques do you use?
- Is there an opportunity for individual sessions?
- What is your background and training?
- What experience do you have in leading groups?
- Are you licensed as a therapist, and, if not, what are your qualifications as a group practitioner?
- What theoretical model do you use?

5. Ask the leader about matters such as fees, the method of deciding when a member should quit the group (terminate) or when the group should be terminated, follow-up procedures, and the structure of the group.

6. Be cautious about responding to advertisements or to brochures and pamphlets circulated in the mail. Referrals from agencies, from professionals, and most of all from clients who have been in the leader's groups should guide you in selecting a group.

7. The size of the group is another factor to consider. Groups of more than 16 or fewer than 5 members are best avoided. If a group is very small, there are not enough interaction possibilities. If a group is very large, group cohesion is hard to establish, and even a highly qualified leader may have trouble monitoring the interaction. For a group as large as 16, there should be at least two leaders.

EXERCISES

Use the following self-assessment scale to determine your strengths and weaknesses as a group member. Rate yourself as you see yourself at this time. This inventory assumes that you have had some type of group experience. If you have not, you might rate yourself in terms of your behavior in the class you're now in.

After everyone has completed the inventory, the class should break into small groups, each person trying to join the people he or she knows best. Members of the groups should then assess one another's self-ratings.

Rate yourself from 1 to 10 on each of the following self-descriptions.

1 = This is almost never true of me.
10 = This is almost always true of me.

1. I'm able to trust others in a group readily.
2. Others tend to trust me in a group situation.
3. I disclose personal and meaningful material when I'm in a group.

4. I'm willing to formulate specific goals and contracts when I'm a member of a group.
5. When I'm in a group, I'm generally an active participant, as opposed to an observer.
6. I'm willing to openly express my feelings about and reactions to what is occurring within a group.
7. I listen attentively to what others are saying, and I'm able to discern more than the mere content of what is said.
8. I don't give in to group pressure by doing or saying things that don't seem right to me.
9. When I'm a group participant, I'm able to give direct and honest feedback to others, and I'm open to receiving feedback about my behavior from others.
10. I prepare myself for a given group by thinking of what I want from that experience and what I'm willing to do to achieve my goals.
11. While I take an active part in a group, I avoid monopolizing the group time.
12. I avoid story-telling by describing what I'm experiencing now.
13. I avoid questioning other group members and instead make direct statements to them.
14. I'm able to be supportive of others when it is appropriate, without giving pseudosupport.
15. I'm able to confront others in a direct and caring manner by letting them know how I'm affected by them.

4. THE GROUP LEADER:
Personhood and Skills

1. What personal qualities do you think are associated with effective leadership? What personal qualities do you think interfere with effective leadership?
2. Assess yourself with respect to the characteristics you've just listed. What do you see as your strengths? What are the personal traits that might interfere with your effectiveness as a leader?
3. What skills do you think are the most crucial for a group leader to develop?
4. What are some specific steps you could take to develop these leadership skills in yourself?
5. Which do you think are more important in a leader—personal characteristics or learned skills?

PERSONAL CHARACTERISTICS OF THE EFFECTIVE GROUP LEADER

We believe that the personhood of the group leader is the most important determinant of group outcomes. In discussing the personality characteristics of the effective group leader with some of our colleagues, we found that it was difficult to list all of the traits of effective leaders and even more difficult to agree on one particular personality type associated with effective group leadership. The following are some characteristics that we deem important elements of the group leader's personhood.

Courage. One of the most important personal traits of effective group leaders is courage. Leaders show courage in their willingness (1) to be vulnerable at times, admitting to mistakes and imperfections and taking the same risks that they expect group members to take, (2) to confront another, even though they might not be sure that they're right, (3) to act on their beliefs and hunches, (4) to admit it when their perceptions are found to have been inaccurate, (5) to be emotionally touched by another and to draw on their experiences in order to identify with the other, (6) to

53

continually examine their inner selves, (7) to be direct and honest with members, (8) to express to the group their fears and expectations about the group process, and, most of all, (9) to do what they expect others to do in the group situation. Leaders should not use their special role to protect themselves from honest and direct interaction with the rest of the group.

Willingness to model. One of the best ways to teach desired behaviors is by modeling those behaviors in the group. Group leaders should not expect the participants to do anything that they, as leaders, are not willing to do. Thus, if leaders value disclosure, honesty, risk-taking, openness, listening with respect, and so forth, they should exhibit these behaviors in the group. This means that the leaders show respect for members by listening, that they reveal intimate facts about themselves, that they engage in what is risky behavior for them, and that they strive to honestly express what they think and feel about what they experience as the group unfolds.

Presence. The ability to be emotionally present with group members is extremely important, and it involves being emotionally touched by others' pain, struggles, and joys. Some members may elicit anger in a group leader, while other members may evoke pain, sadness, guilt, or happiness. Leaders can become more emotionally involved with others by paying close attention to their own emotional reactions and by allowing these reactions to become intense. This does not mean that they must talk about the situation in their own life that caused them the pain or evoked the anger. It means that they allow themselves to experience their feelings, even for just a few moments. Fully experiencing emotions gives leaders the ability to be compassionate and empathic with their clients. At the same time as they're moved by others' experiences, leaders must remain separate persons with their own experiencing. This mode of relating is extremely important, for group members as well as for group leaders.

To increase his or her presence, it is important for the leader to spend some time alone before leading a group and to shut out distractions as much as possible. The leader can then prepare for the group by thinking about the group members and by focusing on his or her readiness to become involved with others. If this reflection time is not allowed for, the group members will most likely get far less from the leader, for the leader will probably be psychologically detached from the members' experiencing.

Good will and caring. A sincere interest in the welfare of others is essential in a group leader. This means that group leaders must neither abuse their role by using the group mainly for their own purposes nor exploit members to enhance their ego. Good leaders feel that their needs are satisfied to the extent that they can focus on the needs of the participants.

Caring involves respecting, trusting, and valuing people. It may be exceedingly difficult for a leader to care for certain group members, but the leader should at least want to care. It is vital that group leaders become aware of what kinds of persons they care for and what kinds they find it difficult to care for. Leaders can gain this awareness by openly exploring their reactions to members when they become aware of a lack of concern for them.

That the leader cares about the members must be demonstrated to the group; merely saying so is not enough. There are various ways for leaders to exhibit a caring attitude. One way is by inviting a person to participate but allowing that person to decide how far he or she wants to go. Another way is for the leader, aware of discrepancies between a person's words and his or her behavior, to confront that person but to do so in a way that doesn't scare the member off. Another way for the leader to express caring is by giving warmth, concern, and support when, and only when, he or she feels it toward a person. Still another way to show caring is not to tolerate dishonest behavior but rather to encourage people to be what they could be without their masks and shields.

Belief in group process. Some therapists really don't believe that groups can effect significant change in clients, yet they continue to lead therapy groups. We think that a deep belief in the value of group process is positively related to constructive outcomes. We've found that our enthusiasm and convictions are power-ful both in attracting a clientele and in providing an incentive to work. Our belief in group process gives a sense of hope to potential and current group members. We're not suggesting that leaders should uncritically embrace groups as the only means of achieving growth; it would be naive not to recognize the limitations of group process. We are suggesting that, to lead successfully, leaders must believe in the value of what they're doing and trust the therapeutic forces in a group. Group leaders who do not genuinely believe in the value of therapeutic work, and who do it only for money or power, we consider unethical.

Openness. To be effective, group leaders must be open with themselves, open to others in groups, open to new experiences, and open to life-styles and values that differ from their own. Leaders must not only openly reveal their own experiences but also openly show their reactions to members in the group. Openness does not mean that leaders reveal every aspect of their personal lives, though; it means that they reveal enough of themselves to give the participants a sense of the person.

Leader openness tends to foster a spirit of openness within the group; it permits members to become more open about their feelings and beliefs, and it lends a certain fluidity to the group process. Self-revelation cannot be manipulated as a technique, however; it is best done spontaneously, when it seems appropriate.

Ability to cope with attacks. This trait is related to openness. Group leaders who are easily threatened, who are insecure in their work of leading, who are overly sensitive to negative feedback, and who depend highly on group approval will encounter major problems in trying to carry out a leadership function. Members sometimes attack leaders for not caring enough, for being selective in their caring, for structuring the sessions too much, for not providing enough direction, for being too harsh, and so forth. Some of the criticism may be fair—the leader may be inept—and some of it may be unfair—an expression of jealousy, testing of authority, power-seeking, or projection onto the leader of feelings for other significant people. The crucial thing is for the leader to nondefensively explore with the group the feelings that are behind the criticism and to differentiate between feelings that are produced by the leader and feelings that mainly represent transference.

Personal power. Personal power does not mean domination of members or manipulation of members toward the leader's end; rather, it is the dynamic and vital quality of the leader. Leaders have it when they know who they are and what they want and that they have the capacity to become what they want to become. Their life is an expression of what they espouse. Personal power also involves a sense of confidence in self; the group members know that this person knows what he or she is doing. And it involves a certain charisma; the members like the personal qualities of the group leader and would like to develop some of these same characteristics. Rather than talking about the importance of being alive, these leaders express and radiate an aliveness through their actions.

Power and honesty are closely related. In our view, powerful people are the ones who can show themselves. While they may be frightened by certain qualities within themselves, the fear doesn't keep them from examining these qualities. In contrast, powerless people need very much to defend themselves against self-knowledge. Powerless people are very vulnerable and, what's more, can't face this fact. Powerful people recognize and accept their weaknesses and don't expend energy concealing them from themselves and others.

There is often a great need in clients to see leaders not only as powerful but also as having all of the qualities that the members are striving for. Clients may view leaders as perfect, as super people who have "arrived." Such members tend to undercut their own power by giving their leader all of the credit for the insights that they, the members, are in fact responsible for. Powerful group leaders can accept credit where it's due and at the same time encourage clients to accept their own share of credit for their growth. There is a danger that group leaders will become infatuated with clients' perceptions of them as finished products. Group leaders who fall prey to this are likely to stifle their own ongoing growth.

Stamina. Group leading can be taxing and draining as well as exciting and energizing. Thus, a leader needs physical and psychological stamina and ability to withstand pressure, in order to remain vitalized throughout the course of a group. Some novice group counselors begin a group feeling excited and anticipate each session—until the group becomes resistive, or until members begin to drop out, or until members say that they feel the group is going nowhere. At this point, if a leader gives in to fatigue, any possibility that the group will be productive may be lost. This means that group leaders need to be aware of their own energy level and that they need to have outside sources of psychological and emotional nourishment. If they depend primarily on their group's progress for this, they run a high risk of being undernourished and thus of losing the stamina so vital to their success as leaders.

Willingness to seek new experiences. A therapist's personhood is partly determined by his or her experiences with various facets of living. A narrow range of life experiences restricts the capacity of a leader to understand the psychological worlds of clients, who may have different values resulting from different life experiences. If a group leader has lived a fairly sheltered life and has known little pain and struggle, how can he or she empathize with clients who have suffered and have made dramatic life choices? Can those therapists who have never experienced loneliness, joy, anguish, or uncertainty understand these conditions in their clients? While it is not possible for leaders to experience directly everything they may encounter in others, they should at least be committed to seeking a variety of life experiences.

Self-awareness. A central characteristic of any therapeutic person is awareness of self, including awareness of one's goals, identity, motivations, needs, limitations, strengths, values, feelings, and problems. The therapist who has a limited understanding of who and what he or she is will surely not be able to facilitate this kind of awareness in clients. As we've mentioned, being open to new life experiences and divergent life-styles is one way leaders can expand their awareness. Involvement in their own personal therapy, both group and individual, is another way for leaders to become more aware of who they are and who they might become. Awareness of why they choose to lead groups is crucial. What are the needs that are served by being a group leader? Group leaders with dim self-awareness, or leaders who keep themselves blinded for fear of what they might discover, are dangerous people in groups. How can they encourage others to risk finding out who they are if they themselves refuse to do it? Group leaders should be committed to an ongoing process of becoming increasingly aware of their own needs and motivations. Group leaders have a rich source of information about themselves; all they need to do is reflect on interactions they've had with members of their group.

Sense of humor. While therapy is serious business, there are truly humorous dimensions of the human condition. The ability to laugh at oneself and to see the humor in one's own human frailties can be extremely useful. At times people take themselves so seriously that they miss an opportunity to laugh at themselves and to thereby put into perspective the importance of their problems. Groups occasionally exhibit a real need for laughter and joking—simply for release of the tension that has built up. This is particularly true of intensive groups after sustained periods of dealing seriously with weighty problems. This release should not be viewed as an escape, for genuine humor can heal. The leader who can enjoy humor and infuse it effectively into the group process has an invaluable asset.

Inventiveness. The capacity to be spontaneously creative—to approach each group with fresh ideas—is a most important characteristic for group leaders. Freshness may not be easy to maintain, particularly if a therapist leads groups frequently. Leaders must somehow avoid becoming trapped in ritualized techniques or a programmed presentation of self that has lost all life. Leaders who are good at discovering new ways of approaching a group and who are willing to suspend the use of techniques that they know work are unlikely to grow stale. Working with interesting co-leaders is one way for leaders to get fresh ideas. Also, getting some distance from groups—for example, by doing fewer of them or doing other things or taking a vacation—may help a leader gain a fresh perspective.

Inventiveness in leaders involves the ability to detect clues that someone gives them and to create some way of exploring with the person the problem that is hinted at by these subtle clues. In this regard, it is important for group leaders to have a theoretical bias, for this will guide their selection of techniques. For instance, we find that we've been influenced by the psychoanalytic view of development, so that, when we lead groups, we invent techniques that aid people in tapping their memories of early childhood experiences. Thus you can see how, with a certain amount of inventiveness, leaders can use the theory they endorse as a source of fresh techniques.

GROUP-LEADERSHIP SKILLS

In the previous section, we discussed the importance of the group leader's personhood. We emphasized that personality characteristics such as openness, courage, directness, caring, empathy, self-knowledge, and so forth are central to effective leadership. We think it is a mistake, however, to assume that any human being with good will can be an effective therapist. The right personality characteristics are necessary to, but certainly not sufficient for, successful leadership. Basic skills must be learned and practiced. Like most skills, counseling skills can be taught, although there is also an element of art involved in their use. That is, leaders must decide how and when to use these skills, and the ability to do so sensitively is a function of supervised experience, practice and feedback, and confidence in one's use of these skills. Consider now some of the skills that group leaders need to acquire. As you read, keep in mind that, like personal qualities, skills are necessary to, but not sufficient for, effective leadership. Regardless of a therapist's skills, unless he or she is also the kind of person clients will want to emulate, he or she will not be very successful.

Active listening. It is most important to learn how to pay full attention to others as they communicate, and this involves more than merely listening to the words. It involves absorbing the content, noting gestures and subtle changes in voice or expression, sensing underlying messages, and, perhaps most important of all, intuiting what the person is not saying. Group leaders can improve their listening skills by first recognizing the barriers that interfere with paying attention to others. Some of these roadblocks are: not really listening to the other, thinking about what to say next instead of giving full attention to the other, being overly concerned about one's role or about how one will look to others, and judging and evaluating without putting oneself in the other person's place. Like any therapeutic skill, active listening exists in degrees. Some leaders are so intent on being in the spotlight that they can't focus on anything outside of themselves; other leaders have developed a high degree of perceptivity in discerning others' messages. The skilled group leader is sensitive to the congruence (or lack of it) between what a member is saying in words and what he or she is communicating through body posture, gestures, mannerisms, and voice inflections. For instance, a man may be talking about his warm and loving feelings toward his wife, yet his body may be rigid and his fists clenched. Or a woman, recalling a painful situation, may both smile and hold back tears.

Reflecting. Reflecting is dependent upon listening and hearing; it is the skill of reflecting the essence of what a person has communicated so that that person can see it. Many neophyte group leaders find themselves confining most of their interaction to mere reflection. Somehow it seems safe, and, since members continue to talk, leaders continue to reflect. Carried to its extreme, reflection can become a hollow echo, empty of any substance:

> *Client:* "I really didn't want to come to group today. I'm bored and I don't think we've gotten anyplace for weeks."
> *Group Leader:* "You didn't want to come to the group, because you're bored and the group isn't getting anywhere."

There was plenty of rich material here for the leader to respond to in a personal way, or with some confrontation, or by asking the person and the group to examine what was going on in the group. Beginning on a reflective level may have value, but staying on that level produces blandness. The leader might have done better to reply "You feel like quitting the group because you don't sense any involvement; you sound hopeless about getting much from this experience." The leader would then have been challenging the member to look at the emotions that lay beneath his words and, in the process, would have been opening up opportunities for meaningful communication.

Clarifying. Clarifying is a skill that can be valuably applied during the initial stages of an encounter. It involves focusing on key underlying issues and sorting out confusing and conflicting feelings. Thus, a girl might say "I hate my father, and I wish I didn't have to see him anymore. He hurts me so often. I feel guilty when I feel this way, because I also love him and wish he would appreciate me." And the therapist might clarify: "You have feelings of love and hate, and somehow having both of these feelings at once doesn't seem OK." Clarification can help the client sort out her feelings, so that eventually she can experience both love and hate without experiencing guilt. Stronger intervention methods than clarification may have to be used, however, before she can accept this polarity.

Summarizing. The group process can get bogged down or fragmented, and the skill of summarizing is useful. On the basis of a summary, decisions about where to go from there can be made. For example, some members might be arguing that the leader is not providing enough structure and direction, while other members are maintaining that the leader is handling the group correctly. If the interaction seems to be turning into a debate, the group leader might interrupt and have each person state briefly how he or she feels about the issue. The leader can then summarize and offer to the group possible alternatives.

Also, at the end of a session the leader might offer some summary statements or ask each member in turn to summarize. For instance, a leader might say "Before we close for today, I'd like each of us to make a statement about his or her experience in group today and tell where he or she is left." It's a good idea for the leader to make the first summary statement, so that the members will have a model for this behavior. However, sometimes the leader may want to close the session with his or her own reactions, after each participant has given a statement.

Interpreting. Group leaders who are highly directive are likely to make use of interpretation—offering possible explanations for certain behaviors or symptoms. If interpretations are accurate and well-timed, they may result in a member's moving beyond an impasse. It is not necessary that the leader always make the interpretation for the client; in Gestalt therapy, clients are encouraged to make their own interpretation of their behavior. Also, a group leader can present an interpretation in the form of a hunch, the truth of which the client can then assess. For instance, an interpretation might be stated as follows: "Harry, I've noticed that, most of the time when a person in the group talks about something painful, you intervene and become reassuring and in some way try to take that person's pain away. Does this say that you fear painful experiences yourself?" It is important that the interpretation be presented as a hypothesis rather than as a fact. Also important is that the person have a chance to consider the validity of this hunch in the group.

Questioning. In many ways, questioning is not much of a skill, and it is overused by many group leaders. Interrogation seldom leads to productive outcomes, and more often than not it distracts the person working. If a member happens to be experiencing intense feelings, questioning is one way of reducing the intensity. Asking "Why do you feel that way?" is rarely helpful. However, appropriately timed "what" and "how" questions do serve to intensify experiencing. Examples are questions such as: "What is happening with your body now, as you speak about your isolation?" "What ways do you experience the fear of rejection in this group?" "What are some of the bad things you imagine happening to you if you revealed your secrets to this group?" "How are you coping with your feeling that you can't trust some of the members here?" These questions direct the person to heighten feelings of the moment. Leaders should develop the skill of asking these kinds of questions and avoiding the kinds of questions that remove persons from themselves.

Linking. A group leader who has an interactional bias—that is, who stresses member-to-member rather than leader-to-member interaction—in leading groups makes frequent use of linking. This skill calls upon the insightfulness of the leader in finding ways of relating what one person is doing or saying to the concerns of another person. For example, Katherine might be describing her feeling that she won't be loved unless she's perfect. If Pamela has been heard to express a similar feeling, the leader could ask Pamela and Katherine to talk with each other in the group about their fears. By being alert for cues that suggest that members have some common concern, the leader can promote member interaction and raise the level of group cohesion.

Confronting. Beginning group leaders often are afraid to confront group members for fear of hurting them, or of being wrong, or of retaliation. It doesn't take much skill to attack another or to be merely critical. However, it does take both caring and skill to confront group members when their behavior is disruptive of the group functioning or when there are discrepancies between their verbal messages and their nonverbal messages. In confronting a member, a leader should (1) challenge specifically the behavior to be examined, avoiding labeling the person and (2) share how he or she feels about the person's behavior. For example, Danny has been very interruptive, pelting people with "why" questions and offering interpretations. The leader might intervene with "Danny, I really get annoyed with all your questioning and telling people how they are. Most of the time when you enter the group interaction you interpret others' behavior for them, and I still don't know much about you. I fear that, if you don't look at this, when the group ends you'll be a stranger. If that were to happen, I'd be disappointed."

Supporting. The skill in supportive behavior is knowing when it will be therapeutic and when it will be counterproductive. A common mistake is offering support before a participant has had an opportunity to fully experience a conflict or some painful feelings. While the intervention may be done with good intentions, it may abort certain feelings that a given client needs to experience. Another mistake is supporting game-playing behavior. For instance, if a woman is playing helpless and trying to convince everyone of how fragile she is, the leader would, by offering support, in effect foster her dependency. What the leader might do instead is confront the member with fact that she can do for herself what she's pleading for others to do for her. Support is appropriate when people are facing a crisis, when they're venturing into frightening territory, when they attempt constructive changes and yet feel uncertain about these changes, and when they're struggling to rid themselves of old patterns that are limiting. Leaders should remember that too much support can send the message that people are unable to support themselves.

Blocking. Group leaders have the responsibility to block certain activities of group members, such as questioning, probing, gossiping, invading another's privacy, breaking confidences, and so forth. The skill is to learn to block counterproductive behaviors without attacking the personhood of the perpetrator. This requires both sensitivity and directness. Some examples of behaviors that need to be blocked are:

1. *Bombarding others with questions.* Offenders can be asked to make direct statements out of their questions.

2. *Gossiping.* If a member talks *about* another member in the room, the leader can direct the person to speak directly to the person being spoken about.

3. *Story-telling*. If lengthy story-telling occurs, a leader can intervene and ask the person to say how all this relates to present feelings and events.

4. *Breaking confidences*. At times, a member may inadvertently talk about a situation that occurred in another group or mention what so-and-so did in a prior group. This should be stopped by the leader in a firm but gentle manner.

5. *Invasion of privacy*. If a person pushes another, probing for personal information, this behavior must be blocked by the group leader.

Like confrontation, blocking must be done both forcefully and tactfully, without an attack on the personhood of the offender.

Diagnosing. Diagnostic skills involve more than labeling behavior, identifying symptoms, and figuring out what category a person falls into. Diagnostic ability means the ability to appraise certain behavior problems and choose the appropriate intervention. For example, a leader who diagnoses a client as deeply angry must consider the safety and appropriateness of encouraging the client to "let out his pent-up rage." Leaders also need to develop the skill of determining whether a particular group is indicated or contraindicated for a member, and they need to acquire the expertise necessary to make appropriate referrals.

Reality-testing. A group is a place where participants can safely explore new alternatives that open up for them and where they can test the reality of some of their plans. Thus, group leaders should be aware of the importance of encouraging members to realistically appraise their alternatives. If a man spontaneously decides to quit his job, the leader can encourage him to think about what this might mean and what other possibilities are open to him. Or, if an adolescent decides to drop out of school, she can be directed to explore what the decision may mean in terms of her future.

The leader can best implement this process of reality-testing by having the other members give a person feedback on how realistic they consider the person's plans. It is important, however, that the leader caution the group not to tell the person what to do but rather to offer what they see as the possible outcomes of taking various alternative routes.

Evaluating. A crucial leadership skill is that of evaluating the ongoing process and dynamics of a group. After each group session, it is valuable for the leader to evaluate what happened, both within individual members and among the members, and to think about what kinds of interventions might be used next time with the group. Leaders need to get in the habit of asking themselves questions such as: What kinds of changes are resulting from the group? What are the therapeutic and antitherapeutic forces in the group?

Evaluation is a skill that the leader must teach participants, so that they can appraise the movement and direction of their own group. Once the group has evaluated a session or series of sessions, its members can decide what, if any, changes need to be made. For example, during an evaluation at the close of a session, the leader and the members are in agreement that the group as a whole has been passive. The leader might say "I feel the burden of initiating and sense that you're waiting for me to do something to energize you. I'm challenging each of you to examine your behavior and to evaluate to what degree you're personally responsible. Then please think about what, specifically, you're willing to do to change this group."

Facilitating. The group leader can facilitate the group process by (1) assisting members to openly express their fears and expectations, (2) actively working to create a climate of safety and acceptance in which people will trust one another and therefore engage in productive interchanges, (3) providing encouragement and support as members explore highly personal material or as they try new behavior, (4) involving as many members as possible in the group interaction by inviting and sometimes even challenging members to participate, (5) working toward lessening the dependency on the leader, (6) encouraging open expression of conflict and controversy, and (7) helping members overcome barriers to direct communication. The aim of most facilitation skills is to help the group members reach their own goals. Essentially, these skills involve opening up clear communication among the members and helping them to assure increasing responsibility for the direction of their group.

Empathizing. This skill involves sensing the subjective world of the client. In order to sensitively and accurately empathize with group members, a leader must listen actively to, care about, and respect the members. The leader must also have, in his or her background, a wide range of experiences, to serve as a basis for identifying with others. Finally, the leader must be able to discern subtle nonverbal messages as well as messages transmitted more directly. Yet, while it is very important for the group leader to be aware of what the members are experiencing, it is also important for the group leader to avoid blurring his or her identity by overidentifying with the group members. The core of the skill of empathy lies in being able to openly grasp another's experiencing and at the same time maintain one's separateness. It is impossible really to know what another person is experiencing, but a sensitive group leader can make a good guess.

Terminating. Group leaders must learn when and how to terminate their work with both individuals and groups. They need to develop the ability to tell when an individual is ready to leave a group, when a group has completed its work, and when a group session should end, and they need to learn how to handle each of these types of termination. The skill of terminating a single session or a whole group involves (1) providing the members with suggestions for transferring what they've learned in group to the environment they must return to, (2) creating a climate that will foster a willingness in the members to make contracts to do work between sessions or after the group, (3) preparing people for the psychological problems they may face on leaving a group, (4) arranging for a follow-up group, (5) telling members where they can get additional therapy, and (6) being available for individual consultation at the

termination of a group. Follow-up and evaluation activities are particularly important if the leader is to learn the impact of the group as a therapeutic agent.

Summary

Several points need to be emphasized about the group-leading skills we've
discussed. First, these skills can best be thought of as existing to various degrees,
rather than on an all-or-none basis. They can be highly developed and used in a
sensitive and appropriate manner, or they can exist to only a minimal degree.
Second, these skills can be learned and constantly improved—through training and
supervised experience. Third, these skills are not separate and discrete entities;
rather, they overlap a great deal. Active listening, reflection, and clarification are
interdependent, as are the skills of interpreting and diagnosing. Hence, by developing certain skills, a leader automatically improves other skills. Finally, these skills
cannot be divorced from the counselor's personhood, for the choice of which skills to
develop and use is an expression of the counselor's personality.

EXERCISES

Review the first section of this chapter and decide how you stand with respect
to each of the personal characteristics of a good leader. How are your strengths
manifested in your participation in groups? What are some specific ways in which
you need to improve?

Review the second section of this chapter and ask yourself to what degree you
have mastered the skills described. Rate yourself on the following self-assessment
scale for group leaders and then discuss, with a small group of class members, why
you rated yourself as you did. With your group, explore specific things you might do
to develop these skills.

Rate yourself from 1 to 7 on the following items.

1 = I am very poor at this.
7 = I am very good at this.

1. *Active listening:* I am able to hear and understand both direct and subtle
   messages.
2. *Reflecting:* I can mirror what another says, without being mechanical.
3. *Clarifying:* I can focus on underlying issues and assist others to get a
   clearer picture of some of their conflicting feelings.
4. *Summarizing.* When I function as a group leader, I'm able to identify
   key elements of a session and to present them as a summary of the
   proceedings.
5. *Interpreting:* I can present a hunch to someone concerning the reason for
   his or her behavior without dogmatically telling what the behavior means.
6. *Questioning:* I avoid bombarding people with questions about their
   behavior.

7. *Linking:* I find ways of relating what one person is doing or saying to the concerns of other members.
8. *Confronting:* When I confront another, the confrontation usually has the effect of getting that person to look at his or her behavior in a nondefensive manner.
9. *Supporting:* I'm usually able to tell when supporting another will be productive and when it will be counterproductive.
10. *Blocking:* I'm able to intervene successfully, without seeming to be attacking, to stop counterproductive behaviors (such as gossiping, story-telling, and intellectualizing) in group.
11. *Diagnosing:* I can generally get a sense of what specific problems people have, without feeling the need to label people.
12. *Evaluating:* I appraise outcomes when I'm in a group, and I make some comments concerning the ongoing process of any group I'm in.
13. *Facilitating:* In a group, I'm able to help others openly express themselves and work through barriers to communication.
14. *Empathizing:* I can intuitively sense the subjective world of others in a group, and I have the capacity to understand much of what others are experiencing.
15. *Terminating:* At the end of group sessions, I'm able to create a climate that will foster a willingness in others to continue working after the session.

The following evaluation form can be used in several ways. Group leaders can use it as a self-evaluation device, supervisors can use it to evaluate group leaders in training, group leaders can evaluate their co-leaders with it, and group members can use it to evaluate their leader.

Rate the leader from 1 to 7 on the following items.

1 = to an extremely low degree
7 = to an extremely high degree

1. *Support:* To what degree does the group leader allow clients to express their feelings?
2. *Interpretation:* To what degree is the group leader able to explain the meaning of behavior patterns within the framework of a theoretical system?
3. *Confrontation:* To what degree is the group leader able to actively and directly confront the client when the client is engaging in behavior that is inconsistent with what he or she says?
4. *Modeling:* To what degree is the group leader able to demonstrate to members behaviors he or she wishes them to emulate and practice both during and after the session?
5. *Assignment:* To what degree is the group leader able to direct the client to improve on existing behavior patterns or to develop new behaviors before the next group session?

6. *Referral:* To what degree is the group leader able to make available to the client persons capable of further assisting the client with personal concerns?

7. *Role direction:* To what degree is the group leader able to direct the client to enact specific roles in role-playing situations?

8. *Empathy:* To what degree does the group leader demonstrate the ability to adopt the internal frame of reference of the client and communicate to the client that he or she is understood?

9. *Self-disclosure:* To what degree does the group leader demonstrate a willingness and ability to reveal his or her own present feelings and thoughts to clients as it is appropriate to the group-counseling situation?

10. *Initiation:* To what degree is the group leader able to get interaction going among members or between leader and member?

11. *Facilitation:* To what degree is the group leader able to help clients clarify their own goals and take steps to reach these goals?

12. *Diagnosis:* To what degree is the group leader able to identify specific areas of struggle and conflict within each client?

13. *Following through:* To what degree is the group leader able to implement and follow through to reasonable completion work with a client in an area the client has expressed a desire to explore?

14. *Active listening:* To what degree does the group leader actively and fully listen to and hear the subtle messages communicated by clients?

15. *Knowledge of theory:* To what degree does the group leader demonstrate a theoretical understanding of group dynamics, interpersonal dynamics, and behavior in general?

16. *Application of theory to practice:* To what degree is the group leader able to appropriately apply a given theory to an actual group situation?

17. *Perceptivity and insight:* To what degree is the group leader able to sensitively and accurately extract the core meanings from verbal and nonverbal communications?

18. *Risk-taking:* To what degree is the group leader able to risk making mistakes and to profit from mistakes?

19. *Expression:* To what degree is the group leader able to express thoughts and feelings directly and clearly to clients?

20. *Originality:* To what degree does the group leader seem to have synthesized a personal approach from a variety of approaches to group leadership?

21. *Group dynamics:* To what degree is the group leader able to assist a group of people to work effectively together?

22. *Cooperation as co-leader:* To what degree is the group leader able to work cooperatively with a co-leader?

23. *Content orientation:* To what degree is the group leader able to help group members focus on specific themes in a structured type of group experience?

24. *Values awareness:* To what degree is the group leader aware of his or her own value system, aware of the client's value system, and able to avoid imposing his or her values on the client?
25. *Flexibility:* To what degree is the group leader able to change approaches—to modify style and technique—to adapt to each unique working situation?
26. *Awareness of self:* To what degree is the group leader aware of his or her own needs, motivations, and problems, and to what degree does the leader avoid exploiting or manipulating clients to satisfy his or her own needs?
27. *Respect:* To what degree does the group leader communicate an attitude of respect for the dignity and autonomy of the client?
28. *Care:* To what degree does the group leader communicate an attitude of genuine caring and concern for the client?
29. *Techniques:* To what degree is the group leader knowledgeable about techniques and able to use them well and appropriately to help clients work through conflicts and concerns?
30. *Ethical awareness:* To what degree does the group leader demonstrate awareness of and sensitivity to the demands of professional responsibility?

5. THE GROUP LEADER:
Basic Issues
in Group Leadership

1. How responsible are you for the outcomes of a group?

2. What is the value of techniques in groups? When are techniques useful? When do they inhibit?

3. Where are you on the directive/nondirective continuum as a leader? Does your active direction get in the way of the development by the group of a spontaneous and unique direction? When does your leadership squelch the initiative of the members? Does nondirection constitute avoidance of leadership responsibility? Do you ever find that, in attempting to be nondirective, you've let the group flounder?

4. How involved should group leaders become in terms of disclosing their own conflicts and unfinished business in a group that they're leading? Can this be merely a gimmick of leaders to prove to the members that they too are human and have problems? Is it possible for a group leader to be both participant and leader?

5. How do you deal with the fact that you feel differently toward different members? What do you do when you find yourself immediately attracted to a member? When you find a member boring? When you feel indifferent toward, threatened by, or angry with a member? How much do you reveal, and how soon?

6. What do you think is the role of a group leader? Should the leader be a therapist? A facilitator? Just another group member? A guru? A technician? A mother or father figure? An evaluator? A director?

7. What aspects of your behavior would you like members to model? Are you aware, as you lead a group, that you're a role model?

8. What are some of the fears that you, as a new leader, are experiencing? How do you plan to deal with these fears?

9. What is the place of theory in group work? How can adherence to a theoretical model be limiting? Useful? Can you transcend your training and develop your own style of leading? Who has influenced your style as a leader? What kind of a group leader do you wish to

become? How can you begin to develop a style that is consistent with your personality?

As a group leader, you'll find that you need to take a position on some basic issues. You will have to decide who is responsible for the direction of the group and whom to hold accountable for the success or failure of the group, how much and what kind of structure to provide, how much to disclose about yourself, how to recognize and deal with transference and countertransference, what the role and function of the group leader are, how to model for group members, how to develop a theoretical model to guide your practice in groups, and how to deal with various problems that arise in the course of groups. This chapter is designed to encourage you to formulate your own positions on these issues and to provide some guidelines that will help you do so.

THE DIVISION OF RESPONSIBILITY

A basic issue that group leaders must consider is the issue of responsibility for the direction and outcome of the group. If a group proves to be nonproductive, is this due to a lack of leader skill, or does the responsibility rest with the group members? One way of conceptualizing the issue of responsibility is by thinking of it in terms of a continuum. At one end is the group leader who assumes a great share of the responsibility for the direction and outcomes of the group. This type of leader tends to have the outlook that, unless the leader is highly directive, the group will flounder. Such leaders tend to see their role as that of the expert, and they actively intervene to keep the group moving in ways they deem productive. A disadvantage of this form of "responsible leadership" is that it robs the members of the responsibility that is rightfully theirs; if clients are perceived by the group leader as not having the capacity to take care of themselves, they soon begin to live up to this expectation by being irresponsible, at least in the group.

In the days when I (Jerry Corey) had just begun leading residential groups, I burdened myself with every detail. I even shook people out of their sleeping bags and goaded them to hurry during breakfast so that we could begin by 8:00 A.M. sharp! What resulted was a lot of resistance, until one courageous member finally told me "I feel that I don't need to take responsibility for starting on time, because you're so efficient. I really feel that you don't trust me enough to allow me to make the decision of whether I want to get someting from the workshop or not." Finally, I learned to distribute responsibility, and with better results. We then did begin at 8:00 A.M. (or a little earlier or later), but the members took the responsibility of getting themselves ready. This freed me to focus my energy on the more important group-leadership tasks and taught me the value of shared responsibility. I still wanted to start work on time, though. I stated to the group very clearly and unequivocally that I would like to begin on time and that their responsibility was to get themselves ready. In this way, I let my feelings be known and left the decision concerning how to use the workshop time up to the participants.

Leaders who assume an inordinate degree of responsibility not only undermine members' independence but also burden themselves. If people leave unchanged, they see it as their fault. If members remain separate, never forming a cohesive unit, such leaders view this as a reflection of their lack of skill as a leader. If the group is disappointed, these leaders feel disappointed and tend to blame themselves, believing that they didn't do enough to create a dynamic group. This style of leadership is draining, and leaders who use it may eventually lose the energy required to lead groups.

At the other end of the responsibility continuum is the leader who proclaims "I am responsible for me, and you are responsible for you. If you want to leave this group with anything of value, it is strictly up to you. I can't do anything for you—make you feel something or take away any of your defenses—unless you allow me to." This type of leadership frequently characterizes encounter-group leaders. It is not our preferred style. When people are together for a period of time in an intensive group, they need some protection, and we feel that it is irresponsible for the leader not to provide it.

Ideally, each leader will discover a balance whereby he or she accepts a rightful share of the responsibility but does not usurp the members' responsibility. This issue is central because a leader's approach to other issues (such as structuring and self-disclosure) hinges on his or her approach to the responsibility issue. The leader's personality is involved in the determination of the amount of responsibility he or she will assume and what, specifically, this responsibility will include.

THE ISSUE OF STRUCTURING

The proper question is not whether or not a group leader should provide structure but rather to what degree structure is to exist. Like responsibility, structuring exists on a continuum: At one end is the T-group leader, who typically does nothing at the onset of the group except wait for one of the members to assume the leadership. The entire T-group experience is often characterized by this lack of structure, in order that the participants will define their own structure. This style frequently results in negative feelings on the part of group members, who eventually attack the facilitators for not "doing what they're supposed to do."

At the opposite end of the continuum are the leaders who operate with a very structured program. They use structured exercises to open sessions, and throughout the group they employ exercises—to heighten experiencing, to focus members on a particular theme or problem area, to elicit certain feelings, such as anger or closeness, and even to induce states such as extreme loneliness or rage.

We don't believe in passive leadership, even though at times we are passive in a group. We don't prefer simply to wait and let the group go in any direction it happens to go. We believe that, by imposing some structure, we give group members the opportunity to experiment with new levels of awareness and to build new forms of behavior from this awareness. Some specific behaviors we often use to structure a group experience are (1) confronting a member who is blending into the woodwork and asking whether she is content to stay in the background, (2) confronting a person about a manipulative game he is using to get people to take an interest in him or to keep people at a distance, (3) suggesting that all the members take a fantasy journey in which they reexperience some feelings experienced at an earlier period, (4) expressing our impatience or boredom, or our delight and enthusiasm, when we feel it in group, (5) initiating certain nonverbal techniques when they seem appropriate to what someone is feeling, (6) asking each person to give feedback, (7) setting up specific role-playing situations when it seems appropriate, (8) encouraging someone to act out feelings in a symbolic way (such as by talking to her father in an empty chair), (9) confronting the group when it seems to be stuck at an impasse and offering to help the group around the impasse, (10) inviting people to work on problems, (11) providing support and eliciting group support when a member is struggling with some very difficult and scary material, (12) directing attention to nonverbal as well as verbal messages, (13) giving a member feedback on how we experience him, particularly if we see him behaving in a self-defeating way, and (14) pushing a person to test her own limits, without pushing too far.

In brief, we believe that some degree of structuring is essential in a group but that the structuring should not be so tight that it robs the group members of the responsibility of providing their own structure for the group. We don't favor an extremely unstructured style, nor do we feel comfortable with a highly structured and organized style of group leading. We find that we operate best with some general structure that permits member flexibility and encourages members to create their own unique structuring of the group.

SELF-DISCLOSURE AND THE GROUP LEADER

The key question here is not whether leaders should disclose themselves to the group but rather how much and when. What are the effects of leader disclosure on the group? What are the effects on the group leader?

Some group leaders keep themselves mysterious. They're careful not to make themselves personally known to their group, and they strive to keep their personal involvement in the group to a minimum. Some do this because of a theoretical preference, for they view their role as one of a "transference figure" on whom their "patients" can project feelings they've experienced toward parents and other "authority figures." By remaining anonymous, the leader tends to limit the reactions of group members to projections. Through this re-creation of an earlier relationship, unresolved conflicts can be exposed and worked through.

Other reasons why some group leaders don't reveal themselves personally are that they don't want to incur the risk of losing their exalted "expert" image and that they don't want to be uncomfortable. They strive not to "contaminate" the "doctor-patient" relationship, out of their stated concern that this will interfere with effective therapy. There are leaders who, in addition to keeping their personal lives a secret, disclose very little concerning how they feel in the group or how they feel toward different members. Instead of sharing these reactions, they intervene, making interpretations and suggestions, clarifying issues, acting as a moderator or coordinator, evaluating, and imposing structured exercises to keep the group moving. All of these functions are admittedly important, but, at the same time as leaders perform these functions, it is both possible and desirable for them to get involved in these activities by revealing what they are presently experiencing.

What about the leaders at the other end of the continuum, whose ethic is "the more disclosure, the better"? Inexperienced group leaders tend to make the mistake of trying too hard to prove that they're just as human as the members. They freely disclose details of their personal lives and explore their current problems in the groups they lead. These leaders may have submitted to group pressure to stop acting like a leader and become more of a group member. The motivation of the disclosing leader may be a desire to use part of the group time for his or her own development or a need to make himself or herself known in a personal way to group participants. The rationale for high disclosure may be that it is unfair to expect members to disclose and risk unless the leader is willing to do so also. While this reasoning has merit, it is important that the group leaders not fall into the trap of pretending that there are no differences between the roles and functions of leaders and members. That there are differences in function does not mean that one is more human than, or in some other way superior to, the other. It does mean that, even though group leaders can function as participants at times, their primary reason for being in the group is to initiate, facilitate, direct, and evaluate the process of interaction among members. If a leader is uncomfortable in the role of leader, perhaps this is an indication that he or she should be participating in a group as a full-fledged member.

It becomes evident that it is difficult to judge whether a leader's self-disclosure is facilitative and appropriate. To arrive at a decision, one needs to ask questions such as the following:

- What is the theoretical framework of the group leader?
- How genuine is the disclosure on the leader's part?
- What type of group is involved?
- What stage of development is the group at? (Is it the initial session, or have members been together for a time?)
- What is the nature of the disclosure?
- What was going on in the group just prior to the disclosure?

At this point, we will present some guidelines for your consideration in determining your own position on the issue of leader self-disclosure. We use these guidelines in our practice.

1. If group leaders determine that they have problems they wish to explore, they should seek their own therapeutic group, in which they can be fully participating members without the concern of how their work will affect the group. Group leaders have a demanding job and shouldn't make it even more difficult by confusing their role with that of the participant.

2. Leaders should ask themselves why they're disclosing certain personal material. Is it to be seen as regular people? Is it to model disclosing behavior for others? Is it because they genuinely want to show private dimensions to the members? It may be therapeutic for group members to know the leader and the leader's struggles, but they don't need to know it in elaborate detail. For instance, if a member is exploring her fear of not being loved unless she produces and is perfect, the therapist may reveal in a few words that she also wrestles with this fear. A sense of identification can be established in this way. At another time it may be appropriate for this leader to talk at more length about how this fear is manifested in the way she leads groups, particularly if it is manifested in a feeling of pressure to be a good therapist and a fear of not being loved if the group is not helped. Again, the timing is crucial. While this disclosure may be appropriate in the advanced stages of a group, sharing it initially may burden the participants with the fear that this leader is using the group for her own therapy.

3. Disclosure that is related to what is going on in the group is the kind of disclosure that is most productive. For instance, any persistent feeling a group leader has concerning a member or concerning what is happening or not happening is generally best revealed. If a leader feels annoyed at a member's behavior, it is advisable for him or her to let the member know this reaction. If a leader senses a general resistance in the group, it is best for him or her to talk openly about the resistance and about how it feels to experience this resisting. Disclosure related to how a leader feels in the group is generally more appropriate than disclosure of personal material that is not relevant to the ongoing interaction of the group.

4. The possible effects on the members of the disclosure must be considered. For example, in the first session of a week-long residential group, I (Jerry Corey) reported that I had concerns about my ability to be really present with the members. I went on to talk about how drained I felt after the end of that academic year and how I was beginning to grow tired of having the same life struggles. During the week I managed to become more energized, with the help of my two co-leaders. A member came to me at the end of the week and told me how uncomfortable that disclosure had made her—that she had hesitated to burden me with more problems and had wondered whether I would really be interested in helping her work through her confusions. So, leaders need to consider the possible aftereffects of their disclosures.

5. Group leaders have to ask themselves how much they want to reveal about their private lives to the many people they deal with. We regularly co-lead couples' groups, weekend workshops, week-long marathons, and other groups and classes. Do we want to be open books for all of these people? Our position is that we do want to feel the freedom to function openly as persons but that at the same time we want to preserve a measure of our privacy. At times we've been confronted by group members for not revealing more of our personal struggles. They feel they know us as leaders, they say, but want to know more about us personally. We want to take into consideration the fact that, in a given year, we may be exposed to 200 different people, in about 15 groups. If we told everything about ourselves to everyone, not only would we lose privacy; we would also lose spontaneity, for it would probably be impossible, with this kind of repetition, to maintain a fresh and unrehearsed style.

DEALING WITH TRANSFERENCE AND COUNTERTRANSFERENCE

An issue related to leader self-disclosure is how group leaders can best deal with transference and countertransference. Transference consists of the feelings that clients project onto the therapist. These feelings usually have to do with relationships the clients have experienced in the past, and, when they're attributed to the therapist, they're not realistic. Countertransference refers to the feelings that are aroused in therapists by clients—feelings that, again, have more to do with unresolved conflict in a past relationship than with any feature of the present relationship.

As we mentioned earlier, the group leader who places value on dealing with the transference relationship also adopts the position that intimate disclosure should be kept to a minimum. We believe that, regardless of the value a leader puts on exploring transferences, he or she should be aware of the kinds of feelings toward and expectations about their leader that members have. Unless these feelings are dealt with in group, meaningful work may never occur. Participants do have an image of the group leader, and at times this includes unrealistic expectations. We'll now describe some of the more common ways in which clients may initially perceive a group leader.

1. *The expert.* Some members enter a group because they're seeking direction and help. What they hope for is that the therapist will "cure" them—offer them a recipe for happiness or give them some quality that they don't believe they can find in themselves. Thus, they obediently, respectfully, and hopefully place their trust in the leader, waiting to be shown the way. They hope to increase their self-confidence, to know themselves better, to become more assertive, to feel more intensely, to lose their fears, and to gain courage. If they don't move in this direction, they may tend to resent the leader for not doing his or her job.

2. *The authority figure.* It is not uncommon for group members, during the initial phases of a group, to timidly reveal how stifled they feel in the presence of the group leader, whom they view as an authority figure. They say that they feel judged, that they feel inferior and insignificant when they're in the leader's presence, and that they don't see themselves as able to measure up to the leader's standards. These people may be psychologically bringing their parents with them to group; how they feel toward the group leader is much the way they've always felt toward their parents. By elevating the leader to a superior place, they discount their own worth. They can never really love or respect the group leader as a person, for they have too much resentment and fear.

3. *The superperson.* Clients often view their therapist as a superbeing. It is inconceivable to them that the leader may feel inadequate at times, or that his or her marriage may not be perfect, or that he or she does not have all the answers to human suffering. These clients are amazed if they discover that the leader is not a perfectly adjusted, self-actualized being. Perhaps the need here is to believe that the leader has "arrived" and that, therefore, the client can hope to do so too.

4. *The friend.* Some clients resent the professional aspects of a client-therapist relationship. Others experience jealousy over having to share "their therapist" with

others. Some say that the office structure—appointments, fees, waiting room, and so on—interferes with the spontaneity they would like. It may be true that a leader can be a therapist-friend—one who cares for members and is involved with them. However, it is not realistic for members to expect the therapist to be a friend. If clients rely too heavily on this therapeutic relationship for friendship, they may fail to develop friendships on the outside. The dynamics of making a friend out of a group leader are similar to the dynamics of making a parent out of the leader. Clients hope that the leader will care for them in a special way, that they will be approved of and even loved unconditionally, and that they will be seen as desirable by the leader.

5. *The lover*. Some group members want to convert the therapeutic relationship into a romantic one. In many ways, they may attempt to attract and seduce the group leader. They may feel that, if they succeed in getting the leader's special attention, they will hold a special place in the group. Chances are that they'll be disappointed, because they're usually searching for love that they never received as a child or for love that they don't now receive from others. So that, no matter what they experience with the leader, their expectations will not be fulfilled. Of course, seductive behavior often generates countertransference, which the group leader must deal with. This is true of all of the projections—whether a group leader is made into the expert, the authority figure, the superperson, the friend, or the lover. Unless the therapist is well aware of his or her own motivations and unresolved conflicts, there is a likelihood that the member-leader relationship will be antitherapeutic.

How can the group leader deal with transference? The answer is complex and depends on the circumstances under which the relationship develops. What follows are general guidelines.

First, the feelings should be brought out openly in the group. This also allows for consensual validation. In other words, if all the members see the leader as an aloof and distant expert, it may be that the leader indeed presents himself or herself that way and that this is not a transference situation.

Once these feelings are revealed, they can be explored, like any other problem that a member chooses to deal with in group. The best way for a member to resolve an "authority hang-up" is for him or her to confront the leader who represents this authority and to examine the intimidation experienced in the leader's presence. The member might simply talk about the feelings he or she has toward the leader. In addition, the leader might assume the role of the person's father or some other authority figure in the person's life. Roles can be reversed—the member becoming the parent and the leader becoming the member. This can be a useful feedback device; that is, the member can see how he or she is viewed by the leader. Also, while the member continues in the authoritarian role, the leader (or another group member) might take an assertive stance. In this way, an alternative response to authority is offered. The members might now resume dialogue with the "parent/leader," this time experimenting with the more forceful position that was demonstrated. Still another approach to this problem would be to use the Gestalt empty-chair approach, in which the member plays out both parts—the underdog and the top dog. These are but a few illustrations of how transference problems can be worked out. The important elements are (1) that the feelings are recognized and expressed and (2) that the feelings are then dealt with therapeutically.

A more delicate issue is how the leader can best deal with his or her own feelings toward a group member. Even in the Freudian tradition, which dictates that therapists spend years in analysis in order to understand and resolve blocked areas, countertransference is a potential problem. So it can be a very big problem for the beginning group leader. Some people are attracted to this profession because, on some level, they imagined that as a helper they would be respected, needed, admired, looked to as the expert, and even loved. Perhaps they have never experienced the acceptance and self-confidence in their ordinary lives that they experience while "helping others." Such leaders are using groups to fulfill needs that would otherwise go unmet.

The issue of need for power is germane here, for, as group members elevate the group leader to the level of expert, or perfect person, or demanding parent, they also give away most of their power to the group leader. A self-aware therapist who is interested primarily in the client's welfare will not encourage the client to remain in an inferior position. However, the insecure leader who depends on the underdog position of clients to give him or her a sense of adequacy and power will tend to keep the group member powerless.

Countertransference feelings are likely to develop in the romantic/sexual realm, particularly when an attractive group member indicates an attraction to a group leader. A group leader may never have felt attractive before becoming a group leader; he or she may even have felt ugly and rejected. Now, in the leader role, he or she feels desirable. The danger is that he or she will depend on group members for this feedback.

Dealing with countertransference openly in a group can compound the complexities of group process by generating negative feelings toward the group leader. At times it may be important that this is done. One of the advantages of working with a co-leader is that the partner can offer valuable feedback from an objective viewpoint and can help the other partner see things in himself or herself that had been blocked from awareness.

Group leaders who are in training may have the opportunity to explore with a supervisor feelings of attraction or repulsion toward certain members. Leaders who are conducting groups independently and who become aware of a pattern that indicates possible countertransference problems should seek consultation with another therapist or become a member of a group, to work through these problems.

Three additional points need to be emphasized to leaders:

1. Don't be gullible and believe uncritically whatever group members tell you—particularly initially. It's easy to become enamored with feedback that tells you how helpful, wise, perceptive, attractive, powerful, and dynamic you are; don't be swept away by the unrealistic attributions of group members.

2. Don't be overly critical and thus discount genuine positive feedback. All members who see a leader as helpful or wise are not suffering from "transference disorders." Members can feel genuine affection and respect for group leaders, and

this may be a function of the person of the therapist that they experience, not merely a transference reaction. By the same token, just because a participant becomes angry with the leader does not mean that this person is transferring anger toward the parents onto the leader. Participants can feel anger and have negative reactions toward the group leader personally. It may be true that the leader radiates a distant, know-it-all manner, or manipulates the group toward his or her own ends, or is seductive with certain members. In short, all feelings that members direct toward the group leader should not be ''analyzed'' as transferences to be ''worked through'' for the client's good. If a group leader hears consistent feedback, such as that he or she doesn't seem caring, then it is imperative that this feedback be seriously examined for its validity and, if deemed valid, acted upon.

3. Recognize that not all of your feelings toward members can be classified as countertransference. Some leaders operate under the misconception that they should remain objective and care for all members equally—that they should not be attracted to anyone in particular. Such leaders expect themselves to be superhuman. Counter-transference is indicated by exaggerated and persistent feelings that tend to recur with various clients in various groups. You can expect to enjoy some members more than others and to be sexually attracted to some members. Again, this is not some disease to be cured. What is important is that you recognize your own feelings for what they are and that you not get into emotional entanglements that are antitherapeutic.

THE ROLE OF THE GROUP LEADER

The demands of the group leader's role are often conflicting. When leaders structure and direct a group they are sometimes criticized for being controlling. Then, when they allow the group to exert more influence on the group's direction, they may be told that they're not providing enough leadership. If leaders use techniques, they may be told that these methods are contrived and gimmicky. Leaders who share their own problems with a group may sense that this burdens some participants, and leaders who act only as leaders may be told that they're not sharing enough of themselves. To be sure, the role of the leader is difficult.

We feel that a group leader's job is to initiate certain types of interaction, to direct the activities of the group, and to create a climate conducive to exploration of personally significant experiences. The leader is largely responsible for establishing an atmosphere in which people can trust one another, can behave in new ways, can question many of their basic beliefs and assumptions, and can risk making themselves known.

We see the group leader as demonstrating to others by example the way to more effectively relate. Thus, a leader needs to be more than a sterile embodiment of a role. He or she must be a person and be willing to share that personhood. If the leader hides behind professionalism (retreats into the role), then the group is also inhibited.

But leaders definitely have functions and responsibilities, too. For one thing, they must set limits. Although leaders don't need to prepare a lengthy list of ''dos'' and "don'ts," they do need to establish and explain to the members certain ground rules. We like to emphasize to members the importance of confidentiality, of deciding for themselves what they'll work on, and of not interacting in small groups when the entire group is working.

Group leaders have the responsibility of providing some direction and general orientation during the initial phases of a group. Leaders can emphasize early in the group that members should: allow themselves to experience their feelings; openly share their feelings; concentrate on how they feel at the present moment; respect their own and others' right to privacy and to decide what to work on in group; allow themselves to reexperience some old hurts, or moments of loneliness, or conflicting feelings; and learn how to deal with the parents that are still inside of them.

Group leadership involves subtly, sensitively, and *actively* leading. One leadership function involves being sensitive to whether an individual wants to work and what he or she wants to work on. Here the leader's job is to invite the individual to explore and to help the member experience more fully what he or she is presently feeling.

A leader needs to be tuned in to the mood changes of a group; the leader is also largely responsible for setting the tone in a group. For example, if a leader is emotionally involved in the group work, chances are that the members will also be involved. There are times when it appears that the entire group is resisting and no productive movement is occurring. It is the leader's responsibility to assist the members in exploring their resistance, but it is not the leader's responsibility to do anything to or for the members to get them working.

Effective leaders are protective, although not in a maternalistic way or paternalistic way. Rather, they are aware of certain dangers, and they try to minimize the chances of people being unduly hurt, psychologically or physically. For example, if a woman indicates a desire to "pass" on a given activity, or chooses not to explore a particular issue, her right to refuse should be protected. That is, the leader should intervene if some or all of the members pressure this individual to do what she has said she doesn't want to do. If several members gang up to confront an individual, the leader should intervene in this scapegoating. If nonverbal exercises are used, particularly ones that involve aggression (pushing, wrestling, holding down), the leader ought to be prepared to cope with the possible outcomes and is responsible for preventing the members from injuring themselves or one another.

Clarification, summarization, and integration of what has gone on and what has been learned are part of the leader's job. Leaders need to direct attention to ways in which people can profit maximally from the group experience and to help members crystallize their new feelings.

Group leaders have the important function of helping the group become aware of its own dynamics. They can do this by encouraging the members to consider what directions the group is taking, how cohesive the group is, what barriers are preventing the group from working effectively, and whether any unspoken contracts or conspiracies exist among the members.

Helping participants to discover at what point they stopped is another function of leadership. Often a person will delve into a struggle and then stop at a certain point, without having experienced that struggle fully. It is the leader's task to help the person become aware of when and why and how he or she short-circuited the feeling.

The Group Leader as Model

There is, of course, controversy over what the primary role of a group leader is, and the answer depends largely on the theoretical orientation of the person asked. In our judgment, modeling is one of the most important functions of leadership. Group leaders would do well to recognize the extent to which their behavior influences the group. Through their behavior, and the attitudes conveyed by it, leaders can create such group norms as openness, seriousness of purpose, acceptance of others, and the desirability of taking risks. Leaders exercise this influence on the group process by virtue of their position as leader.

We believe that group leaders teach largely by example—by doing what they expect members to do. They must realize that their role differs from that of the group member, but they mustn't hide behind a professional facade. By engaging in honest, appropriate, and timely self-disclosure, group leaders can both participate as members in group process and fulfill the leadership function of modeling.

PROBLEMS AND ISSUES FACING BEGINNING GROUP LEADERS

Those who are just beginning to lead groups typically feel overwhelmed by the number of potential problems. New leaders ask themselves questions such as:

- Will I be able to get the group started? How?
- What techniques should I use?
- Should I wait for the group to initiate?
- Do I have what it takes to follow through, once something has been initiated?
- What if I make mistakes? Can I cause someone serious psychological damage?
- Do I know enough theory? Can I apply whatever I do know in groups?
- Should I share my anxiety with my group?
- How much should I participate as a member?
- What do I do if there is a prolonged silence?
- What if the entire group attacks me?
- How do I know whether the group is helping people change?
- How can I work with so many people at one time?

These are but a few of the concerns of inexperienced leaders. (Seasoned leaders often wrestle with the same issues.) Before they begin, group leaders cannot be guaranteed effectiveness. Hence courage is a necessary characteristic of group leaders—the courage to function under conditions of uncertainty. Group leaders will make mistakes, and, if they can admit them, they will learn from them. It is important that leaders not be harshly critical of themselves—that they not work under self-imposed standards of perfection.

One problem that new group leaders will probably be confronted with is receiving negative reactions from group members. If a leader structures a group by using techniques, he or she may be accused by members of constricting their freedom, and the members may rebel by refusing to cooperate with the structure. On the other hand, members may direct negative reactions toward a nonstructuring leader for allowing them to flounder, and they may wait passively for the leader to initiate some exercise. Group leaders need to learn how to confront the members with these reactions in a nondefensive way. If leaders become tight and defensive, the members may become increasingly defensive. Thus an undercurrent of unresolved hostility will develop that will muddle up any further work.

Beginning group leaders would do well to realize that it will take time to develop leadership skills to the point that they feel they're effective leaders. Many feel like quitting after leading only a few sessions; such people usually want to be accomplished leaders without experiencing the self-doubts and fears that may be necessary to the development of a leader. Some feel devastated if they don't receive an abundance of positive feedback. It probably cannot be mentioned too many times that some struggle and uncertainty are almost surely going to be a function of learning how to lead well. Nobody expects to perfect any skill (skiing, playing the guitar, making pottery, and so on) in a few introductory lessons. Those who finally experience success at these endeavors are the ones who have the endurance to progress in increments. The same can be said of group therapists, although their success depends not only on native skill and supervision but also on involvement in their own personal therapy. There is probably no better teacher than experience, but unguided experience may be less than helpful. Immediate feedback, from a supervisor, from co-leaders, or from other leader trainees in a training group, enables leaders to profit from their experience.

THE GROUP LEADER'S THEORETICAL MODEL

The group leader who attempts to function without an explicit theoretical framework is like the pilot who flies without a map and without instruments. To operate successfully, leaders must operate on the basis of certain specifiable assumptions regarding the nature of the person, the goals of a group, and the role of both leader and member.

It is beyond the scope of this book to survey the various group theories (except as done in Chapter 1), but we want to stress that group leaders seeking to develop professional competency need exposure to various and even contrasting theories of counseling. We aren't advocating rigid entrenchment in one theory; rather, we encourage leaders to read about and study various group models, so that they can develop a rationale for organizing a group and for functioning in a certain way in the group. Unfortunately, too many leaders are practice oriented, which means that they use certain techniques but can't say why. By thinking about the different therapeutic group models, leaders may be stimulated to examine questions such as:

1. What is the nature of human beings?
2. How can I incorporate my philosophy of human nature into the way I lead groups?
3. Can people be trusted to determine their own direction in a group, or do they need strong intervention from the leader to keep them moving productively?
4. Who should determine the goals of the group? The members? The group leader?
5. How specific should goals be?
6. What is the group leader's role? Facilitator? Director? Expert? Consultant? Resource person?
7. How much responsibility for the ongoing process lies with the group leader? With the members? To what degree should the group be structured by the leader?
8. Should the leader have an individual focus or a group-interaction focus? That is, should the leader work with one person at a time or encourage maximum interaction among members?
9. How much personality change is desirable? Should the focus be on attitude change or on behavior change?
10. What are the functions of group members?
11. What techniques are the best? Why?
12. What are the criteria for measuring the success of a group?

These are examples of issues that group leaders can clarify to their satisfaction by reference to a chosen theory. Ultimately, the most meaningful perspective of group is one that is an extension of the values and personhood of the group leader. A theory is not something divorced from the essence of the person; at best, it is an integral part of the person and an expression of the person's uniqueness. It is unrealistic to expect group leaders in training to have integrated a well-defined theoretical model with their practice. This may take years of extensive reading and practice in leading groups. Group leaders should devote considerable time to thinking about and discussing with others their ideas about issues in group practice.

The process of developing a personalized group model that guides one's practice is obviously an ongoing one; the model continually undergoes revision. With increased experience, the leader develops new questions. Experiments are tried, clinical hunches put to the test. By talking to fellow group leaders, leaders can get ideas for modifying old practices to fit new knowledge. The good group leader constantly questions his or her mode of operation and makes changes over time.

As we've suggested, in developing a personalized approach to group practice, leaders can select certain features from various models and combine them into a method that is appropriate to their personality and to the kind of group they lead. For example, a given group leader might rely heavily on the following concepts:

• *from TA:* the contract; early decisions and the client's capacity for redeciding; confrontation about games that prevent intimacy; and becoming aware of scripts that people are living out by following parental injunctions.

• *from Gestalt therapy:* focus on polarities within the person and on unfinished business from the past that interferes with the present; emphasis on the here-and-now; direct experiencing of feelings rather than talking about feelings; reexperiencing earlier events as though they were occurring now; use of role-playing in which a member plays each of the parts in a conflict; and use of exercises to heighten experiencing.

• *from psychoanalysis:* focus on resistance, transference, and other unconscious mechanisms and attention to the events of the first five years of life as important influences on current personality structure.

• *from existential therapy:* focus on people's capacity to make choices; stress on human conditions of loneliness, despair, guilt, and anxiety; emphasis on expanding awareness; and stress on risk-taking.

• *from behavior therapy:* contracts that delineate concrete client goals; desensitization activities, use of reinforcement procedures to decrease undesired behaviors and increase desired ones; role-training, coaching, behavior rehearsal, and other methods of assertiveness training; immediate feedback to direct new learning; and learning new behavior by experimenting in group.

• *from rationale-emotive therapy:* the concept that people indoctrinate themselves with irrational beliefs; learning to rigorously challenge one's belief system to determine the validity of one's assumptions; and homework assignments in rational behavior.

• *from reality therapy:* emphasis on accepting what is and emphasis on making decisions about the quality of one's behaving and committing oneself to a new course of action.

• *from client-centered therapy:* emphasis on trust, acceptance, empathy, genuineness, and understanding and the use of listening, reflecting, clarifying, and being fully present.

As you can see, each therapeutic approach involves certain concepts that can be valuable in a group leader's practice. By learning about these group perspectives, new leaders can lay a foundation on which to build their own theory of practice. We highly recommend that, in addition to reading, group leaders experience a range of types of workshops. In this way, the practitioner can gradually refine his or her leadership approach.

The reader who wants to pursue in more depth the ways and means of creating a personalized theory can refer to *Theory and Practice of Counseling and Psychotherapy,* by Gerald Corey.

EXERCISES

Attitude Questionnaire on Group Leadership

Below are some statements concerning the role and functions of a group leader. Indicate your position on each statement, using the following scale:

1 = strongly agree
2 = slightly agree
3 = slightly disagree
4 = strongly disagree

1. It is the leader's job to actively work at shaping group norms.
2. Leaders should teach group members how to observe their own group as it unfolds.
3. The best way for a group leader to function is by becoming a participating member of the group.
4. It is generally wise for leaders to reveal their private lives and personal problems in a group that they are leading.
5. A group leader's primary task is to function as a technical expert.
6. It is extremely important that a good leader have a definite theoretical framework that determines how he or she functions in a group.
7. A group leader's function is to draw people out and make sure silent members participate.
8. Group leaders influence group members more through modeling than through the techniques they employ.
9. Generally, it is best for the leader to give some responsibility to the members but also to retain some.
10. A major task of a group leader is to keep the group focused on the here-and-now.
11. It is unwise to allow members to discuss the past or to discuss events that occurred outside of the group.
12. It is best to give most of the responsibility for determining the direction of the group to the group members.
13. Group leaders should limit their self-disclosures to facts that have to do with what is now going on in the group.
14. If group leaders are basically open and engage in disclosing themselves, transference by members will not occur.
15. A leader who experiences countertransference is not competent to lead groups.
16. Group leaders should develop a personalized theory of leadership based on ideas drawn from many sources.
17. To be effective, a group leader must recognize his or her reasons for wanting to be a group leader.

18. Part of the task of group leaders is to determine specific behavioral goals for the group participants.
19. A group leader's theoretical model has little impact on the way people actually interact in a group.
20. If group leaders have mastered certain skills and techniques, it is not essential for them to operate from a theoretical framework.

After you have completed this self-inventory, we suggest that your class break into small groups to discuss each item.

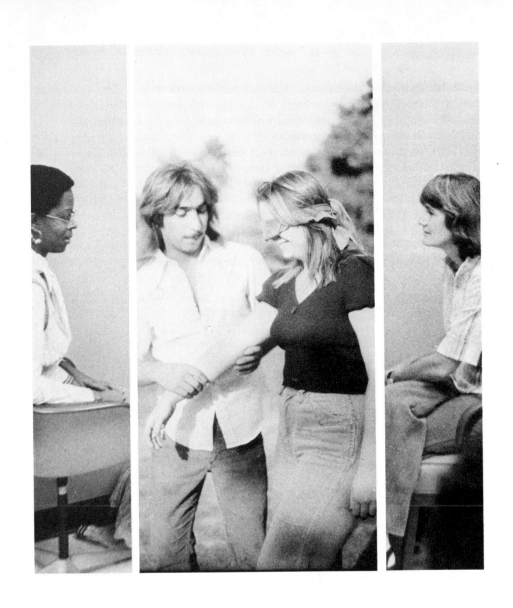

6. THE FORMATION AND
INITIAL STAGES OF
A GROUP

1. What kinds of issues do you think leaders should consider in organizing a group?

2. What kind of criteria would you use to select members for a group?

3. What are some crucial things that you would want to do during the
   initial stages of a group?

4. How would you, as a group leader, help to create a trusting climate
   within a group?

5. What importance do you place on preparing members for a group
   experience? What are a few of the things you might do by way of
   preparation?

In forming a group, one must begin by clarifying the rationale for the particular
group. The group leader needs to devote considerable time to planning, if the
experience is to be a successful one. In our judgment, planning should begin with the
drafting of a detailed proposal. The issues that need to be thought through carefully
are: what type of group it will be, what population it will serve, what the goals will
be, why this type of group is needed, what leader qualifications are required, what
screening and selection procedures are appropriate, what the ground rules will be,
what the structure and format will be, what techniques might be useful, and what
follow-up and evaluation procedures will be appropriate.

We cannot overemphasize the importance of the preparatory period, for,
if leaders make thorough preparations, the risks that we described earlier will be
reduced. The more clearly group leaders can state their expectations, the better they
will be able to plan, and the more meaningful will be the experience for the
participants.

OUTLINE FOR DEVELOPING A PROPOSAL
FOR A GROUP

Many good ideas for groups are never put into practice, because they are not
developed into a clear and convincing proposal. If you are going to create a group
under the auspices of an agency, you probably will have to explain to representatives

of the agency your proposed goals and methods. The following questions are the kind you should consider in preparing your proposal.

1. What type of group will it be? A personal-growth type group or a group designed to treat people with certain disorders? Long-term or short-term?
2. Whom is the group for? For a specific population, such as college students or married couples? For people seeking a certain thing, such as personal growth or help with a personal problem?
3. What are your goals for this group? That is, what will members gain from participating in it?
4. Why do you feel that there's a need for such a group?
5. What are the basic assumptions underlying this project?
6. Who will lead the group? What are his or her qualifications?
7. What kind of screening and selection procedures will be used? What is the rationale for using these particular procedures?
8. How many members will be in the group? Where will the group meet? How often? How long will each meeting last? Will new people be allowed to join the group once it has started?
9. How will the group members be prepared for the group experience? What ground rules will be established by the leader at the outset?
10. What kind of structure will the group have? What techniques will be used? Why are these techniques appropriate?
11. How will you handle the fact that people will be taking some risks by participating in the group? What will you tell the members about this, and what will you do about it? Will you take any special precautions with participants who are minors?
12. What evaluation procedures do you plan? What follow-up procedures?
13. What kinds of topics will be explored in this group? To what degree will this be determined by the group members and to what degree by the leader?
14. What do you expect to be the characteristics of the various stages of the group? What is the function of the leader at each stage? What might the problems be at each stage, and how will the leader cope with them?

SELECTION PROCEDURES

After a group proposal has been designed and accepted, the next step is the selection of members. This raises the questions: What kind of screening method should be used? Who should be included in and who excluded from the group?

The type of group should determine the kind of members accepted. A person who can work well in a group that meets once a week for an hour and a half might not be ready for an intensive weekend marathon group. Psychotics would probably be excluded from a personal-growth workshop yet might benefit from a weekly group for outpatients at a mental-health center. The question that needs to be considered is:

Should this particular person be included in this particular group at this time with this group leader?

We endorse screening procedures that include a private session between the candidate and the leader. During the private session, the leader might look for evidence that the group will be beneficial to the candidate. Some questions to consider are: Is this person motivated to change? Is this a choice of the individual or of someone else? Why this particular type of group? Does he or she understand what the purposes of the group are? Are there any indications that group counseling is contraindicated for this person at this time?

Group applicants should be given the opportunity, at their private session, to interview the group leader. They should be invited to ask questions concerning the procedures, basic purposes, and any other aspect of the group. This questioning is important not only as a means of getting information but also as a means of developing a feeling of confidence in the group leader, which is necessary if productive work is to take place. In other words, we believe that screening should be a two-way process and that potential members should be encouraged to form a judgment about the group and the leader. Given enough information about the group, a member can make a wise decision about whether to enter it.

In addition to the private screening session, a pre-group session for all of the candidates is extremely valuable. At a preliminary session, the leader can outline the reason for the group and the topics that might be explored. This can be most helpful for people who are uncertain whether they want to invest themselves in this group. Potential members can meet one another and begin to explore the potential of this kind of group.

We admit that screening and selection procedures are subjective and that ultimately the intuition and judgment of the leader are crucial. We are less concerned with whether candidates will benefit from a group than we are with whether they'll be psychologically hurt by it and whether they'll drain the group's energies excessively. Certain members, while unaffected by a group, sap its energy for productive work. This is particularly true of hostile people, people who monopolize, extremely aggressive people, and people who act out. The potential gains of including certain of these members must be weighed against the probable expense of a fragmented group. Some other types of people for whom we feel group counseling is contraindicated are the suicidal, the extremely fragmented or acutely psychotic, sociopathic personalities, people in extreme crises, the highly paranoid, and the extremely self-centered.

GROUP COMPOSITION

The choice of the composition of a group must depend on the type of group. The solution to the problem of heterogeneity versus homogeneity is found in the goals of a particular group. Some groups are by their very nature relatively homogeneous, such as groups for children, adolescents, the aged, the overweight, alcoholics, professionals, couples, and so on.

In general, for a specific target population with given needs, a group composed entirely of members of that population is more appropriate than a heterogeneous group. Consider a group composed entirely of old people. It can focus exclusively on the unique problems that characterize their developmental period, such as loneliness, isolation, lack of meaning, rejection, deterioration of the body, and so forth. The likeness of the members can lead to a great degree of cohesion, which in turn allows for an open and intense exploration of this life crisis. Members can express feelings that have been kept private, and their age can give them a bond with one another.

However, a case can sometimes be made for combining people from different populations in a single group. In one of her "Death and Dying" seminars, Dr. Elisabeth Kübler-Ross shared her dream of having children on every ward for the elderly. She maintains that this would give the elderly a chance to share their lives and experiences with children and to get the meaning from life that comes from taking care of children. The children would benefit by getting the opportunity to experience older people. Thus, a combination of these two age groups could have some unique therapeutic results for members of both age groups.

But, as we've shown, homogeneity fosters cohesion. Examples of homogeneous groups are Alcoholics Anonymous, Synanon, Recovery Inc., Parents without Partners, and Weight Watchers. It is common to hear people claim that, unless one has actually experienced what it is like to be, for example, an alcoholic, one cannot fully understand, and thus cannot help with, an alcoholic's unique problems. We don't accept the premise that in order to have a therapeutic impact on a client the group leader must have experienced every problem of the client. It is important only that a group leader be able to identify with the feelings of clients—his or her loneliness, fear, and anxiety. However, when a specific problem exists, group cohesion can help, and so homogeneity is appropriate.

On the other hand, sometimes a microcosm of the outside social structure is desired, and in that case a heterogeneous group is, of course, called for. Personal-growth groups and certain therapy groups tend to be heterogeneous. Members can experiment with new behavior and develop interpersonal skills with the help of feedback from a rich variety of people in an environment that represents out-of-group reality.

PRACTICAL CONSIDERATIONS IN THE FORMATION OF A GROUP

Group size. What is a desirable size for a group? This depends on several factors: the age of the clients, the experience of the leader, the type of group, and the kinds of problems to be explored. For instance, a group composed of elementary-school children might be kept to 3 or 4, while a group of adolescents might be made up of between 8 and 10 persons. For a weekly ongoing group of adults, about 8 people with 1 leader may be ideal, but, for a week-long residential workshop with co-leaders, 15 people make a good working group. A group of this size is big enough to give plenty of opportunity for interaction and small enough for everyone to be involved and to feel a sense of ''group.'' A group of this size can also be broken up into subgroups with co-leaders.

Frequency and duration of meetings. How often should a group meet? For how long? Should a group meet twice weekly for one-hour sessions? Or is an hour and a half to two hours once a week preferable? With children and adolescents, it may be better to meet more frequently and for a shorter period, to suit their attention span. If the group is taking place in a school setting, the meeting times can correspond to regularly scheduled class periods. For groups of college students or relatively well-functioning adults, a two-hour weekly session might be preferable. This two-hour period is long enough to allow some intensive work yet not so long that fatigue sets in. Of course, you can choose any frequency and duration that suit your style of leadership and the type of people in your group.

Length of group. What should the duration of a group be, and is it wise to set a termination date at the beginning of a group? We believe that, with most groups, a termination date should be set and announced at the outset, so that the members will have a clear idea of the time limits under which they are working. Our college groups typically run about 15 weeks — the length of a semester. With high school students, the same time period seems ideal, for it is long enough for trust to develop and for work toward behavioral changes to take place but not so long that it seems to be dragging on interminably.

Place for group meetings. Where should the group hold its meetings? Many places will do, but privacy is essential; the members must feel that they will not be overheard by people in adjoining rooms. We like a group room that's not cluttered up with chairs and tables and that instead allows for a comfortable seating arrangement. We prefer a setting that allows the group to sit in a circle and that allows enough freedom of movement that the members can spontaneously make physical contact with one another.

Voluntary versus involuntary membership. Should a group be composed of volunteer members only? Or can work with involuntary members sometimes be productive? Obviously there are a number of advantages to working with a group of clients who wish to invest themselves in the group process and who are motivated to change and committed to working. If a group experience is presented in a favorable light to members who are forced, for example by the mental-health facility in which they reside, to participate in a group, then the chances of productive work taking place will be increased. Counseling involuntary clients presents a number of problems, for, although clients can be required to attend sessions, they can't be forced to work. If the motivation for change is lacking, a group counselor may experience great frustration.

Open versus closed groups. Should a group be open or closed? Regardless of the decision, the issue needs to be clarified at the initial session. There are some advantages to incorporating new members into the group as certain members leave, for this can provide new stimulation. However, this practice makes cohesion difficult, particularly if too many clients drop out or too many new clients are introduced at once. In an ongoing group, we prefer to bring in new members one at a time as openings occur. In a closed group, the expectation is that the entire group will remain as a unit until the termination date. If a person decides to leave, the group merely becomes smaller. It is a good idea to discuss with the members at the initial session whether they would prefer an open or closed group.

THE INITIAL STAGES OF A GROUP

The Group Intake, or First Session

At the initial group session, the leader can explore the members' expectations, clarify the goals and objectives of the group, discuss procedural details, impart some information about group process, and answer members' questions.

The structuring of the group, including the specification of procedures and norms, should be accomplished early in the history of the group. Some of this structuring should have been done during the individual intake session, but a continuation of the structuring of the group should be the focus of the first few sessions.

What kinds of procedural issues need to be explored at this initial session? Group counselors should either establish ground rules or ask the group to do so. Rules need to be outlined concerning such issues as confidentiality; regular attendance and promptness; eating, drinking, and smoking during the sessions; the availability of private sessions in conjunction with group meetings; subgrouping, or formation of cliques; socializing outside of the group; physical expression of aggression; attempting to stay in the here-and-now; and in-group sexual behavior. All expected behavior—being direct, avoiding excessive questioning, disclosing personal material, and so on—needs to be specified.

Dealing with Resistance

Regardless of the type of group, there is likely to be some resistance, often arising from fearful expectations. If these fears can be put to rest at the outset, the whole group will benefit.

Because we recognize that anxieties exist, we begin by encouraging the members to openly share and explore them. It sometimes helps in the building of a trusting atmosphere to ask people to split up into pairs and then to join pairs and make a group of four. In this way, members can choose others with whom to share their expectations, get acquainted, discuss their fears or reservations, and so forth. For some reason, talking with one other person and then merging with others is far less threatening to most participants than talking to the entire group. This subgroup approach seems to be an excellent icebreaker, and when the entire group gets together again there is generally a greater willingness to interact.

What are some fears that clients typically experience? The following anxieties do not seem uncommon:

- I'm afraid I'll look stupid.
- What if I find I'm abnormal?
- Will I tell too much about myself?
- Will I be accepted by the group?
- What if I find out what I'm really like?
- What if everyone rejects me?
- I'm afraid I'll be withdrawn and passive.
- I fear being hurt.
- What if the group attacks me?
- I'm afraid of seeing my problems magnified.
- What if I become dependent on the group?
- What if I find out things about myself that I can't cope with?
- Will I physically hurt someone if I'm really open to my feelings?
- What if I go crazy?
- What will my spouse feel/think if I talk about him/her?
- What if I'm asked to do something I don't want to do?
- What if I stutter and shake?

During the initial phase of a group, the members typically appear rather resistant. This resistance needs to be faced and the factors contributing to it discussed. In some cases, the participants are highly suspicious of the group leaders, fearing being manipulated. The participants may doubt that counseling groups can be of any real value in helping them solve their problems. There are some clients who will not believe that they have the freedom to talk about whatever they want in whatever manner they choose, so they will sit back and wait, almost expecting to be lectured at.

Trust versus Mistrust

The issue of trust versus mistrust is one of the most basic issues in group process. If a basic sense of trust and security is not established at the outset, serious problems can be predicted. People can be said to be developing trust in one another when they can express their feelings, no matter what they are, without fear of censure; when they are willing to decide for themselves specific goals and personal areas to explore; when they focus on themselves, not on others; and when they are willing to risk disclosing personal aspects of themselves.

In contrast, a lack of trust is indicated by an undercurrent of hostility and suspicion and an unwillingness to talk about these feelings. Other manifestations of lack of trust are participants' taking refuge in being abstract or overly intellectual, talking endlessly about others but refusing to focus on themselves, and being vague about what they expect from the therapeutic group. Before a climate of trust is established, people tend to wait for the leader to decide for them what they need to examine. Any disclosures that are made tend to be superficial and rehearsed, and risk-taking is at a low level.

The Struggle for Power

Conflict frequently characterizes the beginning stages of a group. It is common for negative feelings to be expressed as the participants attempt to form a group identity. The group may look to the leaders and demand that they become more directive and guide them in making progress. If the group leader is directive, initiating certain structured exercises, the group members may accuse him or her of not giving them enough freedom to shape the direction of their own group. Power struggles among the members may occur.

Attacking the leader is very often a vital part of the power struggle of a group; the manner in which the leader responds is crucial. It is a mistake for the leader to become overly defensive or to hide behind the leader role. The leader must realize that, if a group feels safe enough to challenge its leader, it may very well be in transition to a more meaningful working stage. During this transitional period, the group leader must have a clear picture of his or her role, not slipping into a detached, guarded, professional stance and not pretending that he or she is just another member. What is important is that leaders demonstrate, through appropriate self-disclosure, what they expect of the members. By discussing his or her feelings about the power struggle going on, the leader can both initiate discussion of the problem and model appropriate group behavior.

Self-Focus versus Other-Focus

One characteristic we observe in members of most beginning groups is a tendency to talk about others and to focus on people and situations outside of the group setting. At times, story-telling participants will deceive themselves into believing that they are really working, when in fact they're resisting speaking about and dealing with their own feelings. They may talk about life situations, but there is a tendency to focus on what other people in their lives are doing to cause them difficulties. The skilled group leader helps the members who have an other-focus to develop in such a way that they become willing to examine their own reactions to others. Leaders do this by teaching participants that they are responsible for their own problems and that they're free to make choices.

The demanding job, during the initial phase of a group, is to get the group members to focus on themselves. Of course, trust is a prerequisite for this openness about oneself. When members deviate from a self-focus and use other-focus as a method of resisting deeper exploration of self, then leaders should remind them of the value of focusing on themselves. Leaders need to learn to confront members who are using this defense, in such a manner that the members will not defensively close themselves off from what the leader or other members are saying. An awareness of proper timing is essential; the readiness of a client to accept certain interpretations or observations must be considered. Leaders must be skilled not only in helping people recognize that their other-focus is defensive but also in giving them the courage to work through their resistance.

HOW WE PREPARE FOR GROUPS

Because we believe that involvement, enthusiasm, inventiveness, and caring are important in group leaders, we believe that we need to be physically and psychologically ready for every new group or workshop that we lead. We have found that, in order to avoid becoming programmed group leaders, or programming a certain course for our groups, we must spend some time, away from our daily routines, thinking about the group that will shortly be convening.

Whether the group is a weekend workshop of skills training for counselors and teachers, a couples group, or a week-long intensive personal-growth group, we generally arrange to spend a day or at least several hours together before we begin. Not only is it important for us to reflect on the goals and structure that we would like a particular workshop to have; it is also important for us to talk about ourselves with each other. How are things between us? Are there any sources of friction between us that might interfere with the progress of the group? Do we feel good enough about ourselves and each other to devote our energy to the demanding tasks of group leadership, or will our unspoken conflicts drain off our vitality and energy? Are we feeling nurtured by each other and excited by the prospect of working together?

Our summer residential workshops come after a busy school year, and so we feel a need to shift gears and become psychologically ready for them. Sometimes at the end of spring we realize that we've both been so involved with the demands of our separate projects that we've neglected to make contact with each other or failed to resolve certain grievances between us. Even though we may not work through all of our conflicts, we do attempt to air our grievances so that our needs will be known to each other.

We don't want to give the impression that a married couple who lead groups together must present an ideal image of togetherness and self-actualization. We find that being ourselves, with our individual problems and interpersonal differences, doesn't necessarily block our effectiveness in leading groups. In fact, by being honest with each other and our groups about our strengths and limitations, we're able to provide a model of behavior that facilitates group movement. However, we do mean to emphasize that our job is taxing; it requires our full attention. We can't afford to divert energy to an unspoken resentment between us. If there were a crisis state in our relationship, it would be very difficult for us to function effectively and be there fully for the group. And we don't believe we would be justified in using the group time for our therapy. In our judgment, to bring our unfinished business into a group we are leading and attempt to work it through there would be to unfairly burden the group. If there are major difficulties or differences between us, we evaluate the wisdom of attempting to co-lead at that particular time.

We believe that, not only should our relationship be in good shape, but we must also feel in good psychological shape as individuals. If we're feeling ineffectual, overworked, overtired, unappreciated, depressed, highly anxious, or in a state of personal crisis, then our effectiveness as leaders will be seriously diminished. We know how much physical and emotional energy leading an intensive group workshop generally takes, and, if we're not personally nourished before the group, the danger exists that, lacking the energy to lead, we'll only use the group to satisfy our own needs. If, on the other hand, we feel ready when we enter a group, we've found that we derive additional energy from our giving and receiving. The questions we ask ourselves before we begin a new group are:

- Am I really looking forward to beginning this group?
- Do I feel alive and enthusiastic?
- How personally effective have I been feeling lately?
- Have my projects been rewarding?
- Are there certain internal conflicts that are haunting me and that need to be resolved before I attempt to work therapeutically with others?
- Am I liking the quality of my own life and the direction it's taking, or am I dissatisfied with the choices I've made?
- Am I willing to do for myself what I might be encouraging group members to do in their lives?
- Am I willing to face myself honestly, accept what I see, make decisions to change, and act on my decisions?

Before a group, we ask the members to write a paper telling about significant aspects of themselves, about their personal goals for the group, and about the nature of the personal struggles they hope to explore in the group. Not only does this writing exercise help the group members get a clear focus on the areas they most want to understand and change, but their written reports also provide us with their subjective view of what they want for themselves from this group. Part of our preparation for a group involves reading these papers. We discuss our reactions to what we read, and we begin to develop some ideas regarding how we will open the particular group. We focus on some of the unique problems that members write about, and we think about some of the ways we might work with the various members.

Most of all, we want to be looking forward to the experience at the initial session. We hope to direct our full attention to effectively and creatively leading a group, and we find that preparing ourselves pays off for both the group and ourselves. We have spoken mostly about the preparation stages of a group, but we would like to say a few words about our experience during the first few sessions with a new group.

Many times we have asked each other ''Why are we doing this? Are all this effort and work really worth it?'' The first day of residential workshop, for example, is usually very demanding. People are overly polite, and there is the general fumbling around that most groups experience. Participants may tend to reveal only surface thoughts and feelings, and, although everyone has been told the value of trust and the importance of risking, they tend to wait for the other person to risk first. Building trust is a slow process, and we must remind each other that instant intimacy is not our goal. Even though we know that the participants need to get acquainted before they open themselves to others and show their vulnerabilities, we often become impatient, longing for the time when these preliminaries will be done with and people will be relating in ways that are more deeply meaningful. We need to remind ourselves that there is a period of transition between leaving the real world and fully participating in a group experience. People's trust and care must be earned. Our job is to create a climate in which the group members can risk shedding facades. This process is trying and demands that we accept people's fearfulness and suspiciousness during these early sessions.

EXERCISES

Group-proposal exercise. Write up a brief proposal for a specific type of group with a specific target population and present it to your class. Some members of the class may take the role of the director of an agency, some may role-play fellow workers, and others may play prospective clients or parents of clients. The exercise can be varied, but the main idea is for you to practice presenting your group proposal and to get feedback on how you come across and how your proposal can be improved.

Screening-interview exercise. One person in the class volunteers to play the role of a group leader conducting a screening interview for group members for a particular type of group. The group leader conducts a ten-minute interview with a potential member, played by another class member. After ten minutes have passed, the prospective client tells the group leader how he or she felt and what impact the group leader made on him or her. Then the group leader shares his or her observations about the prospective group member and tells whether the person would have been accepted into the group, and why or why not. This can be repeated with another client so that the group leader can benefit from the feedback and try some new ideas. Several students can experience the role of the interviewer and the role of the interviewee. It is essential that feedback be given so that the person can improve his or her skills in conducting screening interviews. The rest of the class can offer feedback and suggestions for improvement after each interview.

Group member interviews group leader. We have recommended that prospective group members examine the leader somewhat critically before joining a group. This exercise is just like the preceding one, except that in this one the group member asks the questions of the leader, trying to learn things about the leader and the group that will allow a wise decision about whether to join. After ten minutes, the leader shares his or her observations and reactions, and then the member tells whether he or she would join this leader's group and what his or her reservations would be. Again, the class is invited to make observations.

Initial-session exercise. For this exercise, ten students volunteer to play group members at an initial group session and two people volunteer to play co-leaders. We suggest that the co-leaders begin by giving a brief orientation—explaining the group's purpose, the role of the leader, the rights and responsibilities of the members, the ground rules, or group-process procedures, and any other pertinent information they might actually give in the first session of a group. The members then express their expectations and fears, and the leaders try to deal with them. This lasts for approximately half an hour, and the class members then describe what they saw occurring in the group. The group members describe how they felt during the session, and they offer suggestions for the co-leaders. The co-leaders can discuss with each other the nature of their experience and how well they feel they did, either before any of the feedback or afterward.

Introducing-yourself exercise. This exercise consists of telling the class what you would tell a group about yourself if you were the group leader. About four people volunteer, and each person is given five minutes. When this is completed, the four talk among themselves first, and then the class offers input regarding the impact made by each person.

The issue of voluntary versus mandatory group membership. This is an issue that most group leaders will wrestle with, so it is best to clarify your position now. This exercise makes use of the inner and outer circle. First, five to eight people form the inner circle, and they discuss all the reasons why all membership should be by free choice. Then they become the outer circle, and a new group of five to eight students argues the position that required group membership is called for at times.

Exercise for the beginning stage of a group. This exercise can be used to get group members acquainted with one another, but you can practice it in class to see how it works. The class breaks into dyads. Select a new partner every five or ten minutes, and, each time you change partners, consider a new question or issue. The main purpose of the exercise is to get members to contact all of the other members of the group and to begin to reveal themselves to others. We encourage you to add your own questions or statements to our list.

1. Discuss your reservations about the value of groups.
2. What do you fear about groups?
3. What do you most want from a group experience?
4. Discuss how much trust you have in your group. Do you feel like getting involved? What are some things that contribute to your trust or mistrust?
5. Decide which of the two of you is dominant. Does each of you feel satisfied with his or her position?
6. Tell your partner how you imagine you would feel if you were to co-lead a group with him or her.

7. THE WORKING STAGE
OF A GROUP

1. What do you think are the major differences between an effective and an ineffective group?

2. How can a client who has gained insight into the reasons for a problem be helped to act on this insight?

3. What is your position on the values and limitations of catharsis in groups?

4. As a group leader, what do you think you can do to assist participants in making constructive choices about how they will behave in the group?

5. What is your position on the use of techniques and exercises to facilitate communication and interaction?

It is difficult and somewhat arbitrary to divide the history of a group into phases or stages. The borderlines become blurred, and in actual practice there is considerable overlap of the stages that we term *initial, transitional, working, final, evaluation,* and *follow-up*.

The purpose of this chapter is to focus your attention on the characteristics of groups that have successfully reached a working stage, to examine some of the core conflicts and crises of the working phase of groups, and to present some guidelines for group leaders to follow in trying to help participants learn the most from the group.

We'll begin this chapter by contrasting the characteristics of a working group with those of a nonproductive group, and then we'll describe in greater detail the characteristics of effective groups.

CONTRASTS BETWEEN A WORKING GROUP AND AN INEFFECTUAL GROUP

Working Group	*Ineffectual Group*
Members trust other members and the leaders, or at least openly express	Mistrust is evidenced by an undercurrent of unexpressed hostility. Mem-

Working Group	*Ineffectual Group*
their lack of trust. There is a willingness to take risks by sharing meaningful here-and-now reactions.	bers withhold themselves, refusing to express feelings and thoughts.
Goals are clear and specific and are determined jointly by the members and the leader. There is a willingness to direct in-group behavior toward realizing these goals.	Goals are fuzzy, abstract, and general. Members have unclear personal goals or no goals at all.
Most members feel a sense of inclusion, and excluded members are invited to become more active. Communication among most members is open and involves accurate expression of what is being experienced.	Many members feel excluded or cannot identify with other members. Cliques are formed that tend to lead to fragmentation. There is fear of expressing feelings of being left out.
There is a focus on the here-and-now, and participants talk directly to one another about what they're experiencing.	There is a there-and-then focus, people tend to focus on others and not on themselves, story-telling is typical, and there is a resistance to dealing with reactions to one another.
The leadership functions are shared by the group; people feel free to initiate activities or to suggest exploring particular areas.	Members lean on the leaders for all direction. There are power conflicts among members and between members and the leader.
There is a willingness to risk disclosing threatening material; people become known. The interactions are honest and spontaneous. Members are willing to risk disclosing their reactions to others.	Participants hold back, and disclosure is at a minimum. Many members remain unknown. Game-playing is more evident than spontaneous interactions.
Cohesion is high; there is a close emotional bond among people based on sharing of universal human experiences. Members identify with one another. People are willing to risk experimental behavior because of the closeness and support for new ways of being.	Fragmentation exists; people feel distant from one another. There is a lack of caring or empathy. Members don't encourage one another to engage in new and risky behavior, so familiar ways of being are rigidly maintained.
Conflict among members or with the leader is recognized, discussed, and often resolved.	Conflicts or negative feelings are ignored, denied, or avoided.

Working Group	*Ineffectual Group*
Members accept the responsibility for deciding what action they will take to solve their problems.	Members blame others for their personal difficulties and aren't willing to take action to change.
Feedback is given freely and accepted without defensiveness. There is a willingness to seriously reflect on the accuracy of the feedback.	What little feedback is given is rejected defensively. Feedback is given without care or compassion.
Members feel hopeful; they feel that constructive change is possible—that people can become what they want to become.	Members feel despairing, trapped and helpless, victimized.
Confrontation occurs in such a way that the confronter shares\ his or her reactions to the person being confronted. Confrontation is accepted as a challenge to examine one's behavior and not as an uncaring attack.	Confrontation is done in a hostile, attacking way; the confronted one feels judged and rejected. At times the members gang up on a member, using this person as a scapegoat.
Group norms are developed cooperatively by the members and the leader. Norms are clear and designed to help the members attain their goals.	Norms are merely imposed by the leader and/or are not clear.
There is an emphasis on combining the feeling and thinking functions. Catharsis and expression of feeling occur but so does thinking about the meaning of various emotional experiences.	The group relies heavily on cathartic experiences but makes little or no effort to understand them.
Group members use out-of-group time to work on problems raised in the group.	Group members think about group activity very little when they're outside of the group.

THE WORKING STAGE

During the working stage, it becomes very important for the group leader to realize that the clients are the ones who are responsible for their lives. The clients must be encouraged to filter the feedback they receive and make their own decisions concerning what to do about it. Neither the group leader nor the other members should attempt to be helpful by giving abundant suggestions or by deciding a course of action for that person; these actions only undermine the individual's autonomy.

Practice for Behavior Change

Emotional and intellectual understanding of one's basic conflicts may be considered necessary for behavioral change but not sufficient to produce it. For behavior change to take place, action is necessary. Clients must make decisions on the basis of their increased self-awareness, and they must act on these decisions. A new behavior cannot become a part of one's repertoire without considerable practice.

A way for leaders to help clients act on insights is by initiating role-playing exercises when they seem appropriate. For example, consider the client who comes to realize that he submerges his autonomy in his desperate efforts to please his boss and that he would like to establish a more equal relationship and thereby gain a sense of integrity. While someone else plays the role of the boss, he can try out more assertive behavior. Others can model behavior he might try and give him feedback about how they perceive him in this situation. Additionally, he can be given, or can give himself, homework assignments designed to help him practice more effective behavior. Through the group process, he has become aware that he doesn't assert himself, and he has decided to make his feelings known; now it is important that he force himself to practice his desired behavior, so that it can become a part of him.

Contracts and homework assignments can be helpful to members who want to transfer what they've learned in a group setting to their life in the outside world. But these techniques should not be used until participants have had a chance to fully experience their feelings and to work through resistances and unfinished business. Clients can be expected to feel ambivalent about abandoning familiar ways, and this ambivalence must be expressed before lasting behavior change can take place.

The Use of Catharsis

Depending on the type of group, catharsis, or an explosive release of buried feelings, may occur during the more intensive working phases. We think that some type of emotional release is valuable, but we prefer it to be a natural expression of a client's needs rather than something that a group leader induces or forces out of members. In therapy groups, marathon groups, some encounter groups, and other intensive groups, catharsis may be valued for its own sake, as a full experiencing of feelings that were buried. But catharsis is only a part of the therapeutic experience. While catharsis may at times be necessary to the fulfillment of member goals, we strongly believe that it is not by itself sufficient. As members engage in deep exploration of unfinished business that is interfering with their present functioning, they need not only to experience buried feelings but also to think about what these feelings signify. Otherwise substantial behavior change cannot take place.

Exploration of Alternatives

Often those who seek therapy complain of feeling trapped, stuck without options, and destined to live out their existence miserably. Likewise, many clients in group settings do not see viable alternatives to their unsatisfying mode of being. One function of a group is to assist such persons to discover that they are not stuck with their early decisions—that there are options open to them and that, by taking advantage of those options, they can enjoy a more satisfying life.

For example, Susan felt very isolated and lonely, and through a group experience she became aware that she had isolated herself in the past and that she was cutting herself off from meaningful encounter with others in the group. Through feedback, she became aware of which of her behaviors were contributing to other members' not reaching out more to her, and she began to accept the responsibility for her loneliness. She came to realize that, because her parents had rejected her, she was avoiding intimacy, for fear of further rejection. She came to feel that she was lovable, and so she began to feel free to develop a wider range of behavioral responses. Since she no longer made others into her rejecting parents, she was able to let people know her needs for intimacy.

As another example, Hank came to realize that the only way he could feel OK about himself was controlling his wife and blocking any effort on her part to change. When he came to the group, he felt that, either his wife would remain the compliant person he had married, or he would divorce her. In the group, he gained self-confidence and thus lost the need to keep his wife inferior. And he discovered a new option—he could enjoy watching his wife change.

Choices to Be Made in the Working Stage

In discussing the initial stages of the group's evolution, we described several critical issues, such as trust versus mistrust, the struggle for power, and self-focus versus other-focus. During the more intensive working period in the evolution of a group, certain other key issues are at stake, and again the group as a whole must resolve the issues for better or worse. We will now discuss each of the choices that the group must make at this stage. Remember that a group's identity is shaped by the way its members resolve these critical issues.

Disclosure versus anonymity. People can protect themselves through anonymity; yet the very reason many become invested in a therapeutic group is because they want to make themselves known to others and to come to know others in a deeper way than they have allowed themselves to do in their daily lives. If the group process is to work effectively, the participants must be willing to reveal themselves, for it is through self-disclosure that they begin to learn about themselves.

Individuals can decide to disclose themselves in a significant and appropriate way, or they can choose to remain hidden, for fear that if they were to reveal themselves to others they would be rejected.

Honesty versus game-playing. There are those who believe that, in order to survive in the real world, they must sacrifice their honesty and substitute deceit, game-playing, and manipulation. They may say that in order to "get ahead" they have to suppress what they really think and feel, figure out what others expect from them, and then meet these expectations.

It is fundamental to the success of a therapeutic group that honesty prevail and that a person not have to be dishonest to win acceptance. If these conditions hold, participants can both be themselves and learn to accept the true selves of others. Group interaction can deteriorate into another form of game-playing unless the participants choose to be honest with themselves and one another.

Spontaneity versus control. Unfortunately, some encounter-group proponents have glorified being impulsive and doing one's "thing," without regard for the consequences to themselves or to others. One problem arising from this glorification is that members and leaders alike may force themselves to be "spontaneous," thereby producing behavior that seems contrived or rehearsed.

We hope that group participants will make the choice to relinquish some of their controlled and rehearsed ways and allow themselves to respond more spontaneously to events of the moment. We encourage spontaneity indirectly, by making clients feel that it's OK to say and do many of the things they've been preventing themselves from saying or doing.

Acceptance versus rejection. Throughout the entire course of a group, the members must deal with the acceptance/rejection polarity. We sometimes hear a member say "I'd like to reveal more of myself and be more active in this group than I have been, but I'm afraid that if I'm me in here I'll be rejected." This fear can and should be explored, and those who feel this way must choose to take the risk of looking foolish and of not being universally accepted.

We find that many clients are frightened more by acceptance than by rejection. It's as though some say "If you accept me, or love me, or care for me, then I won't know how to respond; I'll feel burdened with a debt to you."

We hope that group members will recognize their own role and responsibility in the creation of an accepting climate and come to understand that, by contributing to a climate either of acceptance or of rejection, they can help determine whether they as individuals will be accepted or rejected.

Cohesion versus fragmentation. As we mentioned earlier, cohesion is an essential characteristic of a group. Our conviction is that cohesion is largely the result of the group's choice to actively work at developing unifying bonds. Members do this mainly by choosing to make themselves known to others, by allowing caring to develop, by initiating meaningful work, and by giving honest feedback to others.

If a group chooses to remain comfortable or to stick with superficial interactions, then there will be little group togetherness. If enough members choose not to express their fears, suspicions, disappointments, doubts, and so forth but rather to bury or avoid these reactions, then fragmentation will result. Cohesion results only from working with meaningful, if painful, problems.

Responsibility versus blaming. In individual therapy, the client must accept the responsibility for his or her behavior if any significant behavior changes are to take place. Likewise, group members must stop viewing themselves as victims of external factors, including other people, if they are to become more effective persons.

At some point in therapy and group work, clients usually focus their anger on others, whom they blame for their unhappiness. But, during the more intensive phases of group work, clients generally come to accept the fact that a blaming style will get them nowhere. When they stop playing the game of "poor me," they find that they can act on the alternatives that are becoming more apparent.

WHAT WE DO DURING THE WORKING STAGE OF A GROUP

When we co-lead groups or intensive workshops, we become energized if the group is motivated to work and to engage in meaningful self-exploration. In effective groups, the members do the bulk of the work, for they bring up subjects they want to talk about and demonstrate a willingness to be known.

Between group sessions, we devote time to discussing our reactions to group members, to thinking of ways of involving the various members in transactions with each other, and to exploring possible ways of assisting participants to understand their behavior in group and to resolve some of their conflicts. We think that it is essential for us to look critically at what we are doing as leaders and examine the impact of our behavior on the group. It is also essential that we talk with each other about the process and dynamics of the group. If we find that we have differing perceptions regarding the group process, we discuss our differences. In this way, we challenge each other, and we grow.

When a group seems very resistant, and productive work seems to emerge very slowly, we wonder whether we want to continue doing group work. At times like this, we experience a sapping of our energies. If we have persistent feelings that the group is avoiding doing meaningful work, we will express these feelings, and the perceptions they're based on, to the group. We try to express honestly to the members what we see occurring and how we are feeling as members of the group, but we avoid chastizing the members and telling them that they're not meeting our expectations. At the same time, we challenge the group to assess its own processes. If resistance is the general rule in a group, then it is imperative that we challenge the group to recognize the barriers that are standing in the way of effective work.

EXERCISES

Most of the exercises that follow are not, as the exercises in previous chapters were, intended solely for group leaders in training. Most of these exercises can also be introduced by you into the groups that you eventually lead. You'll have to decide for yourself which of these exercises are appropriate for your particular group and when they should be introduced. Some good exercises backfire because the group leader has failed to consider questions such as: What will happen if I use this technique with these people at this time? Are they ready for such an exercise?

Are they receptive, or will they resist it as an attempt on my part to control them? Is there sufficient trust for this exercise to work? Is there adequate time to complete the exercise? Will there be time for the members to discuss their reactions to the exercise?

We hope that your classroom group will allocate time to discuss and evaluate the various exercises you do in your class. What are your personal reactions to each of the exercises you experiment with, and how did they affect you? What was the effect on the group of a given exercise? If you spend time processing your experiments in this way, you'll have a basis for judging how effective these exercises will be in groups you lead.

We want to emphasize that these techniques are not to be considered tools that a group leader can arbitrarily select from a kit and impose on a group. It is important for you to prepare group members for exercises and equally important for you to know why you're using them. We have seen too many group leaders frantically use technique after technique to keep a group moving; in these cases, exercises have become devices for allaying leader anxiety. There are many times when introducing exercises will increase the resistance level of groups instead of facilitating deeper communication. Part of the art of group leadership consists of knowing when and how to suggest certain interaction exercises, as well as when to avoid them. As a guideline, you might remember that it is better to avoid using structured exercises when you feel stuck and don't know what to do. It is at such times that a technique is bound to fail. Rather, you might openly state that you feel uncertain about what to do to get the group moving, or you might initiate exploration of the reasons for the group's immobility.

It may help to continually remind yourself that these exercises are always means to the end of facilitating significant interaction and never ends in themselves. Further, group leaders should not force themselves to use techniques that don't suit their personhood and their unique style as leaders. It is crucial that you feel comfortable using a particular structured exercise and that you adapt these exercises to suit your personality, for they won't work well if they're not extensions and expressions of you.

Brainstorming exercise. With your class, spend ten minutes or so brainstorming about what you might do as a group leader if your group were ineffective. Mention anything you can think of that you might do to change your ineffective group into an effective one. At this point, don't comment on any of the suggestions being made. Someone takes notes and, when the brainstorming is over, reads back some of the suggestions, which are then discussed and evaluated.

Forming contracts. Each class member writes a contract detailing something new that he or she is willing to do within a specified time period. The contract might be related to behavior in the classroom. For instance, a person who tends to be a questioner might make a contract stating "For one week I will not ask anyone any questions in this class. Instead, I will make direct statements." The person who rarely participates in class verbally but who would like to do so can promise "For the rest of this semester, I will verbally participate at least once in each class session."

Of course, your contracts can be more personal. The object of the exercise is to make you think of concrete changes you'd like to make and to give you the experience of trying to stick to a contract.

I have a secret. Think of a secret—the one that you would least like the rest of your class (group) to know. Don't reveal the secret, but imagine yourself disclosing it to everyone in your class (group). What is this like for you? What do you imagine people would think about you?

You are your past. An egg timer is used for this exercise. Think about certain experiences from your past that you judge to have been significant in making you the person you are now. Share these experiences with the class (group) until the sand runs out. Then give the egg timer to another person. This exercise continues until everyone has had a turn. The instructor (group leader) might begin the exercise for modeling purposes.

Draw your past, present, and future. You need a large piece of paper, crayons, and about 15 minutes to complete this exercise. Draw or sketch your entire life on this sheet of paper in any way you want to. Depict your past as you recall it, your life at this time, and your projection of your future. After everyone has completed the sketch, choose a partner, and describe to him or her what your sketch signifies about your life.

Reconstruct your past. Write a brief description of your past as you wish it had been. Then choose a partner. Tell your partner how you imagine your life would be different today if your past had been as you fantasized it.

Honesty versus game-playing. The class breaks into small groups. Share with your group your fantasies of how your life would be different if you were completely honest. Would you want it that way? Then discuss with your group the games you now play that you played as a child, and ask yourself whether these games still "work" for you. Finally, each group makes a list of the games its members most often play. Each group can briefly report its findings to the class.

Rejection exercise. Group participants often claim that they fear being rejected. This exercise is designed to enable members to experience and explore these fears. First, the entire group sits with eyes closed imagining being rejected by the entire group. In fantasy, allow yourself to see each person rejecting you, until you are left alone. How does it feel? Then, after a few minutes of silence, each person in turn takes the egg timer and shares what the experience of being totally rejected was like. Members might eventually discuss the things they do (and don't do) because of their fear of group rejection.

Acceptance exercise. Fantasize yourself being valued, respected, loved, and accepted by every person in your group. Hear what each person says, and see what each does. What are you feeling as you imagine this? Again, pause for a few moments of silence after the fantasy. Then describe to the class your experience for as long as it takes the sand in the timer to run out. After everyone has had a turn, the group can discuss the contrasts between the ''rejection'' exercise and this one.

Closeness/distance exercise. Often group members express feelings of loneliness, saying that they feel distant from others and from their own feelings. At other times, the same members may report feeling close to the other members. With your class, explore how connected you feel with others. Do you ever feel lonely in your group, and, if so, how do you cope with it? Select the person in the group whom you feel the closest to and tell that person in what ways you experience this closeness. Then select the person you feel the most distant from and express why you sense this and what it is like for you.

Contact exercise. Get together with four other people. Then address each member in turn, completing the following sentence: ''I can make contact with you by . . . . '' You might think of other sentences to complete. When each member has done this, discuss with the others how your ways of either making or avoiding contact with people in your group are similar to the ways you do this outside of the group.

A personal-identity road map. Draw a road map of the incidents that have shaped your personal identity. Consider questions such as the following:

- Who am I now? What has made me this way?
- What are some of my earliest recollections?
- What are some key decisions I made at various points?
- What choices did I make for myself, and what choices did others make for me?
- What are some risks I took recently that led to a change in my life?
- What do I want from life? What kind of identity do I want to develop?

Creating a new religion. Working with four other people, plan a new religion. What will your religion be like? What will it hold as virtues, and what as vices? When you complete your task, join the rest of the class and share your results.

Exchange of qualities. Each member in turn tells every person in the group what qualities he or she has that the speaker would like to have. The speaker offers to each member one of his or her qualities in exchange. This procedure can be modified in several ways. A person can simply mention what traits he or she likes in others or tell individuals in the group what desirable quality he or she has that they could benefit from.

Guided fantasy. Several people volunteer to guide the class on a fantasy journey. Of course, one person at a time leads the group. It is best for the participants to lie on the floor (if it is carpeted) or sit comfortably with their eyes closed. Some relaxation exercises may be helpful as a prelude, and participants should clear their minds and allow themselves to go with the exercise. The purpose of the fantasy is to stimulate the class members to reexperience certain periods in their life, such as times of closeness, fear, or loneliness.

8. TERMINATION,
EVALUATION, AND
FOLLOW-UP

1. What are some guidelines that a leader might follow in closing each group session?

2. If a member wants to leave a group before its termination, how should the leader handle it?

3. What activities are important during the closing phases of a group?

4. What kinds of questions might you as a leader ask members in order to determine how the group had affected them?

5. What are some subjective and objective measures you might use to assess the results of a given group experience?

6. How important do you think it is to hold some type of follow-up session? What might you want the group to discuss at a follow-up session?

The initial phase of a group's development is extremely crucial, for during this time, if all goes well, participants are getting acquainted, basic trust is being established, norms are being established that will govern later intensive work, and a unique group identity is taking shape. The final stages of group evolution are also vital, for during this time members have an opportunity to clarify the meaning of their experiences in group, to consolidate the gains they've made, and to revise their decisions regarding what newly acquired behaviors they want to transfer to their everyday life. As group members sense that their group is approaching a termination point, there is a danger that they will begin to distance themselves from the group experience and thus fail to closely examine the ways in which their in-group learning might affect their out-of-group behavior. For this reason, group leaders must learn to help group members put into meaningful perspective what has occurred in the group.

In this chapter, we'll discuss ways of terminating both individual sessions and the entire group experience. We'll show how leaders can help members evaluate the meaning of their behavior in the group. Questions we'll explore are: How can the members be encouraged to evaluate the degree of their satisfaction with each session? How can leaders get participants to actively prepare themselves for the following session, or for a follow-up session after termination of a group? How can a group complete its unfinished business? How can the members best be prepared for leaving the group and carrying their learnings into the real world? What are the difficulties in saying good-bye, and are they avoidable? Are there any ways of preparing the members to cope with their tendency to regress to old ways or to discount the meaning of their experience in the face of the outside world's pressures and skepticism? Are follow-ups necessary, and how should they be designed? How can members and leaders evaluate the group experience?

CLOSING GROUP SESSIONS

For groups that meet on a weekly basis, it is important to summarize at the close of each session what occurred in that session. At times it is useful for the leader to stop the group halfway through the session and say "I notice that we have about an hour left today, and I'd like to check out with you how each of you feels about what you've done so far today. Have you been as involved as you want to be? Are there some issues you'd like to explore before this session ends?" This does not need to be done routinely, but sometimes such an assessment during the session can help the members focus their attention on problem areas, especially if the leader senses that the members are not doing and saying what they need to do or say.

If a group has reached the tenth of 20 weekly sessions, it's a good idea for the leader to initiate evaluation by members of both their own and the group's progress. To our groups, we say something like "Well, we've been together for about 20 hours, and we have another 20 hours to go. Could we go around and have each of you say something about how it would be for you if this were our last session? How do you feel about the work you've done in here during the past 10 weeks? What kinds of changes have you noticed in the way you are in group and in the way you are in your daily life? In what ways would you like to be different in the next half of this group? What have these group sessions been like for you so far?"

The purpose of this line of questioning is to help the participants evaluate the degree of their investment in the group and the extent of the gains they've made. If members can realize at this point that they've merely been showing up and listening to others, there is still time for them to change. Because members don't usually come to such a realization spontaneously, it's a good idea for the leader to guide the members into reflecting on the time limitations of their group and on whether they're getting what they hoped for when they joined the group.

In closing a weekly group session, consider the following guidelines.

1. It is good for clients to leave a session with some unanswered questions. We think it's a mistake to try to ensure that everyone leaves feeling comfortable. If clients leave feeling that everything is nicely closed, they will probably spend very little time during the week reflecting on matters raised in the group. However, if transactions have occurred that need clarification, or if undercurrents of certain feelings persist, these things should be considered, not left dangling.

2. Some statement from the members concerning their level of investment of energy is useful. If clients report boredom weekly, they can be asked what they're willing to do to relieve their boredom.

3. Members can be asked to briefly tell the group what they're learning about themselves through their relationships with other members of the group. The participants can briefly indicate some ways in which they've changed their behavior in response to these insights. If participants find that they would like to change their behavior even more, they can discuss with the leader contracts and homework assignments they can do before the next session.

4. Members can be asked whether there are any topics, questions, or problems that they would like to explore in the next session. This creates a link between one session and the next. By prompting the members to think about the upcoming session, it also indirectly encourages them to stick to their contracts during the week.

TERMINATION OF THE GROUP EXPERIENCE

Premature Termination

When should a member leave the group? If a group begins with eight members and the decision is made to remain a closed group for a specified period of time (say, 20 weeks), then the time of a member's termination is, theoretically, predetermined. However, members may decide to drop out early, for a variety of reasons—work-schedule conflicts, lack of time, lack of enthusiasm for the group, and so on. Of course, the option of withdrawing from a group must exist. A practice that we have found helpful is requesting that a person discuss openly his or her reasons for planning to leave the group. In some cases, it is very wise for a person not to continue in a group. At times, the leader may even feel it necessary to ask a group member to leave. In any case, we think that a premature departure should be explored in the group setting.

Closing a Group

Throughout the history of a group, the members have been giving and receiving feedback, and this feedback has helped them assess the impact of their behavioral experiments on others. However, during the closing session we like to emphasize a more focused type of feedback for each person. We generally begin by asking members for a brief report on how they've perceived themselves in the group, what the group has meant to them, what conflicts have become clearer, and what (if any) decisions they've made. Then the rest of the members give feedback concerning how they've perceived and how they've felt about that person. Here we want to point to a potential problem: too often people give only positive feedback at this time, particularly if they feel a closeness with the others and some misgivings about the termination of the group. Favorable comments may give a person a temporary lift, but we question their long-term value. We do value positive feedback and deem it important that members disclose what they see as strengths and what they like about other members. However, we also like members to express doubts or concerns, in ways such as the following:

- My greatest fear for you is . . . .
- My hope for you is . . . .
- I hope that you will seriously consider . . . .
- You block your strengths by . . . .
- Some things I hope you will think about doing for yourself are . . . .

During this feedback session, we emphasize that participants can make some specific contracts in areas they want to further explore after the group. We suggest some type of group follow-up session at a later date, which gives the members added incentive to think about ways to keep some of their new decisions alive.

During the final stages of a group, we think that certain questions need to be raised: What has this experience meant? You have shared your struggles, but is this enough in itself? You have experienced and expressed emotions, but so what? What does all of this mean in terms of your living in the world? Where can you go from here?

The final phase in the life of a group is extremely critical, for this is when group members must consolidate their learnings. It is a difficult time because the members are aware that their community is about to dissolve, and they mourn the loss of it in advance. Sometimes the intensity tapers off during the final sessions because participants, aware that their time together is limited, are reluctant to bring up new business to explore. It is important that the group leader focus on the feelings of loss that may permeate the atmosphere. These feelings need to be identified and explored, although they probably cannot be alleviated. It is important that members face the reality of termination and that they learn how to say good-bye. If the group has been truly therapeutic, they will be able to extend and continue their learning outside, although they may well experience a sense of sadness and loss.

EVALUATION OF THE GROUP EXPERIENCE

Before the follow-up session, which we schedule for a few months after the last group session, we often send out a questionnaire to the group members. In answering the questions, the members are preparing themselves for the follow-up session by evaluating their group experience. The responses also serve to tell us whether we succeeded in our therapeutic efforts.

The following is a sample questionnaire.

1. What general effect, if any, has your group experience had on your life?
2. What were the highlights of the group experience for you? Some of its most meaningful aspects?

3. What were some specific things that you became aware of about yourself, in terms of your life-style, attitudes, and relationships with others?
4. What are some changes you've made in your life that you can attribute at least partially to your group experience?
5. Which of the techniques used by the group leaders had the most impact on you?
6. What perceptions of the group leaders and their styles do you have?
7. What kinds of problems did you encounter upon leaving the group and attempting to do what you had decided to do in the outside world?
8. Have the changes that occurred as a result of your group experiences lasted? If so, do you think the changes are permanent?
9. What kinds of questions have you asked yourself since the group? Were questions of yours left unanswered by the group?
10. Did the group experience have any negative effects on you?
11. What kinds of individual and/or group experiences have you been involved in since this particular experience?
12. What effects do you think your participation in the group had on the significant people in your life?
13. Have there been any crises in your life since the termination of the group? How did they turn out?
14. How might your life be different now had you not experienced the group? Do you feel that you would have made any significant changes in your behavior?
15. Have you become more aware, since the termination of the group, of the part you played in the group process?
16. If a close friend were to ask you today to tell in a sentence or two what the group meant to you, how would you respond?
17. In retrospect, are you skeptical about the value of the group process or about the motivations of other people in the group?
18. Since the group, have you encouraged others to become involved in a group or in some other kind of growth experience?
19. How do you evaluate this form of group experience? What is its potential for helping people change in a positive direction? What are its limitations? Its risks? How would you recommend it be used? Do the potential gains outweigh the risks?
20. What are some other questions you think we should ask in order to get a complete picture of the meaning the group had for you? Do you have anything else to say about yourself and your experience either during or since the group?

THE FOLLOW-UP SESSION

After the evaluation questionnaire has been completed, we schedule a follow-up session for open discussion of the results of the questionnaire. By holding this session, we believe, we maximize the chances that the members will get a lasting benefit from the group experience.

At the follow-up session, the members report on whether and how they're using their expanded self-awareness in their relationships in the outside world. They tell what the reentry into the real world was like and how the people they live and work with responded to them. Often the people a member lives with have grown comfortable with the way the member was and resist his or her changes. The member is no longer predictable and may even expect other people to change. This can produce anxiety in others, which often leads to hostility toward the member. At the follow-up session, the group can reinforce the member's new style of behavior at a time when his or her will to change may be weakening.

We ask members at the follow-up session whether they are continuing to reach out for what they want. Are they taking more risks? What kinds of results are they getting from their new behavior? Frequently at follow-ups people will report "The outside world isn't like this group. I've been honest with some people out there, and they don't know how to take me!" At this point, we usually emphasize that people do need to be selective about whom to be completely honest with, since many people will resist directness and openness or will not desire intimacy. The follow-up can thus help the members become more realistic about their expectations.

Related to this problem of expectations is the fact that people leaving any intensive group experience usually report feeling high, or supercharged. These peak feelings are pleasant but usually transient. When the person faces the real world, he or she generally feels less and less powerful. If the follow-up session comes several weeks after the intensive group session, we have a somewhat deflated, but more realistic, individual to work with. It is at this point that the person may be able to do some really fruitful planning.

Finally, a follow-up session offers us one more opportunity to remind people that they are responsible for what they become—that they must take risks in order to grow but that the option of growth is indeed theirs.

EXERCISES

We think that exercises are important as catalysts during the initial stages of a group and that, applied at appropriate times in the course of a group, they can intensify a person's experience. For instance, role-playing can be very effective during the working stages of a group. There are fewer exercises appropriate to the final stages either of a session or of a group; however, there are a few activities that we find useful at these times. Again, most of the exercises we suggest are suitable both for a classroom and for a therapeutic group.

Summarizing exercise. At the close of a class (group) session, each person makes a statement concerning how he or she experienced the session. It is important that discussion of the statements not occur, for the purpose of the exercise is quick assessment of what the session was like for each member.

Future-projection exercise. It is important to encourage group members to devote time after a session to reflecting on what they want for themselves in the coming session. To get practice with such reflection, each person completes the sentence "At our next session, I would most like . . . . "

Discounting exercise. After a group experience, participants may find ways of discounting that experience, or old patterns may erupt and block the establishment of new behavior. For example, when she left her encounter group, Jane felt close to many people and decided that it was worth it to risk getting close. She tried this at work, was rebuffed, and then began telling herself that what she had experienced in the group was not real. In this exercise, you are asked to imagine all the things you might say to yourself to sabotage your plans for change. The idea here is to openly acknowledge tendencies you have that will interfere with your establishing new behavior.

Feedback exercises. A student sits with his or her back to the group, and the members express their hopes and fears for the person as though he or she weren't there. Or, the class details which traits, attitudes, or behaviors will interfere with, and which will increase, the person's effectiveness as a group leader. For these exercises, instead of being treated as absent, the person who receives feedback can sit in the center of the circle, and people can speak directly to him or her.

Group-termination exercise. Students take turns pretending that they are leaders and that the class is a group that is about to terminate. The idea is for students to consider how to prepare members for leaving a group.

Termination-interview exercise. A person in the class volunteers to become a group leader and to conduct an interview with a group member (also a volunteer) as though they had just completed a group experience together. For about ten minutes, the group leader interviews the client regarding the nature of his or her group experience. After the exercise, the client reacts to the interview.

9. ETHICAL AND PROFESSIONAL ISSUES

1. What will an ethical group leader be sure to tell prospective members about a group?

2. Would you ever lead a group made up of members who were required to attend? If so, how would you handle the problems that would probably arise?

3. What are some measures you might take as a group leader to ensure confidentiality in your group?

4. What psychological risks do you think are associated with group membership? How can these risks be minimized?

5. What do you feel is the place of nudity in groups? Of sexuality? Of drugs? Of nonverbal exercises?

6. What kind of educational and training backgrounds do you think a person needs in order to be a competent leader?

7. What kind of training and supervision would you like to receive as a part of your program in group leadership?

8. What is your position on the issue of private psychotherapy for group leaders? Should group membership be part of a leader's background? If so, should it be required or just recommended?

9. If you were designing a training program for group leaders, what would the main elements of your program be?

10. What do you think are some of the rules that group leaders must follow in order to practice ethically?

For those who are preparing to become group leaders, of central concern should be ethical considerations. In this chapter, our aim is to highlight what we consider the ethical issues of significance to professional group leaders. We believe that you should begin to think about a professional ethical code before you begin to practice. You will undoubtedly develop a code of conduct in the course of leading groups, but it is our hope that, by getting you to think about ethics ahead of time, we can help you to avoid harmful and costly mistakes.

THE SCREENING OF GROUP MEMBERS

In Chapter 6, we discussed why and how to screen group participants. Here the focus is on the ethical aspects of screening. We believe that failure to screen candidates is unethical. A leader needs to develop a system for assessing the likelihood that a candidate will benefit from a group experience. Factors that need to be taken into consideration are the level of training of the leader, the proposed makeup of the group, the setting, and the basic nature of the group. For example, it might be best not to accept a highly defensive individual into an ongoing adolescent group, for several reasons. For one thing, a group may be too threatening for a person so vulnerable and may lead to increased defensiveness and rigidity. For another thing, this person may have a counterproductive effect on group members who want to do serious work.

The key point is that some kind of screening and selection procedure is essential; practitioners who don't pay attention to this phase of group work unnecessarily increase the psychological risk for the members. It is irresponsible for leaders to allow group members to get involved in a group that is not what they wanted. There may be an emphasis on aggression and confrontation that they were not told of, or the purpose of the group may not coincide with their purpose. As a part of the selection process, candidates should be given enough information to be able to decide whether the group is right for them. Thus, they need to be told the goals, procedures, format, and expected outcomes of the group.

THE ISSUE OF INVOLUNTARY MEMBERSHIP

Obviously, voluntary participation is an important beginning point for a successful group experience. The members must want something for themselves, they must be receptive. They will make significant changes only to the extent that they actively participate. Unfortunately, all groups are not composed of clients who have chosen to be in a group. In some mental-health facilities, the main therapeutic vehicle is group therapy, sometimes as often as three times weekly. People from all wards may be required to attend these sessions. This situation is somewhat akin to compulsory education; people can be forced to attend but not to learn.

For those group leaders who work in institutions in which the policy is to require group treatment, the group members should at least be given the opportunity to ventilate their feelings about this requirement. Perhaps many are reluctant to become involved because of misinformation about or stereotyped views of the nature of therapy. They may not trust the group leaders or the process involved. They may think group therapy is a form of indoctrination. Perhaps they view themselves as healthy and the members of the group as a bunch of sickies. Most likely many of them are frightened and have reservations about opening themselves to others. They may be very concerned about others' gossiping or maliciously using information against them. Perceptive leaders will deal with these issues openly, and, while they may not be able to provide the members with the option of dropping out of the group, they can provide the support necessary to enable the members to fully come to grips with their fears and resistances. The members can also be given the freedom to decide how to use the session time. Group leaders can assure members that the degree to which they participate is up to them—that they may remain silent if they wish and that it's up to them to decide what personal topics they will discuss and what areas they will keep private. In other words, they should be clearly informed that they have the same rights as the members of any group, with the exception of the right not to attend.

The issue of mandatory group participation becomes particularly thorny for students enrolled in either graduate or undergraduate programs designed to train counselors or paraprofessionals. Increasingly, colleges and universities that offer degrees in counseling and other human services are requiring participation in either individual or group therapy as an integral part of these degree programs. The rationale for requiring personal counseling for these students is that the students need to be aware of their own motivations, needs, and problems before they attempt to counsel others. There are some faculty members and students who oppose the requirement, on the grounds that any form of counseling should be initiated by the client; they believe that *mandatory counseling* is a contradiction in terms.

Some guidelines can be established. If counseling is a requirement, then the university should provide it for the students. Private and public institutions alike should make psychological services available, either free or at rates adjusted to student income. It is ethically questionable for schools to require therapy and then suggest that the students pay professors on campus for this service. Understandably, students may question the motivation of professors who support this requirement and then encourage students to become their clients. Furthermore, conflict of interest is a consideration when a student is also a client of a professor.

We have found that most serious students who are sincerely interested in becoming professionally qualified as group leaders are very willing to invest themselves in membership in a therapeutic group. They are usually keenly aware of the fact that as leaders they will be called upon to facilitate positive change in others and that they won't succeed unless they've been members themselves. The quality of the group experience is highly related to the degree of acceptance by the students. If a therapeutic group is offered as a resource for the personal development of counselors, and if students are given the freedom to determine their goals and the structure of the experience, we think most students will be eager for a group and will appreciate such a resource. Those who are highly defensive and antagonistic are the ones who may need to reexamine their commitment to becoming counselors.

In examining the question of the ethics of requiring group participation for students in counseling programs, we think that another question should be asked: Is it ethical for group leaders to consider themselves qualified to lead groups if they've never been group members themselves? We think not. Learning from books and lectures is important but has its limitations; certain skills can be learned only through experimentation. Struggling with trusting a group of strangers, risking vulnerability, receiving genuine support from others, feeling joy and closeness, and being confronted are all vital learning experiences for future group leaders. If for no reason other than because it provides a deep understanding of what clients face in groups, we think that group experience for leaders is indispensable.

CONFIDENTIALITY

One of the central ethical issues in group work is that of confidentiality. It is especially important in groups because not only must the group leader keep the confidences of members; he or she must also get the group members to keep one another's confidences.

In certain group situations, confidentiality becomes especially critical and also more difficult to maintain. This is true of groups in various institutions, agencies, and schools where the group members know and have frequent contact with one another and with one another's associates outside of group. For example, in an adolescent group in a high school, great care must be exerted to ensure that whatever is discussed in the group session is not taken out of the group. If some members talk about things that happened in the group in places other than their sessions, the group process will come to a halt. People are not going to reveal facts about their personal lives unless they feel quite sure that they can trust both the leader and the members of their group to respect their confidences. The group leader should emphasize the importance of confidentiality at various stages of the group's evolution. During the private screening interview, this issue should be stressed, and it should be clarified at the initial group sessions. At appropriate times during the course of a group, the leader should remind the members of the need for not discussing identities or specific situations connected with the group. The leader should point out that confidences can be broken by carelessness as well as by malicious gossip. If at any time any member gives indications that confidentiality is not being respected, the leader should as soon as possible explore this matter with the group.

Group leaders may be tested by some members of the group. For instance, a group counselor may tell the participants of a group in a correctional institution for youth that whatever is discussed will remain in the group. The youths may not believe this and may in many subtle ways test the leader to discover whether in fact he or she will keep this promise. For this reason it is essential that group leaders not promise to keep within the group material that they may be required to disclose. Counselors owe it to their clients to specify at the outset the limits on confidentiality. For instance, a counselor working with children may be expected to disclose some information to parents if the parents insist on it, or a leader of a group of parolees may be expected to reveal to the members' probation officers any information they acquire in the group concerning certain criminal offenses. A group leader should let the members know that he or she may be required to testify against them in court unless the leader is entitled to privileged communication. (In general, licensed psychologists, psychiatrists, and licensed clinical social workers are legally entitled to privileged communication. This means that these people cannot break the confidence of a client unless (1) in their judgment, the client may do serious harm to himself or herself or (2) in their judgment, the client may do serious harm to someone else.)

A particularly delicate problem is safeguarding the confidentiality of minors in groups. Parents may inquire about what their child discusses in a group, and it is the responsibility of the group leader to inform them in advance of the importance of confidentiality. Parents can be told about the purpose of the group, and they can be given some feedback concerning their child, but care must be taken not to reveal specific things that the child mentioned in group. One way to provide feedback to parents is through a session involving one or both parents, the child, and the group leader. This can be particularly helpful when a child needs to communicate certain feelings to the parent, or when certain issues need to be brought out into the open. For example, in a group a girl may talk about her reaction to the breakup of her parents' marriage. She may want to discuss her feelings with her parents yet be reluctant to do so on her own. A conference could be arranged so that, in the presence of the counselor, the child could tell her parents how she feels about the divorce. In this way, the child could have the support of the counselor's presence but tell her parents her feelings directly, without calling on the counselor to do it.

THE ISSUE OF PSYCHOLOGICAL RISK

The forces at work in a therapeutic group are powerful ones. They can be constructive, effecting positive change, but their unleashing always entails some risk. It is essential that group leaders inform the prospective members of some of the risks; a leader mustn't assume that the participants are aware of them. Leaders must also make serious attempts to reduce the risks. Members of a group may be subjected to scapegoating, group pressure, breaches of confidence, inappropriate reassurance, and hostile confrontation. The group process may even precipitate a crisis in a member's life. These hazards should be discussed with the participants during the initial session, and the leader should examine with the group ways these dangers can be avoided.

What are some other psychological risks that might be explored? A person may enter a group feeling relatively comfortable and leave feeling vulnerable and defenseless. Areas of personal conflict may be exposed for the first time, causing much pain and leading to a new self-awareness that is difficult to cope with. A person's outside life may be drastically affected, for family members may have adverse reactions to changes. Participants may be left, at the conclusion of a group, in a condition no better than the one they were in when they began the group; they may even feel less equipped than ever to cope with the demands of daily life. A person may feel misunderstood or rejected by the other members and may leave the group angry, determined never to join another group. Some groups—short-term intensive workshops in particular—may arouse strong, previously hidden feelings, and it is important that people be given means of understanding, or even resolving, the unresolved issues that are behind these feelings. Participants sometimes leave a group with conflicting feelings, wanting to continue with individual or group counseling yet afraid of going further. In a follow-up session, these members can get the support they need in order to be able to examine the ambivalence and decide what to do.

Sometimes, rather than being unaware of the dangers of participating in a group, members invent dangers of their own and are very fearful. These fears should be explored early, so that the members can determine how realistic they are and, it is hoped, put some of them to rest. For example, some members believe that if they allow themselves to feel their pain they'll go crazy or sink into a depression so deep they won't be able to climb out of it. Some are convinced that if they give up their self-control they won't be able to function. Others are frightened of letting others know them, because they think that they'll be rejected. There are those who are reluctant to experience their anger, because they fear physically hurting another.

Not only do certain risks need to be identified and dealt with in group, but safeguards against these risks also need to be established. It should be stressed by the leader that group members have the right to decide for themselves what to explore and how far to go. Group leaders must be alert to group pressure and block any attempts of members to get others to do something they choose not to do. Members can be invited or asked rather than ordered to participate in certain exercises or techniques. Group members should be assured that they have the option of declining to participate in group activities they find extremely threatening. If members want to express their aggression physically, precautions are necessary if sprains and bruises are to be avoided. Symbolic actions—such as beating a pillow—are safer than direct expressions of aggression and may be just as valuable. It is essential that group leaders learn how to cope effectively with whatever may arise as the result of an exercise. It may be easy to provoke someone into experiencing rage, but it is another matter to know what to do when this person releases some long-standing controls.

After a group experience—particularly an intensive weekend or week-long experience—participants may make rash decisions that affect not only their lives but also the lives of members of their family. What the individual may see as the result of newfound spontaneity or decisiveness may be due merely to a burst of energy generated by the group. For example, a woman who has been married for 20 years and who becomes aware in the group of her extreme alienation from her husband may leave the group with a resolve to get a divorce. The group leader should caution her of the danger of making decisions too soon after the group. If this woman has changed in the group, she may be able to relate to her husband differently; if she acts too soon, she may not give this a chance to happen. It is not the leader's responsibility to stand in the way of members' decisions, but it is his or her responsibility to warn members against acting on a "group high."

Another risk members face is having difficulties when they attempt to be outside the way they were in the group. As we warned in Chapter 8, the resistance they meet on the outside may cause some members to discount entirely the value of the group experience, and hence provisions should be made for follow-up sessions. At a follow-up session, members can get support for their new behavior, which can help them overcome their setbacks.

CONTROVERSIAL ISSUES

We will briefly comment on four controversial issues related to group practice: nudity, drugs, sexuality, and physical exercises. These areas warrant special attention because they are associated with some emerging group practices. These issues relate primarily to the encounter-group movement, but the way they are resolved will have implications for other types of groups.

Nudity and groups. In many growth centers, there is an increasingly strong trend toward nude encounter sessions. In some growth centers, nudity is considered an option for any of the groups offered, and the brochures make reference to the individual's responsibility to decide on this matter. Some groups, though, are announced as "nude encounters." Nude encounter was pioneered by Paul Bindrim and accounted for a rapid increase in the number of people wanting a personal-growth experience. Bindrim views the shedding of one's clothes as symbolic of the shedding of outworn masks. While space does not allow for an extended discussion of this hypothesis, we do wish to point out some ethical considerations. First, we do see value in the experience of nudity in certain groups for certain clients. Many people are ashamed of their bodies, or have a distorted picture of what constitutes normalcy, and the experience of nudity with others may help them. Many group members who experience being nude with others find this a freeing experience and one that is more sensual than sexual. Some cautions need to be voiced, however, concerning nudity in groups. The appropriateness of nudity depends largely on the type of group, the setting, and the nature of the participants. While it may be appropriate for adults, who have been told of it in advance, in a privately run encounter group, it would surely not be appropriate for an adolescent group in a school setting. Members should be given advance notice that nudity may be part of the group sessions, so that they can take this into consideration when deciding whether to become a member of the group. It is important that members not be pressured to take off their clothes simply because some members have done so and that individual choice be respected.

Sexuality and groups. Participants in groups should be encouraged to explore their sexual feelings just as openly as they would any other feelings. We think that sexual intercourse between members in a group is counterproductive, however, and that as part of the therapeutic contract members should avoid sexual contact. This becomes a concern in private ongoing group therapy where extra-group socialization occurs. Also, it is a concern in weekend encounter groups, marathon groups (groups that last from 12 to 48 hours), and residential groups (groups in which the members live together for a week or so and meet for ongoing therapy sessions). We feel that participants feel safer about expressing their sexual feelings if there is a policy of no sexual intercourse. In addition, this policy prevents the participants from avoiding important issues by seeking sexual relationships with one another. Quite often participants will disclose the difficulty they encounter in being intimate with their spouse and define this as a problem that they want to solve. If they escape facing this problem by "falling in love" with a stranger for a weekend, they may leave the group feeling "high" but without having solved their problem. In short, we think that any kind of therapeutic group should be a place where persons are enabled to view themselves from a new vantage point—not a place where they can make sexual conquests.

Drugs and groups. Our hope is that group participants will be able to experience a "high" without the aid of drugs or chemicals. One reason many people seek a personal-growth group is that they hope to discover ways of feeling alive and intense. Taking drugs during group sessions or coming to sessions under the influence of drugs or alcohol seems to defeat the essential purpose of a group, which is to intensify one's genuine experiencing. We generally encourage participants to refrain even from taking aspirin for a headache during sessions; we encourage them instead to deal with the tension that is producing the symptom. If a group member habitually comes to group sessions stoned, this behavior should be discussed in the group.

Some people use marijuana routinely, as part of their life-style. We have had several participants make contracts to abstain from this habit in order to see how this would change the quality of their interpersonal relating. This abstention had some significant effects, particularly for those who were typically withdrawn and isolated. For instance, one member found for the first time that he could enjoy sex without the help of drugs.

Nonverbal exercises and groups. In many encounter groups, participants engage in a variety of nonverbal exercises, ranging from touching others affectionately to fighting. Typical activities are falling backward and trusting to be caught by a partner, arm wrestling, pushing and shoving, fighting with bataccas (soft, felt-covered clubs), wrestling, beating pillows, holding a person down, milling around with eyes closed and making body contact, touching and caressing, and massaging, to mention just a few.

Regarding the use of aggressive exercises, we think group leaders have a responsibility to use caution. Release of anger on a symbolic object is recommended. Group leaders should be equipped to cope with powerful feelings, including uncontrolled aggression, that can be triggered by certain role-playing activities. As a general rule, leaders should not introduce a technique that will encourage the aggressive expression of anger unless they feel quite certain that they can handle the consequences—both physical and psychological. A female leader might thus do well to be more cautious than a male leader or a woman co-leading with a man about allowing physical expression of anger. We have come to trust our intuition concerning when it is safe to allow certain activities, and we've found that members respond with self-control when they sense that we don't want them to let themselves go.

Concerning the nonaggressive physical techniques, such as touching and embracing, the following precautions are suggested. First, it is important that members choose to participate in touching exercises and that those who have reservations have the option of abstaining from the activity. People should be reminded, however, that forcing themselves to do something that makes them uncomfortable may be the only way of overcoming their discomfort. Second, group leaders and members should not simulate affection. It should be expressed only when it is felt, for otherwise members may come to distrust any affectionate gesture as a form of role-playing.

Group leaders should use discretion in introducing nonverbal exercises. The participants should have an opportunity to share their reactions to the activities.

THE ISSUE OF GROUP LEADERS' COMPETENCE

Who is qualified to lead groups? What are some criteria by which to determine the level of competence of group leaders? How can leaders recognize their limits?

Concerning the issue of who is qualified to lead groups, several factors must be considered. One is the type of group. Different groups require different leader qualities. The basic question can thus be restated as: Who is qualified to lead this type of group with this type of population? Some professionals who are highly qualified to work with college students are not competent to lead a children's group. There are professionals who are trained to lead personal-growth groups but who lack either the training or the experience necessary to administer group therapy to an outpatient population. Some may be very successful with groups for alcoholics or drug addicts yet unequipped to lead couples' groups or to work with families.

There are many ways of becoming a professional group leader. Some of the fields of study that prepare people to become leaders of therapeutic groups are:

- counseling psychology,
- clinical psychology,
- psychiatry,
- educational psychology,
- school counseling,
- marriage and family counseling,
- clinical social work,
- pastoral psychology or pastoral counseling, and
- child and adolescent psychology.

Other disciplines that can help prepare professionals for group work are sociology, philosophy, literature, and the behavioral sciences. Course work in personality theory, human growth and development, abnormal psychology, clinical techniques, theories of counseling, and vocational and career development can also be helpful. The main point we want to make is that no one discipline has a monopoly when it comes to offering valuable information and training to potential group leaders. The various types of therapeutic groups each call for a different type of training and experience. We think it is good for group leaders to have a mixed background; we believe it adds depth to their group work. Thus, a group leader who works with children might do well to have training in both general psychology and marital and family counseling.

During the professional education of counselors who hope to work as group leaders, at least one course in the theory and practice of group counseling is essential. Unfortunately, it is not uncommon to find only one such survey course available to students in a master's-degree program in psychology or counseling.

Another issue related to competence is that of licenses, degrees, and credentials. In our judgment, the training that leads to the attainment of such certification is usually valuable, but degrees alone do not indicate that a person is a qualified leader. A person may hold a Ph.D. in counseling psychology and be licensed to practice psychotherapy yet not be equipped, either by training or by personality, to practice *group* work. At the same time, we can conceive of a paraprofessional, without degree or license, who can competently lead or co-lead certain types of therapeutic groups. This issue becomes even more complicated and serious when one considers the number of unqualified people who call themselves experts or who consider themselves qualified to lead any type of group, without benefit of formal training. There are those who organize and conduct intensive encounter groups or marathons on the basis merely of their attendance at a few such sessions as participants. These are the leaders who can bring severe harm to participants.

Group leaders need to recognize their limitations. Toward this end, they might well ask themselves:

- What kind of clients am I capable of dealing with?
- What are my areas of expertise?
- What techniques do I handle well?
- How far can I safely go with clients?
- When should I refer a client to someone else?
- When should I consult another professional about a client?

Professional group leaders know their limitations and recognize that they can't lead all kinds of groups or work with all kinds of clients. They familiarize themselves with referral resources and don't attempt to work with a client of a type they're not trained to work with. Furthermore, a responsible leader is keenly aware of the importance of periodically continuing his or her education. Even a licensed and experienced professional will attend conventions and workshops, take courses, and get involved in special training programs from time to time. This desire to keep abreast of innovations grows out of the recognition that one can always profit from learning new skills and attitudes.

Truly competent group leaders also have an awareness of the reasons for most of the activities they suggest in a group. They are able to explain to their clients:

- the theory behind their group work,
- their goals in the group,
- the relationship between the way they lead the group and their goals, and
- how to evaluate how well the goals are being met.

Effective group leaders try to conceptualize the group process and to relate their operations in group to some conceptual model. They continually refine their techniques in light of this model. This does not mean that they rigidly adhere to one specific approach. As we've pointed out before, a leader may synthesize several group models into a personalized approach.

Finally, we believe it is essential for prospective group leaders to undergo extensive training. Before we present a description of one training program, we'll discuss three types of experiences that we highly recommend as adjuncts to a training program and that we feel are invaluable to the person who seeks to become a competent leader: personal (private) psychotherapy, group therapy, and participation in a training group.

Personal Psychotherapy for Group Leaders

Should group leaders have personal therapy (not *group* therapy) prior to and/or during their internship period? Should this experience be required or merely strongly recommended? What is the rationale for expecting leadership candidates to experience their own personal therapy? What are the possible values of such an experience?

Our strong conviction is that it is the ethical and professional responsibility of those who plan to become group therapists to seek their own private therapy before they attempt to become therapists of others. During the course of their sessions, it is hoped that they will come to a greater understanding of their motivation to become a leader of therapeutic groups. They can also explore: the biases of theirs that might hamper their receptiveness to clients; any unfinished business that might lead to distortions in their perceptions of group members; their philosophy of life—which directly relates to the way they view human beings—and the need they may have to impose this philosophy on clients; the needs they have that may either facilitate or inhibit the group process; current conflicts; their character (aspects of their personhood such as courage, enthusiasm, integrity, honesty, and caring); and the impact their character traits will have on others. In short, our conviction is that group therapists should demonstrate the courage and the willingness to do for themselves what they expect members in their groups to do—expand their awareness of self and of how that self affects others. The rationale here is that a group counselor cannot effectively assist clients to explore in depth conflicts that the counselor has not recognized in himself or herself. We are not implying that therapists must have experienced every personal problem of the clients they work with but that they must have the courage to honestly search within themselves and face what they find.

Self-Exploration Groups for Group Leaders

We have discovered that participation in a self-exploration group (or some type of therapeutic group) is an extremely valuable adjunct to a group leader's internship training experiences.

Beginning group leaders typically experience some anxiety regarding their adequacy, and their interactions with group members frequently lead to a surfacing of unresolved past or current problems. As we've said before, we think it is inappropriate for group leaders to use the group they're responsible for leading as a place to extensively examine their own problems. Leaders who find themselves doing this should join a therapeutic group as a member and use this group for continuing their growth. Besides being of therapeutic value, such a group can be a powerful teaching tool for the intern. Many group leaders have claimed that by actively working on themselves as a group participant they were better able to give empathy to and work in a meaningful and intense way with others.

Training Groups for Group Leaders

In addition to participating in a therapeutic group as a member, the beginning group leader must, we feel, join a training group—that is, a group of leader trainees. The training group can lead to insights and awareness without becoming a therapy group. The interns can learn a great deal about their response to criticism, their competitiveness, their need for approval, their jealousies, their anxieties over being competent, their feelings about certain members of the group they lead, and their power struggles with their co-leaders or the members of their group. These are but a few of the issues that are appropriate for work in a training group.

There is a subtle difference between a training group and a therapeutic group: the focus of a training group is on the skills necessary for efficient intervention. In such a group, new group leaders can become aware of values and attitudes they hold that influence their leadership style. For example, leaders who have an exaggerated need for approval may avoid being confrontive, may assume a passive stance, or may become inappropriately supportive in their groups. Their need for approval thus hampers their potential effectiveness by preventing them from effectively encountering others. Another example is the person who is attracted to being a group leader primarily by the power inherent in this position. This person's exaggerated need to control and direct others and to inspire the adulation of the group members may lead to mechanical use of a repertoire of techniques designed to impress the group participants with the therapist's prowess. Styles such as these can be detected and worked with during the sessions of a training group. Examples of questions that a supervisor might raise with the members of a training group are:

1. What were you feeling and thinking when your group sat silently for ten minutes? How did you deal with this silence? What do you suppose it meant?
2. How did you feel when Jim, one of your group members, openly challenged you on your qualifications to lead a group of college students, many of whom are older than you are?
3. Why did you keep pushing Sally to "work," when she had given several indications that she would rather be left alone?
4. Do you think that there was adequate closure for your group today? Did you allow yourself enough time to summarize what had happened in your group?
5. What did you feel when your co-leader openly disagreed with your perception of George, a group member?
6. Do you think you were confrontive enough with John when he continued with his long-winded story-telling? Why did you allow him to go on as long as you did?
7. Your group today seemed very lethargic, and several members finally stated that they were bored. What do you think was contributing to this situation? How do you and your co-leader feel about the way you dealt with the group's lethargy?
8. For several weeks you seem to have been extremely quiet in your group, and your co-leader has been assuming all of the leadership responsibility. What kind of thoughts run through your mind as you work with your co-leader? Are you satisfied with your participation level?
9. How did you feel when you invited Sue to participate in an exercise and she flatly refused, saying "No, I won't role-play, because that seems phony to me"? Did you like your response to her?

A PRACTICUM IN GROUP LEADERSHIP

During the past five years, I (Jerry Corey) have devoted about half of my working time to the training and supervision of group leaders. To illustrate some of the issues that have been discussed related to the training of leaders, I'd like to describe a practicum in group leadership that I lead. This practicum is for students who are interested in developing skills as a group leader, and it attracts students from a wide range of majors—human services, psychology, sociology, criminal justice, philosophy, and education. It is possible for mental-health and community clinics to establish similar training programs, both for interns and for seasoned professionals who seek to expand their group-process skills. The use of this kind of program thus need not be restricted to schools. And the format of a practicum in group leadership need not be restricted to the one I will describe—that is, two beginning students co-leading. Beginning students may co-lead with advanced students, co-lead with a supervisor, attend groups as a participant-observer, or lead groups alone, under supervision.

Weekend Training Workshop

As a regular part of the group-leadership practicum, which is open to both graduates and undergraduates, I conduct weekend workshops. The weekend consists essentially of a laboratory learning situation in which the participants become both group members and group leaders. Although I experiment with various structures, these workshops typically involve two people co-leading for an hour or two, initiating and facilitating group interaction. Then the group stops and evaluates what has occurred. The co-leaders discuss how they felt and evaluate how they did. The rest of the members give feedback concerning what they liked or disliked and the strengths and weaknesses of the co-leaders' approaches. The group also explores alternative approaches. Basically, the entire group examines its own process, each person learning about group process both as a member and as a leader.

Usually, the co-leaders are given preparation time, which may be in advance of the workshop. I have found that a topical approach is useful in this kind of workshop. Thus, the weekend may be divided into sessions on such topics as autonomy, loneliness, death, meaning in life, love, sexuality, masculine/feminine roles and behavior, and marriage and intimate relationships. (Of course, other topics can be substituted, depending on the nature of the training group.) Prior to the workshop, the co-leaders choose a topic from among a number that I suggest and prepare themselves to deal with it by reading and by getting together and discussing their goals and techniques.

Another way of structuring the workshop is by having each session focus on a particular theoretical approach to group work. The co-leader format is still used. Thus, one set of leaders might act as leaders of a Gestalt group would. Their job would be to illustrate how a Gestalt group functions, introducing appropriate exercises and employing appropriate techniques. After the session, which typically lasts two hours, group members discuss their experience and give feedback to the leaders. At this point, the leaders may also take a didactic approach, explaining to the group the rationale for some of the exercises. The next pair of leaders then leads a session according to the tenets of another group model. Like the topical format, this format gives members practice in co-leading. In addition, the group benefits from the opportunity to study its own process within the context of a given theoretical framework.

Weekly Training Sessions

The weekend workshop is merely one part of the practicum in group leadership. In addition, the counselors-in-training lead weekly groups. A trainee might lead a counseling group for fellow college students, a group formed in a community clinic, a group of adolescents, a group organized by a mental-health agency, or some other type of group.

Many of the group leaders whom I train and supervise gain experience by co-leading small groups on the university campus. These groups are part of a self-awareness and personal-development course that is described in Chapter 12. I spend time observing the trainees leading these groups (I do not observe trainees who lead any other type of group), and then I give feedback during weekly training sessions.

While there are many ways of structuring these weekly sessions, I prefer to meet each week with all of the group leaders before they meet with their own groups. This pre-session allows the students to demonstrate and experience group techniques, to share ways of opening their group sessions, and to exchange ideas that will increase their readiness to lead. After their group sessions, a post-session is held that provides for immediate feedback. During this session, the students and I might do a number of things, including: discussing ways of dealing with resistances encountered in various members; engaging in role-playing to see how alternative approaches might have worked; and recognizing and examining the personal blocks or conflicts that are inhibiting students' effectiveness as group leaders.

Whatever the format, the important thing is that co-leaders have an opportunity to discuss what happened in their groups. This is a time for them to raise questions about significant issues, to share insights, and to learn by examining the dynamics of the group they're leading.

Assessment can be a vital part of the weekly sessions. There are many approaches to evaluation, but somehow the group leaders should be given input about their strengths and weaknesses. I favor the use of multiple forms of leader evaluation. Each week, the co-leaders discuss each other's strengths and weaknesses, and three times during the semester they rate themselves and each other on the forms given in the "Exercises" section of Chapter 4. As their supervisor, I give each leader a written assessment three times during the semester, and my evaluations are often discussed in the training sessions and/or in individual conferences. Group leaders in training thus benefit from input from various sources and at various times and can look for patterns in their evaluations.

I require the trainees to keep an ongoing journal in which they record their experiences in the group-leadership program, including their experiences with the group they're leading. Putting into words what they've experienced can teach the trainees a great deal. I also encourage the trainees to develop a reading program, since readings can offer leaders a great variety of ideas that they can apply to their practice. Finally, I tell the trainees about workshops in psychodrama, music or art therapy, Gestalt therapy, TA, nonverbal techniques, and so on.

The Co-Leader Format as a Training Device

In this leadership-training program, I use a co-leader format in order both to safeguard the group members and to enrich the group leaders' learning experience. In determining the co-leader pairs, I attempt to pair off people of differing sex, differing level of experience, and complementary personal characteristics. I also take into account people's preferences in partners. A particular leader may feel somewhat threatened by another person's dynamic quality and talent, yet also feel that he or she could learn by working with this person and so be willing to cope temporarily with discomfort. I have paired a very spontaneous, active, and directive leader with a person who tends to be reflective, supportive, and inclined to let the group find its own direction. My rationale was that each could learn from the other's style and that the differences could be worked out in a way that would be in the group's interest.

Obviously, the choice of a co-leader is crucial. The decision should not be based merely on personal attraction, or the degree of comfort one might experience in leading with another, but rather on what would be of maximum value to the group. It is also obvious that the co-leaders need to establish a relationship based on cooperation, trust, and support—a relationship in which the persons can be autonomous and yet work together as a team. This is no easy task; it is very difficult for co-leaders to develop a good working relationship, such that they can focus on the group process and the members instead of on each other. This is why it is essential that the co-leaders meet frequently to discuss their differences and their views of the members in their group.

Major advantages of the co-leading model are that each person can provide the other with valuable feedback after each session and that the two leaders can share impressions of the group process. Further, the entire burden of responsibility for the group doesn't fall on one leader. While one leader works intensively with one member, the other leader can monitor the group process and look for ways of bringing other members into the interaction.

Demands and Commitments: Some Concluding Remarks

This group-leadership program is a demanding one—for both the intern and the supervisor. I take the responsibility of training group leaders very seriously, for the psychological welfare of group participants is at stake. Even though the type of training I've described is time-consuming and demands a significant personal commitment, I believe that shortcuts, because they may allow inadequate training and supervision, generally produce disastrous results. Groups frequently are viewed with suspicion and cynicism, and I think one reason is that those who design and lead groups are frequently inadequately prepared, both personally and professionally, to assume the numerous responsibilities of a group counselor.

The investment of time and energy required by a weekend workshop and weekly training sessions is considerable, but it can pay off in terms of the mental health not only of the group members but also of the interns, and even of the supervisors; it is extremely taxing to work with a group of inadequately trained and highly anxious group leaders. Therefore, in the long run, I have found this investment of energy well worth it.

ETHICAL GUIDELINES FOR GROUP LEADERS

A mark of professional group leadership is the establishing of a set of guiding principles. What follows is not a rigid set of policies but rather guidelines that we think will help group leaders clarify their own values and encourage them to take a position on some basic professional issues. We have struggled with these issues in our work with groups, and these guidelines make sense to us. We fully realize that other group leaders will have to develop guidelines that are appropriate for them. Our aim, in presenting these guidelines, is to stimulate you to design a personalized code of conduct.

1. It is good for leaders to reflect often on their personal identity. They can think about their needs and behavior styles and about the impact of these factors on group participants. They need to have a clear idea of what their roles and functions are in the group, and they need to communicate this idea to the group members.

2. Leaders need to have a clear idea of the type of group they're designing. This means that they must be able to express what the purpose of the group is and what the characteristics of the people who are admitted will be.

3. Group leaders must develop a means of screening that will allow them to differentiate between suitable and unsuitable applicants.

4. It is a group leader's responsibility to ask a potential group member who is undergoing psychotherapy or intensive counseling to consult his or her therapist before becoming involved in a group.

5. Prospective group members can be told what is expected of them as members and encouraged to develop contracts that call for them to satisfy these expectations. In other words, members can be told that they will be expected to: develop concrete personal goals, make appropriate self-disclosures, experiment with new interpersonal behaviors, examine their interpersonal style in terms of the impact they have on others, express their feelings and thoughts, actively listen to others and attempt to see the world through their eyes, show respect for others, offer genuine support, engage in confrontation of others as a way of developing an honest relationship with them, and be willing to experiment with new behaviors outside of the group.

6. It is important that prospective participants be made aware of the types of techniques that will be employed and of the types of exercises that they may be asked to participate in. They should be made aware of the ground rules that will govern group activities.

7. Group leaders should avoid undertaking a project that is beyond the scope of their training and experience. Furthermore, they might write a statement of their qualifications to conduct a particular group and make it available to the participants.

8. Leaders might make clear at the outset of a group what the focus of that group will be. For example, some groups have an educational focus, and so a didactic approach is used. Other groups have a therapeutic focus, and these take an emotive/experiential tack. Some groups have a developmental focus, with the aim being to get members to fully utilize their potential, while other groups are more remedial in nature and stress treatment of disabling symptoms or elimination of faulty behavior patterns. Participants need to be fully aware of the primary focus of the group they are about to enter.

9. Group leaders can protect group members' right to decide what to share

with the group and what activities to participate in. Group leaders should be sensitive to any form of group pressure that violates the self-determination of an individual and to any activity, such as scapegoating or stereotyping, that unfairly undermines a person's sense of self.

10. It is good for group leaders to develop a rationale for using the group exercises they do and to be able to verbalize this rationale. Further, group leaders should use only those exercises that they are competent to employ. It is best if leaders have experienced as group members the techniques they use.

11. Every attempt can be made to relate practice to theory. A group leader must develop a unique style of leading based on a personalized theory of group. Leaders might also keep themselves informed about research findings relating aspects of group process to certain outcomes and might use this information to increase the effectiveness of their group practice.

12. Group leaders should avoid exploiting the members of their groups. There is a tendency on the part of some members to glorify and idealize the group leader and to lessen their own power in the process. Ethical group leaders do not take advantage of this tendency and manipulate the participants. They don't enter into sexual relationships with group members, for to do so would be to misuse their power—to exploit clients in the service of their ego needs.

13. The psychological and physical risks involved in group participation can be pointed out to members before they enter a group and also when appropriate during the course of a group.

14. The importance of confidentiality may be stressed to members before they enter a group, during the group sessions when relevant, and before a group terminates.

15. Although group leaders might, when it is appropriate, be open with the group about their values, they should avoid imposing their values and beliefs on clients. It is good for them to respect their clients' capacity to think for themselves and to be sure that members give one another the same respect. Members often impose their values on others by telling them what to do, under the guise of being helpful.

16. Group leaders can be alert for symptoms of psychological debilitation in group members, which may indicate that participation in the group should be discontinued. Referral resources can be made available to persons who need or desire further psychological assistance.

17. It is important that group leaders not just allow but actually encourage participants to discuss their functioning in the group and their reactions to their experiences in the group. Time can be set aside at the end of each session during which members can express their thoughts and feelings about that session.

18. Participants might be prepared for the negative response they may encounter when they try to implement their group learning in their daily lives. Problems likely to be encountered can be openly discussed, and ways of dealing with these problems can be explored in group before the termination of the group. Members can be taught that change is not necessarily automatic and that difficulties in implementation are to be expected.

19. Follow-up sessions might be planned, so that members can see how they've done and so that the leader can evaluate the effectiveness of the group as an agent of change. Also, members can give feedback at this time that can help leaders improve their leadership. Individual follow-up sessions can be available to those individuals who feel a need to confer with the group leader after a group is terminated.

EXERCISES

Exercise in Group Planning

Select a particular type of group (encounter, counseling, or other) and a target population (children, adolescents, or adults). Keeping in mind the type of group you've selected, answer the following questions. The purpose of the exercise is to give you an idea of the kinds of questions you need to ask yourself if you are to practice ethically.

1. What is your role in this group?
2. What do you most want to occur in your group? State your purposes simply and concretely.
3. Would you form a contract with your group, and, if so, what would be the essence of the contract? Would you expect each member to develop a contract?
4. Mention a few ground rules or policies you feel would be essential for your group.
5. How can you determine whether you have the skills necessary to lead this particular type of group?
6. What is the focus of your group? (Didactic? Experiential? Remedial? Developmental?)
7. Would you accept only volunteer group members? Why or why not?
8. What characteristics would people have to have to be included? What is the rationale?
9. In what ways might you, if you wanted, exploit the members of your group?
10. How would you reveal your values without pressuring the members to accept them as theirs? Which of your values might create problems in the group?
11. How would you evaluate the effectiveness of your leadership? How would you assess the degree of progress made by the group members?

Other Exercises

1. Assume that you will be leading an encounter group composed of volunteers from a psychology class. The students chose this option because they preferred an experiential/interactional approach to a lecture/discussion approach. What do you

tell these students regarding the risks involved in experiential learning? What do you say to them about their rights and responsibilities as group members?

2. Assume that you are co-leading an ongoing personal-growth group with college students on campus (and that you and your co-leader are qualified to lead this kind of group). The members request an overnight marathon, and you and your co-leader agree to lead it. The director of the college counseling center, under whom you work, approaches you and asks whether there are any risks posed by a marathon. What do you answer?

During the all-night marathon, one of the students becomes very agitated and tells you of her frequent impulses to hurt herself. She also describes her suicide fantasies. Finally, she gets so upset that she storms out of the room, crying hysterically. What do you do?

After this incident, one member becomes very frightened. His body becomes tense, and he stares vacantly into space, immobile and apparently oblivious to his surroundings. What does this mean, and what do you do?

3. It comes to your attention that certain group members have been gossiping about matters that were dealt with in a high school group that you're leading. Do you deal with the offenders privately or in a group? What do you say?

4. Assume that you are about to begin leading a high school counseling group and that the policy of the school is that any teacher or counselor who becomes aware that a student is using drugs is expected to report the name of the student to the principal. How do you cope with this situation?

5. You are conducting a self-exploration group with children in a family clinic. The father of one of the children in your group meets with you to find out how his child is doing. What do you tell him? What do you not tell him?

6. Assume that you are a private practitioner who wants to co-lead a weekend assertiveness-training workshop. How would you announce your workshop? How would you screen potential members? What kind of person would you exclude from your workshop and why?

7. You are employed as a counselor in the adolescent ward of a county mental hospital. As one of your duties, you lead a group for the young people, who are required to attend the sessions. You sense resistance on the part of the members. What are the ethical problems involved? How do you deal with the resistance?

ANNOTATED READING LIST FOR PART 1

Alberti, R. E., & Emmons, M. L. *Stand up, speak out, talk back!* New York: Pocket Books, 1975. An easy-to-read overview of assertiveness-training concepts.

Bates, M. M., & Johnson, C. D. *Group leadership: A manual for group counseling leaders.* Denver: Love Publishing, 1972. A useful manual for group leaders—particularly those who work with groups in elementary and high schools. Includes discussions of: the role of the group leader, tools for forming a group and orienting the members, catalysts of interaction, practical considerations in organizing groups in the schools, and the various group approaches and models.

Blank, L., Gottsegen, G. B., & Gottsegen, M. G. (Eds.). *Confrontation: Encounter in self and interpersonal awareness.* New York: Macmillan, 1971. A book of readings about the experience of encounter. Deals with marathons; techniques and approaches; innovations in group work; applications to education, business, and industry; and theory and research.

Brown, G. *Human teaching for human learning: An introduction to confluent education.* New York: Viking, 1971. Provides an excellent introduction to confluent education—that is, education that addresses both the cognitive and the affective aspects of the student. Describes many techniques and exercises based on Gestalt awareness that are applicable to groups in elementary and secondary schools.

Burton, A. (Ed.). *Encounter: Theory and practice of encounter groups.* San Francisco: Jossey-Bass, 1969. Excellent readings for the group leader on key issues in encounter-group practice.

Corey, G. *Teachers can make a difference.* Columbus, Ohio: Charles E. Merrill, 1973. Tells how teachers can make a difference by being therapeutic persons. Group leaders can easily adapt these ideas for their own use.

Corey, G. *The struggle toward realness: A manual for therapeutic groups.* Dubuque, Iowa: Kendall/Hunt, 1974. A manual for participants in personal-growth groups, this book advocates a theme-oriented approach to group work. Autonomy, love, sex, marriage, loneliness, death, and values are among the themes discussed.

Corey, G. *Theory and practice of counseling and psychotherapy*. Monterey, Calif.: Brooks/Cole, 1977. Describes eight models of therapy and counseling that are applicable to both individual and group therapy. Contains chapters on the basic issues in counseling, ethical issues, and the counselor as a person. Designed to give the reader an overview of the theoretical basis for the practice of counseling. A student manual is available to assist readers in applying the concepts to their personal growth.

Corey, G. *Manual for theory and practice of counseling and psychotherapy*. Monterey, Calif.: Brooks/Cole, 1977. A student manual designed to accompany the textbook *Theory and Practice of Counseling and Psychotherapy*. Consists of exercises and self-assessment devices designed to make the theories more meaningful by showing the student how they can be applied. Many of the exercises can be used in group-oriented classes.

Diedrich, R. C., & Dye, H. A. (Eds.). *Group procedures: Purposes, processes, and outcomes*. Boston: Houghton Mifflin, 1972. A comprehensive book of readings, with articles on concepts and procedures in groups, group leadership, group membership, and group process and development. Also included are readings on applications of principles of group process to group practice, research and evaluation, and ethical issues.

Dinkmeyer, D. C., & Muro, J. J. *Group counseling: Theory and practice*. Itasca, Ill.: Peacock, 1971. A basic book that can be of help to group counselors —particularly those with a school orientation.

Egan, G. *Encounter: Group processes for interpersonal growth*. Monterey, Calif.: Brooks/Cole, 1970. A thorough treatment (with many references) of the nature of encounter groups. Includes discussions of group goals, group process, leadership, self-disclosure, and personal growth. An excellent theoretical exposition.

Egan, G. *Encounter groups: Basic readings*. Monterey, Calif.: Brooks/Cole, 1971. A book of readings on topics such as structures of groups, goals, leadership, communication processes, self-disclosure, expression of feelings, support, and confrontation.

Egan, G. *Face to face: The small-group experience and interpersonal growth*. Monterey, Calif.: Brooks/Cole, 1973. An excellent guide for beginners in groups, giving a clear picture of the nature and functioning of laboratory groups. Offers a nontechnical description of the theory and processes of small groups.

Egan, G. *Interpersonal living: A skills/contract approach to human-relations training in groups*. Monterey, Calif.: Brooks/Cole, 1976. Contains many exercises for groups at various stages of development. Discusses key concepts of group process.

Ellis, A. *Humanistic psychotherapy: The rational-emotive approach*. New York: McGraw-Hill, 1973. This book presents, in a clear, straightforward manner, most of the key concepts of rational-emotive therapy. Many of the ideas are applicable to group practice.

Fagan, J., & Shepherd, I. L. *Gestalt therapy now: Theories, techniques, applications.* New York: Harper & Row, 1971. Some excellent readings on the theory and techniques of Gestalt therapy. Much of the material is applicable to group work.

Gazda, G. M. *Group counseling: A developmental approach.* Boston: Allyn & Bacon, 1971. A basic book on group process, with a developmental orientation and an emphasis on school counseling. Contains chapters on procedures for groups of preschoolers, of children, of preadolescents, of adolescents, and of adults. Also covered are group-counseling research and ethical and professional issues.

Harper, R. A. *The new psychotherapies.* Englewood Cliffs, N.J.: Prentice-Hall, 1975. A good, although very brief, overview of group therapies. It also briefly deals with family therapies, the behavior therapies, the body therapies, and other types of therapy.

James, M., & Jongeward, D. *Born to win: Transactional analysis with Gestalt experiments.* Reading, Mass.: Addison-Wesley, 1971. An overview of the concepts of TA, along with descriptions of many Gestalt experiments that can be carried out in groups. Very useful for both leaders and members.

Johnson, D. W. *Reaching out: Interpersonal effectiveness and self-actualization.* Englewood Cliffs, N.J.: Prentice-Hall, 1972. Discusses interpersonal skills in both theoretical and practical terms. Some of the topics discussed are self-disclosure, verbal and nonverbal expression of feelings, enhancement of communication skills, constructive confrontation, and resolution of interpersonal conflicts. Many useful exercises for groups are included.

Johnson, D. W., & Johnson, F. P. *Joining together: Group theory and group skills.* Englewood Cliffs, N.J.: Prentice-Hall, 1975. Relates group theory to practice by offering many exercises that can be used in a group setting. Chapters included on leadership, decision-making, use of power, problem-solving, communication within groups, the leading of discussion groups, and the leading of growth groups.

Jourard, S. M. *The transparent self: Self-disclosure and well-being (2nd ed.).* New York: Van Nostrand Reinhold, 1971. The author contends that we have many ways of concealing ourselves and that this concealment leads to sickness; openness is dealt with as one way of increasing self-knowledge. The book contains excellent chapters on encounter groups and outlines a way of being for group leaders. Very highly recommended for anyone interested in groups.

Katz, R. *Preludes to growth: An experiential approach.* New York: Free Press, 1973. A useful manual containing exercises for opening groups and for encountering in groups. Includes a good discussion of the conceptual basis for personal growth. Many guidelines are given for humanistic education.

Kemp, C. G. *Foundations of group counseling.* New York: McGraw-Hill, 1970. A basic overview of the concepts and issues related to group counseling.

Lewis, H., & Streitfeld, H. *Growth games.* New York: Bantam, 1970. A cookbook of techniques based on the Human-Potential Movement. Games and techniques are designed to sharpen senses, expand conciousness, develop breathing, encourage relaxation, and help people break through blocks.

Mahler, C. A. *Group counseling in the schools.* Boston: Houghton Mifflin,

1969. An excellent group-counseling text with an orientation toward groups in the secondary school. Deals with the nature of group counseling, the formation of group, and the various stages in the evolution of a group.

Mann, J., & Otto, H. (Eds.). *Ways of growth: Approaches to expanding awareness*. New York: Viking, 1969. Articles are devoted to such topics as growing self-awareness, breathing therapy, sensory awakening and relaxation, sex and awareness, the encounter group, peak experiences, leaderless groups, and meditation.

Mintz, E. E. *Marathon groups: Reality and symbol*. New York: Avon, 1972. An excellent book for either group leaders or group members who want to understand the dynamics of marathon groups. Included are discussions of the nature of marathons, the process of marathons, the uses of the past, the group as therapist, and how to lead a marathon.

Muro, J., & Freeman, S. *Readings in group counseling*. Scranton, Pa.: International Textbook, 1968. Readings on the rationale for group counseling, group counseling in action, research on groups, operational issues, and ethical considerations.

Napier, R. W., & Gershenfeld, M. K. *Groups: Theory and experience*. Boston: Houghton Mifflin, 1973. A basic book on group process, containing chapters on group membership, group leadership, norms and goals of groups, the evolution of groups, and the current status of groups. Includes discussions of decision-making groups and other experience-related laboratory learning groups.

O'Banion, T., & O'Connell, A. *Shared journey: An introduction to encounter*. Englewood Cliffs, N.J.: Prentice-Hall, 1970. A useful book for both group leaders and group members. Two group leaders discuss their views of encounter groups in a very honest and personal way. Contains a good annotated bibliography.

Otto, H. *Group methods to actualize human potential—A handbook*. Beverly Hills, Calif.: The Holistic Press, 1970. A catalog of techniques for encounter and personal-growth groups. Helpful for the group leader who wants to be exposed to a variety of techniques.

Perls, F. S. *Gestalt therapy verbatim*. Moab, Utah: Real People Press, 1969. Contains excellent discussions of Gestalt techniques. Many of the concepts discussed are applicable to group practice.

Rogers, C. R. *Carl Rogers on encounter groups*. New York: Harper & Row, 1970. A readable book on the basic process of the encounter group. Tells how leaders can be facilitative in groups, what changes occur in the person and in organizations as a result of participation in encounter groups, and when encounter groups can be useful.

Ruitenbeek, H. M. *New group therapies*. New York: Avon, 1970. A comprehensive overview of recently developed approaches to group therapy. Includes discussions of marathon groups and of styles of conducting encounter groups.

Schultz, D. *Theories of personality*. Monterey, Calif.: Brooks/Cole, 1976. A clear text giving an overview of the various theories of personality, including Freudian, neo-Freudian, humanistic, and behaviorist theories. A valuable resource for the reader who wants a brief survey of personality theories that are related to counseling theories.

Schutz, W. *Joy: Expanding human awareness*. New York: Grove, 1967. The theme of this book is that joy is the result of realizing one's full human potential. Methods of improving personal functioning and enhancing interpersonal relating compose the core of the book. A good first book for persons thinking about becoming involved in a here-and-now-oriented group.

Schutz, W. *Here comes everybody: Bodymind and encounter culture*. New York: Harper & Row, 1972. A good treatment of what Schutz has termed "the open encounter group." Various types of growth groups are considered. Schutz also discusses group techniques and the group leader.

Schutz, W. *Elements of encounter,* New York: Bantam, 1975. A very useful guide for group leaders. Defines encounter groups, gives a historical sketch, examines the principles of encounter, describes the theory of group development, discusses rules of groups, and shows how encounter principles can be applied to out-of-group situations.

Shaffer, J. B., & Galinsky, M. D. *Models of group therapy and sensitivity training*. Englewood Cliffs, N.J.: Prentice-Hall, 1974. An excellent overview of various types of groups, including psychoanalytic, existential/experiential, psychodrama, Gestalt, behaviorist, T-, encounter, and theme-centered groups. The excellent final chapter takes a broader perspective, showing how the models overlap and diverge.

Smith, M. J. *When I say no, I feel guilty*. New York: Bantam, 1975. A very useful book, offering principles that can be applied by the reader to everyday situations that call for assertiveness.

Stevens, J. O. *Awareness: Exploring, experimenting, experiencing*. Moab, Utah: Real People Press, 1971. Tells how to explore, expand, and deepen awareness. A good source of exercises for group work, this book also offers suggestions to the group leader for using the exercises.

Suinn, R. M., Weigel, R. G. (Eds.). *The innovative therapies: Critical and creative contributions*. New York: Harper & Row, 1975. A good book of readings on a range of topics, including behavior therapy, therapeutic programs, and paraprofessionals. One section consists of eight articles on group procedures.

Verny, T. R. *Inside groups: A practical guide to encounter groups and group therapy*. New York: McGraw-Hill, 1975. An easy-to-read and comprehensive guide to groups, this book provides guidelines for the consumer of groups, raises questions about groups, describes verbal and nonverbal group techniques, and describes the group marathon.

Yalom, I. D. *The theory and practice of group psychotherapy* (2nd ed.). New York: Basic Books, 1975. An excellent, comprehensive text on group therapy. Detailed discussions are devoted to the curative factors in groups, the group therapist, the procedures involved in the organizing of therapy groups, problem patients, research on the encounter group, and the training of group therapists.

Part 2

GROUP PRACTICE:
Some Special Groups

10. COUNSELING GROUPS
FOR CHILDREN

In the first part of this book, we discussed concepts and issues that are basic to most types of groups. Now, in the second part of the book, we hope to show how the concepts we've presented operate in a variety of specific types of groups and how group-process concepts can be used by leaders as they develop and work with various types of clients in various settings.

Recently I (Marianne Corey) participated in a master's-degree program in counseling that involved a variety of internship experiences, including work with children. Because you may find yourself in a similar internship program involving children, either in a school setting or in a community clinic, I want to share with you my own experience and to describe some guidelines that I followed and some methods that I used in my work with children.

THE COUNSELING PROGRAM

The program I applied for was a federally funded project. After an interview, I was hired by the director of a community counseling center, to whom I was then responsible. He assigned me to an elementary school.

Although my work for this project was very rewarding and proved to be an excellent learning experience, I suffered some frustration at first because I didn't know from one month to the next whether the project would remain in existence or whether I would soon be out of a job. I expended a great deal of energy worrying about the future of the project—a fact that affected my work with the children, although I wasn't aware of it at the time. After several weeks, I contacted the principal of my school and ascertained that I could continue working on a voluntary basis if the funding for the project were discontinued. Freed of my worry about the unpredictable effects of politics on the project, I was able to devote all of my energy to the children.

Another initial source of frustration was the fact that I had been given little instruction on what to do. I knew only that I would be working with elementary-school children, ranging in age from 6 to 11 and designated as problem children by their teacher or the principal; yet it was up to me to design a program that would improve the children's behavior in class. Ten to fifteen children would make up my case load, and I was to see each child at least once a week for about an hour, for a total of 24 visits.

To be referred to me, a child would have to be acting out his or her emotional disturbance in some way, such as through aggressive behavior. In this special program, passive and withdrawn children, as much in need of counseling as the children who were expressing their anger, would not be included. (This was yet another source of frustration for me.) If a child showed one of the following behaviors or attributes, he or she would be considered a candidate for referral:

- excessive fighting,
- inability to get along with peers,
- frequent hurting of other children,
- violation of school rules,
- poor attitude toward school,
- stealing from school or from peers,
- violent or angry outbursts,
- neglected appearance,
- hunger symptoms and/or frequent failure to bring lunch to school,
- chronic tiredness,
- lack of supervision at home, and
- excessive truancy.

My job would be to deal with the problems underlying the child's behavior and, by alleviating them, alleviate the child's school problems and prevent more serious problems from developing.

THE INITIAL PHASE

Contact with School Personnel

Being fully aware that counselors are often mistrusted in schools, I set out to earn the trust of the teachers and administrators.

The first thing I did, therefore, was meet with the principal and the teachers. I asked them what their expectations were of me and what they hoped the project would accomplish. I told them that I wanted to work closely with them, providing feedback about the children, making specific suggestions, and getting their suggestions. I let them know that I intended to work with the children individually and in groups and to involve the parents in the treatment process too. I explained that I would have the children play with clay and puppets, tell stories, and role-play—all activities that allow self-expression—during their contact with me.

Accordingly, I developed a program in which I was in continuous contact with the children's teachers, principal, and parents. The teachers and the principal were most cooperative about meeting with me. I also spoke frequently with the school psychologist, the school nurse, and the school secretaries about particular children, gathering as much information as I could. This information turned out to be most helpful.

The School Setting

The setting for my work with the children was not ideal. The school was short on space (a new school was being built), and I was continually looking for a place to meet with the children. Often, weather permitting, I would meet with them on the school lawn, since I needed a place where the children could explore, touch, talk loudly, shout if they were angry, or give vent to any other emotions they were experiencing. If I took them off campus, or did anything special with them, I first obtained written permission from the parents and the school authorities, preferring to be extremely cautious in my dealings with this public institution. Although I never had an ideal place to work, this did not keep me from working effectively with the children, as we often improvised together.

Since I didn't have my own office for much of the time, I had to call for the children at their classrooms. This deeply concerned me. How would the child react to being singled out? Would my special attention to children amid their peers affect them negatively? Fortunately, I found the contrary to be true. The children responded very positively to my coming to pick them up and were always ready to come with me, even during recess time. Frequently, some of their classmates would ask whether they could come see me too.

My Initial Contact with the Parents

After meeting with the school staff, who identified which children I would be working with, I contacted the parents of each child. During my initial contact, I usually explained to the parents that I worked as a special counselor at the school and that their child had been referred to me by the teacher, who had become concerned about the child's behavior in class. The parents knew before I visited them about my intended involvement with their child, because I had asked the principal and the child's teacher to contact the parents prior to my visit. This interview gave the parents a chance to get to know me and to ask me questions and gave me the chance to get the parents' permission to work with their child. At this time, I gathered information regarding any difficulties the parents were having with the child and collected the data I needed in order to complete numerous forms. If parents became anxious over my probing or over the fact that *their* child had been singled out for psychological treatment, I explained to them that, since teachers have to deal with so many children, they can't always provide all of the attention that a child needs. It would be my job, I explained, to provide the extra attention their child needed.

Up to this point, I had counseled only people who had requested my services; therefore, it was a new experience for me to be confronted by the suspicions of parents who had been informed that their child needed my services. But, for the most part, parents were willing to cooperate and gave their consent. I told them that I hoped to see them alone sometimes and sometimes together with their children. In response to my question about any difficulties they might be experiencing with their child at home, which I asked in order to get clues regarding the child's behavior in school, the comments I received were guarded at first but became much more open with time and frequent contacts.

I explained that I wished to keep as confidential as possible what the child and I would be exploring in our sessions; therefore, I explained, I would let them know in a general way how I was proceeding with the child but would not reveal any of the specifics. The parents were agreeable to this. By going into the child's home, I was able to get much information relating to the problems the child was exhibiting that would otherwise have been difficult, if not impossible, to obtain. It was often difficult to schedule further contacts with parents, though, because every one of them, without exception, was employed. Some parents I was unable to see again after my initial contact. However, I was able to make at least some additional contact with most parents.

My Initial Contact with the Children

Prior to participating in this project, I had worked only with adults and adolescents who were able to express themselves verbally. During my initial contact with the children (I saw them individually), I relied very heavily on my verbal skills, expecting that they would be verbal with me in turn. But conversation with the children proved difficult. The children were reluctant to initiate conversation, being accustomed only to answering questions. I introduced myself to them, stating that I was a special type of teacher called a counselor. I explained that their teacher was concerned about their behavior in class and that they would be talking with me several times a week—individually, as a group, and in their homes. I told them that we would be discussing problems they had in school, at home, or with their peers and that we would talk about feelings.

I let them know that I would be talking about them with their parents and teachers but that what they talked about in the group and alone with me was confidential; they were not to talk to others about what other group members had said, and I would not tell anyone what they had said. I told them that they could talk about anything they wanted to in the group or with me but that they would neither hurt other children nor destroy any property. I set up other rules that I felt were also necessary and made the children aware of their responsibility—aware that in order to be part of the group they had to agree to follow these rules. I also discussed with the children the fact that they might sometimes tell me things that would be important to share with their parents, but I reassured them that they and I would decide together whether to talk to their parents. I felt strongly that it was just as important for a 6-year-old child to know that what she told me would be treated with confidentiality as it would be for a 60-year-old adult. Children's rights are too often violated and their need for privacy too often ignored.

There turned out to be little problem with maintaining confidentiality. When others in the children's classes asked them what they did in their sessions, I heard them state that they played games and talked about feelings.

THE WORKING PHASE

Working with the Children in a Group

My goal was not to do intensive psychotherapy, for my time was limited and this would have been unrealistic. I did hope to pinpoint some of the children's maladaptive behaviors, teach the children more effective ways of interacting with others, and provide a climate in which the children would feel free to express freely a range of feelings. It seemed important to teach them ways of expressing emotions without hurting themselves or others. I wanted to convey to the youngsters that negative feelings do not get them into trouble—that it's acting on these feelings that can lead to problems. In an effort to teach them ways of safely expressing negative feelings, I got them involved in a variety of activities, including role-playing, acting out social situations, painting, finishing stories that I began, putting on puppet shows, playing music, and dancing.

I found that the easiest to work with and most productive groups were those composed of three to five children of the same age and same sex. If there were more than this in a group, I found myself (1) unable to relate intensely to individuals, (2) slipping into the role of disciplinarian to counteract the increased distractions, (3) feeling frustrated at the number of children competing for my attention, and (4) without enough time left over from keeping order to pay attention to underlying dynamics. In addition, children between the ages of 6 and 11 tend to become impatient if they have to wait very long for their turn to speak.

I took care to combine withdrawn children with more aggressive children, but I also felt that it was important for the children to be with others who were experiencing similar conflicts. For example, I put two boys in the same group who felt much anger, hurt, grief, and frustration over their parents' divorce and subsequent remarriage. They slowly learned how to express how they felt about not having much contact with the parent they didn't live with. At first, the boys could only express their feelings symbolically, through play; later, they learned to put words to their emotions and to talk about their feelings with their parents.

As I had planned, I provided some time for each child during which he or she could have my attention alone. I noticed that, in the group, all of the children became less jealous of one another about me and trusted me more once I had begun to provide this individual time. Alone, the children were more cooperative, less competitive, and more affectionate than in the group. They felt less need to show off. Having an adult spend time with them individually gave the children a sense of importance.

With the teacher's consent, I also visited the child frequently in his or her classroom and on the playground, sometimes just observing and sometimes making a brief contact, through touch or words.

Our scheduled group and individual sessions took place twice a week and lasted for half an hour to an hour. It would have been a mistake for me to have insisted that sessions always last a certain length of time, because the children differed from session to session in their patience. When a child stated that he or she wanted to leave a group session, I would say in a friendly manner that that was allowed but that I wished he or she would stay until the session was over. Usually the child stayed. Most of the time the children enjoyed the sessions. I learned by trial and error that it was a good practice to let them know in advance that a session was coming to an end and then to be firm about having them leave and not give in to their demands that the group continue.

Most of my groups were open groups; new members could join. The children already in the group handled this very well. They knew the newcomer from school and didn't meet the child with any negative reactions or resistance, contrary to what I have experienced with adults.

At first I was eager to get to work on a child's specific problem, as perceived by teachers, parents, and others. However, I found I needed to go beyond the specific problem area because the children did not perceive themselves as having a problem. For me to talk to a girl about what was going on when she had violent angry outbursts and suddenly struck out was futile. Therefore, I began to relax with the children, let them lead the way, and listen to what they had to say, directly or through the various symbolic means I've described. Quite by accident, playing with puppets was found to be an excellent means of revealing a variety of emotions and dramatizing situations that produce conflict. I made puppets available to the first- and second-grade children but found that even the fourth- and fifth-grade children were able to use them to give vent to their pent-up emotions.

The groups offered the children the opportunity to act out situations that aroused conflicting feelings. Sometimes I would suggest a problem situation, and sometimes the children would select a problem to act out. The children would take the roles of teacher, friend, principal, parent, brother, sister, or whoever was involved. In this way, the children were able to vent their emotions without hurting others.

Many times I had to remind myself to be patient and to allow the children to take their time in expressing themselves. Sometimes several sessions passed before a child would speak freely. I sat close to the children during the sessions. I listened to them attentively, often reflecting for them what they were saying but, more important, communicating to them, usually nonverbally, that I was with them, that what they were saying was important, and that I cared about what they had to say. I insisted that other members in the group listen and assured all of them that each would have a time to speak. This is a very difficult concept to get across, especially to a 6- or 7-year old, who is still very self-centered and still learning to share.

Sometimes, after a session that I felt got nowhere, I would be surprised to hear a teacher comment on a child's changed behavior. After one such session, a boy who had been very destructive and disobedient before the session became cooperative and able to relate to his peers. His pounding of a lump of clay, which I had interpreted as nonproductive, turned out to have been very important for him. It had relieved much of his anger and so reduced his need to strike out at others.

In retrospect, I can see that I trusted my intuition to a great extent. However, I found that it was important to have a good understanding of different theories of personality, including psychosexual and psychosocial developmental theories, and to be familiar with various counseling theories. I discovered that, in order to understand the underlying causes of the child's problem behavior, I would have to include the parents in the treatment process as much as possible.

I often agonized over the question: is my work with the children doing any good? Changes in the children's behavior were slow in coming and sometimes temporary. A child would seem to have improved one week, but the next week his or her behavior would again be very negative. My firm belief that a child can change if afforded the opportunity to change was challenged again and again.

However, most children made definite changes, as observed by the teacher, the principal, the parents, and me. Truants began to come to school more regularly. A boy who was in the habit of stealing and giving his loot to other children so that they would like him learned that this behavior was one of the reasons that others disliked him in the first place and began to get their attention through more positive actions. A girl who had been conditioned not to trust learned to make friends and to reach out first—to do what at one time she had been most fearful of.

These changes, while encouraging, needed to be reinforced at home. I cannot stress enough the importance of involving parents in the therapeutic process. While most parents welcomed many of their child's new behaviors, some found the new behavior threatening. For instance, one girl caused her mother some anxiety by beginning to ask probing questions about her absent father. I encouraged this mother—and other parents facing similar problems—to try to listen to the child nondefensively.

Why the Group Format Was Effective

My clients, aged 6 to 11, were at a stage of growth in which they were leaving mother and home part of the day, expanding their relationships to include other adults, exploring and testing out-of-home environments, and developing peer relationships. Since most of my referrals were children who had deficiencies in relating to others, I found the group an excellent modality, since it allowed for the learning and practicing of relational skills.

In addition, using the group format allowed me to spend more time with each child than would have been possible had I used individual sessions alone, although, since individual sessions are valuable for their own reasons, I preferred having both types of contact with each child.

Another advantage of the group was that it allowed me to experience the child as the teacher did. Thus, the group gave me the opportunity that individual conferences didn't to spot faulty interactions with peers. I could witness interactions firsthand, I could instantly give feedback; in this way, the chances that learning would take place were maximized.

Finally, the group, by its very nature, encouraged the children to discuss, or otherwise deal with, problems that they had in common. After directly expressing emotions that had been bottled up, the children had less need to express these feelings indirectly by withdrawing, fighting, or getting sick.

Termination of the Group

When I began to work with the children, I told them that the sessions would go on only for a limited time during the school year. Several sessions before termination, I reminded the children that the group and individual sessions would be ending soon. We discussed the imminent termination of our meetings, for I had seen some of the children over a period of eight months, and they had formed a strong attachment to me and I to them. It was as difficult for me to leave them as it was for them to see me leave, and we shared this sadness openly.

While I had been affectionate with the children during our time together, I hadn't deceived them by becoming a substitute mother or by establishing myself as a permanent fixture who would totally satisfy all of their needs. By being realistic from the beginning about the limits of my job, I was able to prevent termination from being a catastrophic experience for the children.

PROBLEMS REQUIRING OUT-OF-GROUP ATTENTION

Academic Problems

The children who were referred to me, almost without exception, were identified by the teachers as children with learning problems. Often these learning disabilities were a reflection of their emotional conflicts. Since I was unable to provide the necessary tutorial assistance, I contacted a nearby university and recruited five graduate students to tutor the children for credit in their child-psychology course. In addition to providing tutorial services, they gave the children additional positive individual attention. This tutoring proved very successful for both the children and the university students, and the program was continued after I left.

Nutrition and Health Care

Several of my children repeatedly came to school hungry, tired, sloppily dressed, and emanating strong body odors. These children had poor self-images and were victims of teasing by their peers. To deal with these problems, I taught personal hygiene, secured some nicer clothes, and made arrangements for certain children to receive free lunches at school. The school had a free-lunch program, but many parents had neglected to enroll their children in it. Besides teaching the children personal grooming, I was able to convince some parents of the importance of their child's hygiene in terms of the child's self-image. Often a change in a child's outward appearance had a significant positive effect on his or her behavior at school. When I detected health problems, I referred the child to the school nurse.

Lack of Supervision, Attention, and Affection in the Home

Because both parents of every child I worked with were employed full-time, they had little time for involvement with their children. (This was true not only of the children in my case load; it also applied to the vast majority of the children at that school, which suggests that, in itself, the full-time employment of the parents was not the factor responsible for the children's psychological problems.) Some of these children, as young as 6 years old, spent several hours a day at home alone. In working with the parents of my clients, I became aware that positive contact with the children was almost nonexistent. When the parents did come home, they were tired and burdened with household chores. Many of the parents deceived themselves by saying that the quality, not the quantity, of the time they spent with their children was important. In most cases, I found that the quality was as poor as the quantity was small. Occasionally I discovered that, if I discussed this matter with the parents in a nonaccusatory way, they would accept the fact that they were contributing to their child's school difficulties and realize that their responsibility for their child's healthy development called for them to change. One parent who had many children began to spend a few minutes a day alone with each child. Another parent started regular family sessions during which each family member could discuss his or her concerns about home and school.

Problems Associated with Broken Homes

The divorce rate at this school was extremely high, and all but two of the children I worked with came from broken homes. In the group sessions, I became aware that much of the children's hurt and anger related to the breakup of their homes. I allowed the children to give vent to these feelings of sadness and anger. I discovered that many parents were unaware of their child's conflict, and I encouraged these parents to listen to their children and allow them to openly express their emotions without fear of the parent's becoming defensive. The children were much more likely to resolve their conflicts if the parents permitted them to talk about the divorce.

WORKING OUTSIDE OF THE GROUP

Working with the Families

I've already discussed the fact that I contacted the parents as often as I could in order to involve them in the process of their child's counseling. On several occasions, I also had lengthy family sessions, discussing not only the particular child's problems but also the dynamics of the entire family. The purpose was to explore the conflicts that affected all of the members and to find ways of improving the quality of interaction. Although I felt enthusiastic about working with entire families, it was hard to arrange such sessions, for reasons of time and scheduling. Stopping by a child's home just to visit or to show movies and pictures of the child that I had taken during a trip to the mountains or at a swimming party I found to be just as valuable as "work" sessions. It seemed especially meaningful to show the movies of the children to the families, because this made the children feel special and proud. These visits increased the parents' trust in what I was doing and increased their willingness to cooperate with me.

Working with the Teachers

Throughout the chapter, I've noted my involvement with my clients' teachers. A point I want to emphasize is that I was working with a very enthusiastic and caring staff. We combined our efforts to come up with ways of improving the children's overall school experience. Our enthusiasm was infectious, and we were able to learn much from each other. The teachers implemented classroom procedures that were extensions and continuations of the work I was doing. For instance, a teacher might give a few moments of individual positive attention before the child asked for attention in a negative way. In addition to meeting with the teachers, I also made frequent contacts with the principal, the school nurse, the school secretaries, the school psychologist, and the school librarian.

Tapping Outside Resources

Because a counselor works with the total child, he or she needs to know what services, agencies, associations, companies, and individuals can be contacted for help when counseling is not enough. Many children are undernourished, under-clothed, and in need of medical assistance, recreational opportunities, or supervision after school. Weekly counseling is more likely to have an effect if the basic needs of the child are being met. I found that I had to become actively involved as a kind of social worker to provide for many of the children's physical needs. I learned to rely on myself to do much of the legwork required to obtain food, clothing, money, or special services for the children and their families. Some families resisted turning to outside agencies, because of pride, or because of fear that strings would be attached, or simply because of ignorance about where to go for help. When a family did want help with emotional, economic, or medical problems, I referred them to one of the agencies or associations listed in the chart that follows. I did this rather than deal with problems I wasn't qualified to deal with or take on additional counseling loads that I might not have had time to follow through on. However, I often made the contacts with the agencies and did the paperwork they required.

The chart that follows lists organizations and agencies and shows which services each provides. Some resources will offer other important services, depending on their financial status at the time a request is made. This list is by no means exhaustive but gives a good idea of what is available.

Probably the most important (and most often overlooked) method of obtaining services for children and their families is asking. Private companies, concerned citizens, and the school staff are all potential resources that can be tapped, both for material goods and for suggestions about where else to go for help. I can't stress enough that the total needs of the child must be considered if the emotional needs are to be met.

THE IMPORTANCE OF THE COUNSELOR'S
PERSONAL AND PROFESSIONAL NEEDS

During this internship, I found that ongoing supervision was of great importance. Most colleges and mental-health institutions provide an inexperienced counselor with the supervision of a licensed psychologist; however, I frequently had to seek supervision on my own, and it is not uncommon for interns to have to pay for supervision! Too often I have seen interns hesitate to approach their supervisor because the latter appeared too busy or because the interns feared exposing themselves to the scrutiny of a superior. In institutions especially, supervision often has low priority, since the fully trained staff members are already overburdened with large case loads. Thus, a nonassertive intern's need for supervision can easily be ignored. Yet I found that, when I stressed my need for supervision, supervisors made the time to counsel me.

Talking to a supervisor gives interns the opportunity not only to examine their relationships with clients but also to explore what each client brings out in them. Many times my discussions with my supervisor became personal-therapy sessions, in the sense that I used the time to work with some insights into myself provoked by my work with a client. Dealing with my personal reactions and problems freed me to work more effectively with my clients.

Thus, ongoing supervision can improve not only your counseling skills but also your self-understanding. A session with a supervisor can also be an excellent time in which to examine conflicts arising from your daily life—conflicts independent of your work with your client. To illustrate the importance of supervision to a beginning counselor, I would like to describe a case of mine that caused me to experience feelings that I felt a great need to explore. This example also gives some idea of how public-service agencies handle "problem children."

An 8-year-old boy, whom I shall call Mark, was referred to me for stealing and truancy. It was suspected that he was physically and emotionally neglected, even abused, at home. I worked with him very intensely in group and individually for three months, experiencing delight and excitement as he began to accept himself, respect others, and show a desire to learn and to make friends. I feel that so much progress was made in such a short time because I invested a great deal of time and energy in seeing that all of his needs were met; this pursuit sent me to the school nurse, the school librarian, the teachers, the principal, and the school psychologist for assistance. We worked diligently as a team on Mark's behalf. Unfortunately, Mark's mother, after giving her consent for the counseling, was not available for further consultation.

Organization	Clothing	Food	Summer camp	Money	Counseling for children	Marriage, family, and child counseling	General counseling	Divorce counseling	Clubs for children	Child-abuse counseling	Sports for children	Care for the handicapped	Dental services	Eye care	Medical services	Day and after-school care	Toys	Tutoring	Furniture	Alcoholism counseling	Drug counseling	Legal assistance	Housing
March of Dimes	X																						
Easter Seal Society												X											
American Cancer Society															X								
Leukemia Society of America															X								
City of Hope															X								
County mental-health associations						X	X	X													X		
Crisis-intervention centers							X														X		
Hot lines							X														X		
Church organizations	X	X		X																			
State medical programs															X								
County food-stamp programs		X																					
City and state housing programs (for the elderly and AFDC families)																							X
City assistance leagues	X	X											X										
Lions Club														X									
Kiwanis Club	X	X																					
Altrusa Service Organization[1]		X																					
Police- and fire-department benevolent associations										X				X									

160

Organization														
Salvation Army	×									×	×			×[2]
PTA	×	×								×	×	×		
Local parent-advisory committees	×	×								×	×	×		
School psychologists			×											
Social Security Administration		×						×						
U. S. Department of Social Welfare	×	×						×						
Free clinics								×			×			
Shriners						×								
Federal and state crippled-children's services						×		×						
Planned Parenthood								×						
Well-baby clinics								×						
Child Protective Services				×										
State departments of social service				×										
Juvenile-justice departments				×										
City and county social-services centers[3]	×	×	×	×									×	×
Local colleges, junior colleges, high schools								×[4]		×				
AAA, Alateens												×		
School child-guidance centers		×												
City parks-and-recreation departments							×							
YMCA, YWCA	×	×					×							
Homes for the aged								×[4]		×				

[1] This organization will provide money for any service if the cost is high.
[2] Emergency housing only.
[3] Services provided will vary.
[4] Transportation for the child must be provided.

One night I received a telephone call from a colleague who worked at another school, who informed me that Mark and his brother were being held at the police station pending placement by Child Protective Services in a foster home, because the boys' mother and her lover had deserted them. My colleague and I offered our homes as refuge (the boys had asked to stay with us) but were told that it is not possible for counselors to involve themselves in this way, especially if they're not licensed foster parents.

A Department of Public Social Service (DPSS) agent drove the boys around for much of the evening, seeking shelter for them. I felt helpless and sad, although I tried to reassure Mark by phone that any family that took him in would do its best. It was painful to tell him that I couldn't care for him temporarily. I soon learned that the boys had been placed in a home in another community.

That the DPSS was doing its job did not alleviate my despair at being unexpectedly separated from a little boy whom I had come to care for, make plans for, and feel excited about. We never had a chance to say good-bye. I did as much follow-up as possible on the case, voicing my interest as to the whereabouts and well-being of Mark and his brother. My interest was received with suspicion, however; although I was readily informed by the responsible agency that the children had been placed in a foster home, I was told that investigation into the whereabouts of a client who was no longer in my case load was highly irregular. I was sad to learn, sometime later, that Mark had come to the attention of the authorities of his new school for stealing and truancy.

I found that my feelings of discouragement, defeat, and powerlessness needed to be explored and worked through. I believe that, if counselors' relationships with clients are to deepen and their willingness to risk involvement with new clients continue to grow, they need to take care of themselves and their personal needs by seeking some kind of counseling. Cases like the one I've just described can be emotionally draining; counselors may suffer not only over the child's conflicts but also over the personal conflicts the child's case brings out in them. In order to continue to work effectively, counselors need to discover sources of help for their personal problems.

SOME CONCLUDING COMMENTS

In looking back, I have come to the conclusion that much of what I did with these children could have been done by a sensitive teacher in a classroom.* However, the nature of the school system makes the likelihood that this will happen very

---

*The program I was part of could also be duplicated by any agency that serves children. For example, a child-guidance center at which a colleague of mine works offers a multitude of psychological services to children ages 6 to 12, who have been referred usually by the school or by the parents. The center provides short-term therapy for approximately three months. Each child has group therapy five days a week. In order to have their child accepted, parents must agree to become involved in both the treatment planning and the treatment process.

small; teachers just don't have the time to involve themselves with the children's psychological and social well-being. It is unfortunate that there is such limited contact between parents and teachers and that teachers are so often ignorant of the facts of the child's home environment, to which the child's school problems can usually be traced.

At this point, I would like to share a few of the teachers' reactions to my involvement with the children. The following quotes are from their written reports.

- "These children have emotional and educational problems, and the individual care given each of them has helped them understand better their limitations and assets."
- "Both children were very explosive and lashed out at other children without provocation. The counselor's attitude and positive outlook helped to calm them, and they now are getting along well in the classroom and with their peers."
- "A student with a high absentee record, who seldom communicated with others, began to change after her involvement in the counseling program. She began to initiate conversation, and she no longer preferred sitting alone; rather, she began to want to be with others. She even began to smile."
- "They are fighting less and are better able to talk things out. The special attention these boys received helped make their second year of school a more successful experience than it would otherwise have been."
- "I believe they have developed a stronger sense of identify—a foundation for self-love—and have developed some positive ways of resolving problems."
- "The counseling program has helped me understand the children and has created a valuable link between the school and the home."

From my experience with this counseling program, I learned a great deal about what it is like to be a child nowadays and what it is like for my children in a public elementary school. I also gained many valuable insights into how best to reach children.

SUGGESTED READINGS

Adams, P. L. *A primer of child psychotherapy*. Boston: Little, Brown, 1974.

Axline, V. M. *Play therapy* (Rev. ed.). New York: Ballantine, 1974.

Axline, V. M. *Dibs: In search of self*. New York: Ballantine, 1976.

Baruch, D. *One little boy*. New York: Delta, 1964.

Bates, M. M., & Johnson, C. D. *Group leadership: A manual for group counseling leaders*. Denver: Love Publishing, 1972.

Boy, A. V., & Pine, G. J. *Expanding the self: Personal growth for teachers*. Dubuque, Iowa: William C. Brown, 1971.

Brown, G. I. *Human teaching for human learning: An introduction to confluent education*. New York: Viking, 1971.

Corey, G. *Teachers can make a difference*. Columbus, Ohio: Charles E. Merrill, 1973.

Dorman, L., & Rebelsky, F. *Growing children*. Monterey: Brooks/Cole, 1976.

Gazda, G. M. *Group counseling: A developmental approach*. Boston: Allyn & Bacon, 1971.

Ginott, H. *Between parent and child*. New York: Avon, 1973.

Glasser, W. *Schools without failure*. New York: Harper & Row, 1969.

Gordon, T. *P. E. T., Parent Effectiveness Training: The tested new way to raise responsible children*. New York: New American Library, 1970.

Holt, J. *How children fail*. New York: Dell, 1964.

Holt, J. *How children learn*. New York: Dell, 1967.

Holt, J. *The underachieving school*. New York: Dell, 1969.

Holt, J. *Freedom and beyond*. New York: Dell, 1972.

Holt, J. *Escape from childhood*. New York: Ballantine, 1974.

Hunter, E. *Encounter in the classroom*. New York: Holt, Rinehart and Winston, 1972.

Jackson, N., Robinson, H., & Dale, P. *Cognitive development in young children*. Monterey: Brooks/Cole, 1977.

Janov, A. *The feeling child*. New York: Simon & Schuster, 1973.

Knoblock, P., & Goldstein, A. *The lonely teacher*. Boston: Allyn & Bacon, 1971.

Kohl, H. *Open classroom*. New York: Random House, 1969.

Kohl, H. *36 children*. New York: Signet, 1973.

Lederman, J. *Anger and the rocking chair: Gestalt awareness with children*. New York: Viking, 1973.

Lee, L. *Personality development in childhood*. Monterey: Brooks/Cole, 1976.

Lynn, D. *The father: His role in child development*. Monterey: Brooks/Cole, 1974.

Lyon, H. *Learning to feel—Feeling to learn*. Columbus, Ohio: Charles E. Merrill, 1971.

Moustakas, C. E. (Ed.). *The child's discovery of himself*. New York: Ballantine, 1966.

Moustakas, C. E. *Psychotherapy with children*. New York: Ballantine, 1973.

Moustakas, C. *Children in play therapy*. New York: Ballantine, 1974.

Moustakas, C. *Who will listen? Children and parents in therapy*. New York: Ballantine, 1975.

Neill, A. S. *Summerhill: A radical approach to child rearing*. New York: Hart, 1960.

Ohlsen, M. M. *Group counseling*. New York: Holt, Rinehart and Winston, 1970.

Roedell, W., Slaby, R., & Robinson, H. *Social development in young children*. Monterey: Brooks/Cole, 1977.

Rogers, C. *Freedom to learn: A view of what education might become*. Columbus, Ohio: Charles E. Merrill, 1969.

Rubin, T. *Jordi, Lisa, and David*. New York: Ballantine, 1962.

Schmuck, R. A., & Schmuck, P. A. *Group processes in the classroom* (2nd ed.). Dubuque, Iowa: William C. Brown, 1971.

11. COUNSELING GROUPS FOR ADOLESCENTS

A detailed description of the unique needs and problems of adolescents is beyond the scope of this book. For group leaders who work with adolescents, good courses in the psychology of adolescence are essential. Reading and reflecting on one's own adolescent experiences and perhaps reliving some of these experiences are also valuable means of preparing oneself to counsel adolescents. Those who wish to review the field of the psychology of adolescence can refer to the list of suggested readings at the end of this chapter.

What we do want to do here is explain what features of group counseling and personal-growth groups make these modes of intervention well suited to the unique needs of adolescents. The adolescent period is a time of searching for an identity and developing a system of values that will influence the course of one's life. One of the most important needs of this period is to experience successes that will lead to a sense of self-confidence and self-respect. Adolescents need to recognize and accept the wide range of their feelings, and they need to learn how to communicate with significant others in such a way that they can make their wants, feelings, thoughts, and beliefs known. The adolescent years can be extremely lonely ones; it is not unusual for adolescents to feel that they are alone in their conflicts and self-doubt. It is a period of life in which people feel a desperate need for universal approval yet in which they must learn to distinguish between living for others' approval and earning their own. During these years, the dependence-independence struggle becomes central. While part of the teenager yearns for independence from the parents, another part longs for the security of dependency. Adolescents must cope with making decisions that will influence their future, such as vocational and educational decisions. In order to make these choices wisely, they must have information about their abilities and interests and information about such realities as job opportunities and college entrance requirements. Adolescents are pressured to succeed; they are expected to perform, frequently up to others' standards.

Sexual conflicts are also a part of this period; not only do adolescents need to establish a meaningful guide for their sexual behavior, but they also must wrestle with the problem of their sex-role identification. Teenagers may have real difficulty clarifying what it means to be a man or a woman and what kind of man or woman they want to become. Adolescents need to be trusted and given the freedom to make some significant decisions, and they need the faith and support of caring adults. They also need guidelines and limits.

This brief sketch of some of the main currents flowing through the lives of adolescents should make the need for developmental counseling obvious. And group counseling is especially suited for adolescents because it provides a place in which they can express and experience their conflicting feelings, discover that they're not unique in their struggles, openly question their values and modify those they find wanting, learn to communicate with peers and adults, learn from the modeling provided by the leader, and learn how to accept what others offer and give of themselves in return. Groups provide a place in which adolescents can safely experiment with reality and test their limits. A unique value of group counseling is that it lets adolescents be instrumental in one another's growth; by offering opportunities for interaction, group members help one another in the struggle for self-understanding. Most important, a group setting gives adolescents a chance to express themselves and to be heard.

GUIDELINES FOR GETTING AN ADOLESCENT GROUP STARTED

How best to go about putting your ideas for a counseling group for adolescents into action depends a great deal on whether you are working in a school or in an agency and what you have in mind to do. Still, we'd like to offer some guidelines, which we feel will help you get your group started no matter what your particular circumstances.

1. Become knowledgeable about the legal factors involved in therapeutic work with adolescents. For some types of groups, written parental permission may be a legal requirement. We feel that no harm—and much protection—can come from routinely requiring the written consent of the parents or guardians of any person under 18 who wishes to participate in a counseling or personal-growth group.

2. Develop a clearly stated rationale for your proposed group. This should include discussions of the goals, the procedures to be used, the evaluation devices that will be used to assess the degree to which the goals were met, and the reasons for which a group approach has particular merit. Too many potential groups fail to materialize because the group leader has impulsively decided to lead a group but has put little serious thought into the planning of an effective design. Refer to Chapter 6 for more information on developing a group proposal.

3. Present your proposal to an administrator at the school you want to work in or to a responsible person at the agency you work for. Unless you have cleared your proposal in this way, your program may never be implemented. The support of administrators is essential, and, if your rationale for designing a group is well organized, the chances are that you will receive support and constructive suggestions from the persons you contact. It may be necessary to make certain compromises in your proposal, so keep an open mind. Remember that the school principal or the agency head—not you—will probably be the target of criticism if your counseling

group is ineffectively run, or run in a way that compromises the integrity of the institution. He or she will be the one who, if you've overlooked the need to get parental permission, receives the calls from parents who want to know what right the school has to probe into the personal lives of their children.

4. Prepare the parents for your program. To lessen the chances of negative parental reactions and to enlist active parental support for your endeavors, make direct contact with the parents. You might spend an evening presenting your program to them, or you might send them a letter briefly describing your program. This letter can be the parental-consent letter that parents mail back to you with their signatures.

5. Be careful about what titles and words you use to describe your group. What's in a name? Many creative programs have been torpedoed because of their names. Names such as ''group therapy,'' ''sensitivity training,'' and ''encounter group'' are potential targets of criticism. While the words you use to describe your group should not be misleading, you do need to be sensitive to the preconceptions that many people have about various forms of therapy. We suggest that you select words that will lessen the chances that either administrators or parents will turn down your proposal.

6. We recommend that, before you submit your proposal to parents or adolescents, you present it to several of your friends and neighbors. Expose a good cross section of people to it. Ask the adults how they would respond if they were to receive your proposal. Would they want their adolescent son or daughter to be involved in your group? If so, why? What do they most like about your plan? If not, why not? Do they object to the idea itself, or to the manner in which you make the proposal? How do they respond to your choice of words? Are you leaving something out that should be included? Do they suggest taking anything out? Ask some adolescents the same kinds of questions and get them to tell you why they would or would not want to participate in your group.

7. Of course, announcing your group to potential clients is necessary. We suggest that you do this personally, if possible. For example, if you are a high school counselor and are proposing a personal-growth group for students, try to present the program in person to various classes. Most teachers will be happy to let you talk about your proposal to their class for 15 minutes. Don't just announce the place and time of the sessions. Demonstrate your enthusiasm. Tell the potential group members openly why you designed such a group. Tell them what they can expect to get from being a member as well as what will be expected of them. If you do this well, chances are you'll have many more applicants than you'll be able to accommodate.

8. It is desirable to have a surplus of applicants. This gives you a wide population from which to select the members. An important thing to look for in selecting members is motivation and readiness for the group. In order to make the wisest possible selections, you should arrange an individual interview with each prospective group member. During this interview, you might ask the candidate: • What information do you have about groups? • What are your expectations and personal goals? • What do you think will be expected of you as a group member?

In addition to asking questions, you should let the candidate know what he or she can expect to learn from the group experience. You should also tell the person about the meeting times, the probable age and sex distributions of the group, and how to prepare for the group. The initial group session should be devoted to discussing group goals, personal goals, the need for regular attendance and for confidentiality, procedures for communicating, and other matters of importance (see Chapter 6).

THE EVOLUTION OF AN ADOLESCENT GROUP

In this section, our purpose is to discuss ways of involving and motivating the adolescent to become an active group participant and guidelines for conducting the sessions and keeping the meetings moving in a meaningful direction. We will address the issues of dealing with resistance, facilitating action, making role-playing meaningful to the adolescent, sustaining the interest of the group, involving as many members as possible in the interactions, and other topics relevant to the unfolding of the adolescent group.

From time to time, we will show how these guidelines can be put into practice, using as our example our experiences as co-leaders of a weekly counseling group for adolescents. Our group consisted of students from a local high school. This was an experimental program, offered free to the school district and to the participating members. The members were expected to attend all the sessions, which met on Wednesday evenings from 7:00 to 9:00 for one semester. In addition to these 15 meetings, we held one 10-hour marathon. The group consisted of ten members, all of whom were there by choice. Most of the participants were already functioning relatively well, so the focus of the group was developmental and preventive rather than remedial. In many respects, the group became a personal-growth group; members were encouraged to initiate discussion of matters important to them at this time in their lives.

During the initial sessions, we talked to the members about the need to specify group, as well as individual, goals. We devoted the beginning sessions to encouraging the participants to formulate their personal goals in as concrete a manner as possible. Contracts were useful in this respect. Some of the personal goals that individuals verbalized were: (1) "to feel less self-conscious around members of the opposite sex," (2) "to decide whether or not to go to college," (3) "to increase my feelings of self-esteem and self-confidence," (4) "to learn how to get along with my parents," (5) "to develop a closer relationship with my parents," (6) "to feel less isolated and different," (7) "to learn how to communicate what I really feel," (8) "to learn how to be more assertive without alienating others," and (9) "to learn to distinguish my parents' values from my own." Granted, a few of these goals are not very precise, but this vagueness was one of the reasons these adolescents had joined the group. Part of our ongoing task was to teach the members to translate their broad goals into behaviors that could be practiced in the group.

Establishing Trust and Dealing with Resistance

At a point early in an adolescent group's history, we might say something like "This is a place in which, we hope, you will come to feel free enough to say what you think and feel, without censoring or rehearsing. It is a place in which you can reveal personal struggles and find, with the help of others, a way of recognizing, understanding, and perhaps resolving certain problems. We hope a climate develops in which, because you feel that what you say is important and that you're respected for who you are, you will be able to discover the many selves within you. To a great degree, the value of the sessions depends on your level of commitment. If you merely show up and listen politely, you may leave disappointed. We hope that as the sessions progress you will think about what you want from this group and ask the group to help you get it. Our agenda in this group will include anything about you that you want to explore; there are no forbidden topics. We hope you will take risks here, saying and doing things that you don't feel safe saying or doing in other social settings. In order to make many of the changes you wish to make, you'll have to take such risks." Although this speech suggests that we give group members a great deal of freedom, it's not meant to imply the absence of realistic limits and rules. For example, in our weekly group, we wouldn't permit marijuana smoking, which would have threatened the very existence of the group. Also, we pointed out to members that their freedom to act must be balanced by a respect for the rights of others.

It must be remembered that many of the freedoms a group offers to adolescents typically do not exist for adolescents. Their teachers may not be interested in their personal views or concerns, the atmosphere of their school may be one of oppression and control, and their parents may miss hearing what they say or appreciating them as young adults, instead attempting to fashion them according to a certain set of standards. Thus, we've found that adolescents will test us to determine whether we mean what we say about what can go on in the group. How we respond to their testing tells the members how much they can trust us as group leaders. If we accept their testing in a nonjudgmental and nondefensive way and resist giving lectures about how they should be, we come a long way toward gaining their acceptance. In our work with adolescents, we've found that they're quick to detect phoniness (and sincerity) and that practicing what we preach is the surest way to earn their respect and to generate an atmosphere of trust in the group.

The Influence of the Leader's Personality

Our experience with adolescents continues to teach us how great the influence of the personality characteristics of the group leader is on the evolution of the group. We find that adolescents respond well to leader characteristics such as: a willingness to share one's self with the group, a caring attitude, enthusiasm and vitality, openness, and directness. They do learn from watching the leader model, but the behavior of the leader doesn't have to be perfect in order for them to benefit. In fact, adolescents can relate well to adults who reveal their personal struggles. Adults who genuinely respect and enjoy adolescents will typically be rewarded with a reciprocal respect.

Adolescents are also sensitive to the "adult" who, never having fully experienced his or her adolescence, attempts to experience it now by becoming one of the gang. Some group leaders do this by imitating the slang and manner of speaking of the adolescents. Young people are quick to detect the insincerity of a group leader who uses expressions to impress them and to give the appearance of being "with it." Because of this insincerity, the leader may experience difficulty in gaining the adolescents' trust and respect. Group leaders would do well to remember that they hold a different position and role from that of the member and that clients usually expect their leader to act differently from them. Leaders who are powerful but who don't use their power to control and stifle members are viewed with respect by adolescents.

Finally, adolescents have taught us that we have the most influence on them when we are seriously attempting to be in our lives what we are encouraging them to become. This does not mean that, in order to be effective, we must be ideal people whom the members can imitate. Rather, it means that we are most effective when the members feel that we practice what we preach.

We want to mention why it is sometimes extremely difficult for people to lead adolescent groups. We think that those who work intensively with adolescents experience a reliving of many of their own unresolved adolescent conflicts. For example, an adult who never faced or resolved certain adolescent fears related to his or her sexuality or lovability may find these fears resurfacing as he or she leads an adolescent group. For this reason, it is crucial that those who lead adolescent groups be willing and courageous enough to explore, and perhaps relive, much of their own adolescent experience.

In addition, adolescents may threaten adults, for they are full of energy, they often are free from major responsibilities, they have the capacity to have fun and experience joy, and they are able to feel intensely. Leaders may suffer from the feeling that they have lost some of these lively qualities. They may be faced for the first time with the facts of their aging and their loss of the capacity to savor life. Such leaders can prevent the growth of feelings of resentment by first accepting the fact of their aging and then looking for new meaning and excitement in their lives.

Keeping the Sessions Moving

In our weekly adolescent group, a valuable skill consisted in keeping the sessions moving, which was mainly accomplished by assisting the members to speak for themselves in concrete terms. This was not an easy task; it was hard to get the participants to focus on themselves in the here-and-now. Especially in a beginning adolescent group, members have a tendency to story-tell endlessly, going into every detail. We found that the best way to teach members not to ask questions or story-tell was to make the group aware of this dynamic as it occurred, by saying something like "I'd like to stop for a moment to check out your reactions to Betty and to find out where you are left at this moment." Very often we found that the members felt lost, unsure what the point was, and bored and had tuned Betty out. This feedback served to teach the members that this behavior had a tendency to be nonproductive, both in the group and in their outside life.

We asked members to try to state how they were affected by a situation rather than how other people acted toward them. For instance, a girl began by talking about how she felt misunderstood by her mother. Soon she slipped away from her own feelings and focused on her mother. She told stories about her mother, blamed her mother for her unhappiness, focused on her mother's feelings, and so on. After a while, one of us remarked "You seem to be talking more about your mother right now than about yourself. Why not tell us how you're affected when your mother does so-and-so?"

Another problem frequently encountered during the course of a session with adolescents is the apathy of some members. At times there can be a general lethargy in the group. Participants may wait for the group leaders to do something to get them going. Even though we may suggest certain themes, or use interaction exercises, there are times when the members go through the motions and then wait passively for another exercise. At times like this, one of us might say "It seems that the energy level is very low in this group tonight. I suggest we go around and have each of you state where you've drifted off to and why, as well as what you're willing to do about it."

Another dynamic that commonly keeps a group from reaching an intensive working level is the bombardment of one member by another with questions. When such questioning occurs, it is appropriate for the group leader to make a comment such as "Fritz, instead of questioning Charlene, tell her what it was that provoked you to ask the question." Unless the questioning is stopped in this way, the intensity of Charlene's emotional experience may soon be dissipated. The leader can then try to prevent this from happening again by stressing to the members that it is far better for them to state how they are affected by someone's emotional experience, and in what ways they're identifying with the person, than to distract the member with questions.

Structuring as a way of keeping sessions moving. We favor active intervention and structuring for adolescent groups, particularly during the initial stages. In our judgment, adolescents do not cope with uncertainty as well as do adults, and some structuring can provide the direction needed to keep the sessions moving. Structuring might involve specifying a theme or topic for the group to deal with. Such topics should be related to the interests and needs of the adolescents and not merely issues the leader feels are important. For instance, a counselor might select topics such as: How can we improve our study habits? What can be done to reduce the absentee rate in classrooms? How can we learn to respect our teachers? The group may well have little interest in these topics, and, if so, the sessions are bound to get bogged down.

In our adolescent group, we developed themes with the participants in the sessions. We didn't say "Since this is your group, what do you want to talk about?" Instead, we structured by limiting the choices somewhat, saying "In working with groups like this, we have found that certain themes are of concern to most young people. A few of these are: What do I want from my life, and what is stopping me from getting it? Can I be who I am and be sincerely accepted by my parents? How can I better understand my feelings of loneliness? In what ways am I like others in my struggles? These are only a few of the topics that we might consider. Every group moves in its own direction. What, in particular, would each of you like to see us focus on in this group?" While this structuring can be reserved for the beginning stages of a group, a general agenda for the next session can be decided on at the end of each session. Flexibility should be built into the structuring, though, for often members will spontaneously bring up pressing problems that are not related to the theme scheduled to be considered, and this deviation from the plan can be very fruitful. A theme, like an interaction exercise, is only a means to the end of involving the members in meaningful group work; it is important that topics or techniques not become ends in themselves. Our adolescent group once planned, at the end of a session, to deal with a certain theme the next week; however, a classmate of the group members committed suicide the night before the next session, and the group was preoccupied with this. The session was devoted to exploring the effect that this tragedy was having on each group member, and the topic of death was explored in a very personal way.

Role-Playing in Adolescent Groups

In our adolescent groups, we usually rely heavily on role-playing and other action-oriented methods. We find that this is an excellent way to keep the interest level high, to involve a lot of the members, and to give a here-and-now flavor to the work being done. Role-playing fosters creative problem-solving, encourages spontaneity, usually intensifies feelings, and gets people to identify with others. By role-playing, participants can learn how to express themselves more effectively. They can test reality and practice new behavior.

In our work with adolescents, we've found that it helps members become comfortable with role-playing more quickly if we participate at first. For instance, if a girl has been describing how she views her parents and how frustrated she feels when she tries to talk with them, we might take the part of her mother and father. That will allow her to deal directly, albeit symbolically, with her parents and feel her frustration intensely. We can then stop action and ask her "What are you experiencing now? What would you most like to do now? If you could reach us, make us really hear you, what would you most want to say?" The role-playing may be brief. When it's over, the person should discuss the experience and plan how to handle this situation when it arises in the future.

At times we meet with mild resistance when we suggest role-playing. Members protest that they don't know what to say, or that they feel foolish, or that they think role-playing is artificial. In response to this, we tell the members to relax for a few minutes and not worry about whether they're saying the right thing. Generally, if we approach role-playing in this light and experimental way, the resistance dissipates, and before the participant knows it he or she is playing a role with gusto. Frequently we check with a person to see whether he or she wants to explore a particular problem and whether he or she is willing to use role-playing to do so. One of us might say ''You seem to be unclear as to how your mother really affects you and how you should deal with her. Are you willing to try something?''

There are many variations of role-playing techniques. To illustrate, we'll use the example of Sally, who discloses that she feels she can never please her father and that this hurts her. She says that she and her father are not close and that she would like to change that. She is afraid of her father, for she sees him as critical of her, and she feels that unless she is perfect she cannot win his approval. Several role-playing situations are possible:

1. Sally can play her father. To get a picture of how Sally perceives her father, we can ask her to give Sally a long lecture and tell her all the things that she must become before she is worthwhile in his eyes. Speaking as her father, Sally might say something like ''I know you have a lot more ability than you show. Why didn't you get all A's? Yes, I'm proud of you for getting five A's, but I must confess I'm let down by that one B. If you really put your mind to it, I know that you could do better.'' We would encourage her to stay in her father's role for a time and say things that she imagines he is thinking but not expressing.

2. A group member who identifies with Sally can play Sally while Sally continues playing her father. From the dialogue that ensues, Sally can get an idea of how her father feels with her, and a group member with a similar conflict can benefit from involvement in the situation.

3. A member who feels that he or she can identify with the father can play that role. If nobody in the group jumps at this opportunity, the leader can take the parent role. This situation allows Sally to intensify her feelings and to demonstrate how she deals with her father. As the role-playing continues, Sally may achieve insight into herself that will help her grow.

4. Sally can also play both herself and her father. She can be directed to say (as her father) what she wishes he would say to her. This is a future projection, and it taps the person's hopes.

5. Sally can present a soliloquy, talking aloud as her father, saying what she imagines her father might say about her. Sally can also use the the soliloquy approach when she is in her own role, after she finishes an exchange with her father. She can express many of the thoughts and feelings she generally keeps locked within herself when she talks with her father.

6. Several other group members can sit in for Sally and show how they would deal with her father. This may suggest to Sally options she hadn't thought of.

It is important for members to process these dramas. In order to help them do this, the leader should ask the members to think about the implications of what they observed in themselves in the role-playing situations. At this time, feedback from other members and interpretations from the leader can enable the members to see with more clarity their own part in their conflicts with others.

Getting Group Members to Participate and Initiate

During the sessions, we look for many ways of bringing uninvolved group members into ongoing interactions. After Sally's role-playing, for example, we might encourage other members to tell what they were experiencing as Sally was working with her father. We might request "Can any of you give Sally feedback? What did you see her doing? Did Sally spark any feelings in you?" Adolescents are usually most eager to become personally involved when other members touch vulnerable spots in them. As we've mentioned, one real advantage of group counseling is that the members can be of service to their peers, by giving their perceptions, by revealing similar problems, by suggesting alternatives, by supporting them in times of despair, by reflecting what they hear them saying, by confronting them on inconsistencies, and so on.

Thus, we try to involve as many members as possible in the group process; in addition, we try to shape the group so that we will be required less and less to give direction. In an effective group, the members gradually assume a larger and larger share of the leadership functions. For instance, if a group that usually functions effectively begins to stray aimlessly, a member will probably point this out. If a group member gets bogged down in story-telling and intellectualizing, we expect a member to call the person on this. In short, one of our aims is to teach adolescents to monitor their own group and become less dependent on us for direction.

A MARATHON SESSION WITH ADOLESCENTS

As part of the semester-long weekly group, an all-day marathon took place at our home. The idea was ours, but we checked with the group to determine whether the members wanted such an experience. Everyone in the group was enthusiastic, so, toward the end of the semester, we made the arrangements. We planned the marathon for a time when we would have several regular weekly sessions left, which we could then use for follow-up. The marathon would last about ten hours, with one break, for lunch. Since at this point in its evolution the group didn't have a specific agenda, the structure would be allowed to evolve naturally.

Some of the activities engaged in by the adolescents in this marathon were very similar to the activities of adults in marathon groups. The adolescents: reexperienced childhood events and dealt with unfinished business concerning their parents; expressed pent-up feelings of rage, hurt, fear, guilt, shame, and so on; looked at their fear of having nothing to offer; dealt with their need for intimacy and their fears of loving and being loved; explored sexual conflicts; struggled with the question of their personal identity; figured out the sources of their values; expressed their conflicting desires for independence and dependence; dealt with their needs for approval and acceptance; and dealt with their feelings of powerlessness. In many ways, then, their struggles were very much like those experienced by adults in an intensive group.

The marathon, along with the weekly group, taught us that adolescents have a capacity for depth of feeling and for intimacy, that they can be extremely perceptive, that they are very able to engage in serious work, and that a group can help them a great deal in their quest for maturity. We found that adolescents could come to know themselves better by expressing feelings that had been locked up and that the group encouraged them to do this by providing support and acceptance. The adolescents in our group began to assume increased responsibility for their lives and to blame others less; they began to move from an other-focus to a self-focus in exploring their problems. We found them surprisingly resourceful and, many times, very courageous. We did not perceive them as unrealistic in their demands; nor were they unable to make compromises. Most of all, we were struck by their willingness to critically evaluate the quality of their lives and to seriously question what they wanted from life. We felt extremely hopeful, for we witnessed some of these young people doing what we find many middle-aged people only beginning to do many years later.

USING A GROUP APPROACH IN
HIGH SCHOOL CLASSES

Assuming that school counselors can acquire the necessary training to lead adolescent groups oriented toward personal growth, we see no reason why schools cannot offer growth groups for students who are not identified as problems. Unfortunately, most counseling and guidance programs are remedial in nature; there are generally few substantial programs designed to assist the great number of students who, while not in crisis states, could benefit from an ongoing small group in which they could explore developmental problems under the guidance of a trained group leader. School administrators are reluctant to have such services offered, because they fear negative parental responses and because they believe the function of a school is to educate youth, not provide psychotherapy for them. Giving psychological help is thought to be the function of community clinics and family-service agencies. We do not argue with this position, although we do believe that personal-growth groups are needed by adolescents and have a legitimate claim to a place in schools. Groups in schools, by helping the students work through their normal developmental crises, may be able to prevent school problems.

We believe that there should be a variety of classes in the high school curriculum that deal with the personal concerns of students. Courses in psychology, human relations, family life, and social problems are becoming increasingly popular on many campuses. We propose that some of these courses be conducted along lines similar to those of a counseling group, although perhaps with more structure. We know of several schools that are adapting group approaches to the classroom for certain courses. What follows is a description of one such program that is being offered in a high school in our community.

The course is called "Human Relations," and it is offered to juniors and seniors on an elective basis. There are many more applicants than can be accepted. Before a student is admitted to the class, the teacher obtains the written consent of the parents on a letter that is mailed to them describing the course in detail. The purpose of the course is much the same as the purpose of a counseling group. Students are encouraged to examine and clarify their values, discuss personal problems, learn to communicate effectively with others, learn to accept people with life-styles that differ from their own, and acquire skills in problem-solving. The teacher's function is not mainly to impart information; rather, her role is one of a resource person, a consultant, a facilitator, and an initiator. She determines the structure and content of the course. Reading material on a wide range of topics is available in the classroom. A graduate student with group-leadership skills assists the teacher in conducting group sessions, which center around the topics chosen by the teacher. When the class is not functioning as a group, it is conducted on a discussion basis, although the teacher occasionally gives lectures and guest speakers from the community are occasionally called upon. The following are some of the experiences members of the class have had with outside speakers.

1. A marriage counselor discussed common sources of strain in family life and described the processes of marriage and family counseling.
2. Workers at a free clinic described the psychological services available at the clinic.
3. A birth-control-clinic representative described the clinic's services.
4. A psychologist talked about the various types of psychotherapy.
5. Members of the gay community talked about homosexuality and about society's view of this life-style.
6. A member of Alcoholics Anonymous described his personal experience with alcoholism and told how AA had helped him.
7. An ex–drug addict discussed what she had learned from being an addict and talked about the causes of addiction.
8. A panel composed of a rabbi, a priest, and a minister exchanged views on interfaith marriages, and each speaker discussed the views of his faith regarding marriage and family life.
9. A physician described the process of sexual development that goes on during the adolescent years and discussed sexual problems.
10. A panel consisting of a minister, a doctor, and a psychologist presented various perspectives on the issue of death and dying.

These are only a few of the kinds of presentations that are made to the class and that provide material for group discussion. In addition, the teacher presents short lectures on a variety of topics that are typically dealt with in therapeutic groups, including: formulating a philosophy of life, cultural attitudes toward death and dying, ways of growing, loneliness, creative solitude, meaning and values, parent-adolescent relationships, personality development, emotional and behavioral disorders, child and adolescent development, conformity, game-playing versus authenticity, love, sex, marriage, and so on. As you can see, these topics lend themselves well to meaningful discussion, and they provide adolescents with material to think about and to apply to their own living.

At times, the entire class (about 30 students) participates in a discussion. But frequently the class is divided into groups of about 6 students. In the small groups, students take turns being the group facilitator. Throughout the course, attention is given to group process and responsible membership and leadership, and the graduate student and the teacher visit the small groups to see how well the students have learned these basic principles. At other times, the class is divided into two groups of 15, with the teacher taking one group and the graduate student taking the other. In these groups, many group techniques and structured exercises are used by the leaders to facilitate interaction.

A Commentary

Anyone who teaches high school classes in psychology or human relations can implement a program similar to the one we've just described. Such teachers can update their skills in group leadership and group process by taking a few selected graduate courses, by attending special summer workshops, by participating in in-service-training programs, by attending a variety of weekend didactic/experiential workshops that are offered through most university extension programs, and most of all by participating in personal-growth groups or therapeutic groups that will enable them to better understand themselves and their impact on others.

Many writers have described the psychologically damaging effect of conventional schools on the learner. In the last decade, there has been an increased interest in humanistic education, which aims at combining the affective domain (interests, feelings, values, personal concerns) with the cognitive domain. Training programs for elementary and secondary teachers in methods of humanistic education are being developed in many universities. A number of studies have been done evaluating the outcomes of student-centered education, and the results suggest that it is possible to effectively combine personal concerns with the traditional curriculum. In fact, the results suggest that the integration of the two may produce superior learning of traditional material. This does not surprise us. When students are interested and actively engaged in the learning process, meaningful learning—learning that has an impact on the learner, as opposed to learning that is superficial and soon lost—can occur.

It is our hope that more teachers will get excited by the extent of the possibilities for integrating personal learning with traditional learning. This integration can take place in the humanities as well as in the social sciences. Such programs could be valuable adjuncts to the counseling and guidance programs of schools, reaching many adolescents who might otherwise remain untouched.

AN ADOLESCENT-PSYCHOLOGY COURSE
ON THE COLLEGE LEVEL

The use of a group-oriented and experiential approach does not need to be limited to high school courses. The adolescent-psychology course, which is offered by most colleges and universities, lends itself to the utilization of a self-exploration type of approach.

I (Jerry Corey) have taught adolescent psychology several times, and it has always seemed to me that the gains from this course are the most significant when the course combines an experiential group approach with the cognitively oriented features of lectures, reading, and writing. Essentially, this course developed into a counseling group with a special focus—the reexperiencing of one's adolescence for the purpose of better understanding the impact of these experiences on one's current style of behaving. (This personal approach to learning can be applied to other college courses, such as introductory psychology, child psychology, and educational psychology. At various times, I have used an experiential approach with all of these courses.) In focusing on the students' adolescent experiences, I gave special attention to identity formation; the physical, psychological, sexual, social, and moral conflicts of the adolescent years; the development of a philosophy of life and a value system; and the influence of the family, the school, and society on the individual.

A few of the procedures used in the course were:

1. *Small, leaderless groups.* Outside of the class period, students got together in small groups and discussed their readings, their adolescent experiences, and other issues raised in the class sessions. The groups were given considerable freedom to develop their own goals and format.

2. *Readings.* Books about the experience of adolescence can stimulate students to reflect on their own experience. Thus, the students were given an extensive reading list at the beginning of the course and encouraged to select books that they thought might have meaning for them. Issues raised in these readings formed much of the course content.

3. *Journals.* In ongoing journals, the students recalled the events of their adolescence.

4. *Reaction papers.* The students were asked to write papers expressing their thoughts and feelings about the class in general, the issues raised in class, or their readings. The students could also use these papers to share any personal material they had recorded in their journals.

5. *Guest speakers.* A wide range of guest speakers were invited to focus on issues currently facing adolescents. These speakers provided material for discussion in class and in the leaderless groups.

6. *General class discussion.* Lectures on adolescent development were kept to a minimum. Instead, class time was used primarily to discuss the students' readings, their reaction papers, problems and conflicts they recalled experiencing in adolescence, and the influence of their adolescent period on them now. A climate conducive to open sharing and discussion was essential, so students were encouraged to

treat one another's contributions with respect. It is important, in such a class, for a supportive and nonjudgmental atmosphere to prevail and for the students to be willing to listen to one another.

When the course was over, the students were asked to write a statement detailing what they had learned that was of the greatest significance to them and what personal meanings the course had had for them. From these statements, I learned that the majority of the students felt that the course had given them greater insight into their own behavior and into the meaning of their adolescent experiences. "I learned about myself" was one of the most frequently mentioned outcomes of the course. Generally, the members of the class felt that, while it might have been uncomfortable, the critical review of their adolescent years had been extremely significant in terms of generating self-awareness, self-acceptance, and an understanding of how their adolescence had influenced their adult values, attitudes, and behavior. Many said that their values had been challenged and that they had reassessed certain values once they realized that these values had been incorporated in childhood or adolescence. Students said they had learned that they were not alone in experiencing certain feelings during adolescence. Many said that the class had made them recognize the importance of independence and responsibility, and a number indicated that they were now more willing to accept the responsibility for the direction of their lives.

In conclusion, this group-oriented approach to the teaching of adolescent psychology proved to be meaningful and exciting, both for the students and for me. Rather than sitting passively and listening to a lecture about the adolescent, and rather than merely reading about adolescent development, the students became active participants in the class by reviewing the highlights of their own adolescence. To a large extent, they used their own memories and experiences to teach themselves the meaning of this crucial period of life.

A WORKSHOP FOR TEACHERS AND COUNSELORS

During the past eight years, I (Jerry Corey) have offered specially designed workshops and groups for high school teachers and counselors through several university extension programs. In this section, I will describe a particular course that I developed and offered through the University of California, Irvine, and the University of California, Riverside (Extension Division). The course was entitled "The Teacher and Counselor as Facilitators of Personal Growth," and it involved a weekend of 20 hours of group interaction. The catalog description read as follows:

> A week-end workshop to explore ways the teacher can facilitate individual growth and make a difference in the lives of students. Focus is on the personal and interpersonal dynamics involved in the learning process and examination of approaches to personalize learning: our experiences as a learner, what schooling does to us, why people become teachers, struggles in becoming therapeutic persons, personal growth groups, a humanistic approach to education, teachers and counselors who are making a difference, the challenge of

revolutionizing our schools, and where to go from here: alternatives and strategies for change. For teachers, counselors, mental health workers and others in the people-helping professions. *Enrollment is limited to 15.*

The central goal and focus of this course was to explore via group participation the issue that teachers and counselors can make a significant difference (either positive or negative) in the lives of their students and counselees. Because I feel that the most valuable tool that a counselor or a teacher has to work with is himself or herself, I designed the course to focus on the participants as persons with values, personhood, internal conflicts and struggles, and potential power.

The underlying assumption of this group workshop was that the most important resource that teachers possess is their sensitivity as humans. Teachers are usually eager to learn techniques of classroom control, or how to deal with certain behavioral problems exhibited by children, or how to motivate children to learn, or how to set up a resource center in their classroom. But such methods may address only the symptoms and not the underlying problems, which may be rooted in the behavior of the teacher. The point of the workshop was to encourage teachers to learn to recognize their reactions to the children they teach and to discover the impact of their behavior on the behavior and attitudes of students in their classrooms. Many teachers have never been exposed to the issue of their personal impact on students; instead, they have been trained in matters related to curriculum, teaching methods, techniques for classroom control and discipline, and assessment measures. Still, many teachers realize that they must develop their self-awareness and sensitivity to others if they are to be effective at reaching and teaching children and adolescents.

During these workshops, the group members typically try to answer some of the following questions:

1. What kinds of students attract you? What kinds cause you difficulty?
2. What was your own schooling like? What kind of learner were you? What effect has your early education had on you as a teacher?
3. Do you teach in much the same way as you were taught?
4. What kinds of teachers or counselors made a significant and positive difference in your life?
5. What are some ways in which you feel powerless as a teacher? How do you cope with your frustrations?
6. How do you gain a sense of meaning from your work as a teacher (counselor)?
7. Do you experience a sense of power as a teacher? When do you feel this power?
8. What are some obstacles within you that prevent you from reaching students as effectively as you might?
9. What are some obstacles within the school system (or within the community) that block you from doing things you'd like to do with or for students?
10. In what ways can you bring humanistic approaches into your classroom? Can you work within a school system and at the same time find ways of doing what you believe is right for students?

11. What are your core values, and how do they influence your teaching?
12. What are some of your personal problems and conflicts, and what effects do these have on your work?
13. Can you allow your students to openly explore some of their personal concerns, or do you stick rigidly to subject matter? Are you able to integrate academic and personal learning?
14. If you could change the school system in any way you wished, what would you do?

These are some of the questions I ask in the teacher/counselor workshop in order to provoke thought and discussion. The workshop participants are encouraged to bring their specific personal concerns into the sessions, though, and to a large degree the direction of each group is determined by the concerns of its members.

In some of these workshops, I have included either elementary-school children or high school students. For example, in one workshop, there were 15 high school students and 15 high school teachers, and all of the participants remained together all weekend. Smaller groups, each including both students and teachers, were formed, and the members were encouraged to air their concerns freely. Teachers got to hear students specify the conditions under which they learned best and the kinds of teachers who reached them effectively. Students got to express their feeling that school was boring and to tell how teachers soured them on learning. They also told how some teachers inspired them and suggested ways in which the classroom could be made more attractive to students. The students also responded to the teachers' answers to the questions listed earlier.

Not only did the students teach the teachers about how children and adolescents perceive their school experiences, but the teachers also taught the students about themselves. Teachers in the workshop were able to talk about the pressures they felt from other teachers, the principal, parents, and students. They allowed the students to see their personal struggles, and many of the students left the workshop saying that they respected these teachers for the risks they took in showing their humanness. They wished they could experience more of this from their own teachers.

Workshops such as this one can energize teachers and increase their awareness of the critical importance of the human dimension in the teaching/learning process. However, some kind of ongoing in-service-training group in which teachers can continue to explore the issues that surfaced in the workshop is what is most needed. This kind of group can help to bridge the psychological gap that separates students from teachers.

TEACHER-CONSULTATION GROUPS

An important service that can be provided by group leaders who work with high school students is consultation with teachers. One way for a leader to provide this service is by forming a discussion group with teachers for the purpose of sensitizing them to the personal problems their adolescent students are experiencing.

The leader can also discuss such matters as how to detect potential personality problems and how to make referrals. A group for teachers can also be a place in which teacher frustrations are explored and in which teachers learn how to nourish themselves and be nourished by others. Methods of humanely dealing with students on a person-to-person basis can be explored, as can the limitations of disciplinary techniques.

The purpose of the leader of such a group is not to tell the teachers how to teach, even though they may be seeking advice on this, but rather to promote an atmosphere in which they can explore the nature of their difficulties with students. Teachers can bring specific interpersonal problems to the group, and the leader can initiate role-playing exercises so that teachers can become more aware of how they're contributing to their problems with students and can experiment with alternative behaviors. Involvement in such a group can be time-consuming, but we suspect, on the basis of our work with teachers, that many teachers would be willing to be involved in a consultation group with a person who has expertise in working with adolescents.

It is important that these sessions not disintegrate into sessions of bad-mouthing certain students. Unfortunately, this occurs often in teachers' lounges. To keep this from occurring, the group leader must keep the focus on the teacher, not the student. This is the same principle that applies in any group. For instance, Ms. Dalton goes on in detail about how she cannot teach because Tom is continually provoking conflict in the classroom; she tells the group all the horrible things Tom does. The group leader can put the focus on Ms. Dalton by asking her how she feels when Tom misbehaves. Exciting possibilities would open up if Ms. Dalton were to play the role of Tom and allow other teachers and the leader to demonstrate how they might handle the situation.

Those who lead adolescent groups do have valuable insights to offer teachers and administrators. They can point out the major problems adolescents experience, and they can explore with the teachers ways in which they might demonstrate their caring and become significant positive influences on the adolescents they contact.

PARENT-CONSULTATION GROUPS

Group leaders of adolescent groups are potentially as valuable as consultants to parents as they are as consultants to teachers. Most parents care about their children. Yet most parents go through a period during which they would like to divorce their adolescent, for the possibility of any real communication with the youngster seems remote. Like their adolescent children, parents need some assistance. They need more than general information about parent-adolescent relationships or methods of control. They need to talk about their feelings of inadequacy, guilt, resentment, and rejection. Many feel deeply unappreciated and feel that, no matter how sincerely they try to improve relations at home, things won't get better. A consultation group can give parents a chance to express some of their frustration and ambivalence about being parents. A good group leader can sensitize parents to the dynamics of adolescence. The leader can present short, informal talks that widen the perspectives of parents, and parents can raise questions and bring up problems that they would like to discuss with the other parents and with the group leader.

Certain programs can also be designed for the parent willing to invest a lot of time and energy in becoming a better parent. Many group leaders offer parent-effectiveness-training groups. Such groups can be held at the local high school or at one of the parents' homes one evening a week. Parents in such groups are encouraged to read books such as Gordon's *Parent Effectiveness Training* and Ginott's *Between Parent and Teenager* and to discuss them in the group. Role-playing gives parents a chance to examine their relationships with their children and experiment with new, more effective behaviors.

SOME CONCLUDING REMARKS

We've discussed the importance of providing groups and workshops for the teachers and parents of adolescents as well as for adolescents themselves. Now we wish to make a few remarks concerning the importance of offering such services to school administrators. If it is not feasible to do this, or if it is felt that administrators should not be included in a parent or teacher group, then administrators can be approached individually.

Frequently, administrators have anxieties concerning group-counseling programs for adolescents. They may fear arousing the anger of parents, they may be skeptical of the value of group counseling in a school setting, they may be concerned about the abilities of the group leaders, or they may harbor misconceptions about the nature and purpose of group counseling. In order to assuage these and similar doubts and fears, the group leader should inform administrators of the design of the group program and, if practical, include them in some of the group sessions with teachers and/or parents. It may be of real value for administrators to openly state and explore some of their concerns and reservations about group-counseling programs, for in this way all members of the staff can work together for common purposes, and some problems and conflicts that might have arisen can be diverted.

SUGGESTED READINGS

Borton, T. *Reach, touch, and teach*. New York: McGraw-Hill, 1970.

Brennecke, J. H., & Amick, R. G. *The struggle for significance* (2nd ed.). Beverly Hills, Calif.: Glencoe, 1975.

Brown, G. I. *Human teaching for human learning: An introduction to confluent education*. New York: Viking, 1971.

Conger, J. *Adolescence and youth* (2nd ed.). New York: Harper & Row, 1977.

Corey, G. *Teachers can make a difference*. Columbus, Ohio: Charles E. Merrill, 1973.

Corey, G. *The struggle toward realness: A manual for therapeutic groups*. Dubuque, Iowa: Kendall/Hunt, 1974.

Douvan, E., & Adelson, J. B. *The adolescent experience*. New York: Wiley, 1966.

Erikson, E. *Identity: Youth and crisis*. New York: Norton, 1968.

Frankl, V. E. *Man's search for meaning* (Rev. ed.). Boston: Beacon, 1963.

Ginott, H. *Between parent and teenager*. New York: Avon, 1973.

Goethals, G. W., & Klos, D. S. (Eds.). *Experiencing youth: First-person accounts* (2nd ed.). Boston: Little, Brown, 1976.

Green, H. *I never promised you a rose garden*. New York: Holt, Rinehart and Winston, 1964.

Harris, T. *I'm OK–You're OK*. New York: Avon, 1976.

Hesse, H. *Siddhartha*. New York: New Directions, 1951.

Hesse, H. *Demian*. New York: Harper & Row, 1965.

Hodge, M. *Your fear of love*. New York: Doubleday, 1969.

James, M., & Jongeward, D. *Born to win: Transactional analysis with Gestalt experiments*. Reading, Mass: Addison-Wesley, 1971.

Jenkins, G. G., & Shacter, H. S. *These are your children* (4th ed.). Glenview, Ill.: Scott, Foresman, 1975.

Lefrancois, G. R. *Adolescents*. Belmont, Calif.: Wadsworth, 1976.

Levy, R. *I can only touch you now*. Englewood Cliffs, N.J.: Prentice-Hall, 1973.

Lyon, H. C., Jr., *Learning to feel: Feeling to learn*. Columbus, Ohio: Charles E. Merrill, 1971.

Mahler, C. A. *Group counseling in the schools*. Boston: Houghton-Mifflin, 1969.

Matteson, D. R. *Adolescence today: Sex roles and the search for identity*. Homewood, Ill.: Dorsey, 1975.

Mintz, E. E. (Ed.). *Marathon groups: Reality and symbol*. New York: Avon, 1972.

Moustakas, C. E. *Loneliness and love*. Englewood Cliffs, N.J.: Prentice-Hall, 1972.

Postman, N., & Weingartner, C. *Teaching as a subversive activity*. New York: Dell, 1969.

Ralston, N. C., & Thomas, G. P. *The adolescent: Case studies for analysis*. Corte Madera, Calif.: Chandler, 1974.

Rice, F. P. *The adolescent: Development, relationships and culture*. Allyn & Bacon, 1974.

Rogers, C. *Freedom to learn: A view of what education might become*. Columbus, Ohio: Charles E. Merrill, 1969.

Silberman, C. E. *Crisis in the classroom*. New York: Random House, 1971.

Sugar, M. (Ed.). *The adolescent in group and family therapy*. New York: Brunner/Mazel, 1975.

Thornburg, H. D. *Contemporary adolescence: Readings* (2nd ed.). Monterey, Calif.: Brooks/Cole, 1975.

Weinstein, G., & Fantini, M. (Eds.). *Toward humanistic education: A curriculum of affect*. New York: Praeger, 1970.

White, K. M., & Speisman, J. C. *Adolescence*. Monterey, Calif.: Brooks/Cole, 1977.

12. GROUPS FOR
COLLEGE STUDENTS

On university and college campuses, a variety of groups are available to students and to the community. If you are training to be a counselor, you might get a chance to lead such a group. For this reason, we will focus in the first part of this chapter on some methods of designing counseling groups to be offered at a college counseling center. Both of us have led such groups. In the second section of the chapter, I (Jerry Corey) will explain how a college course can be created in the form of a personal-growth group.

COUNSELING GROUPS IN THE COLLEGE COUNSELING CENTER

The Need for Therapeutic Groups on Campus

A common complaint we hear from students is that it is easy to feel isolated on the university campus. Students feel that, while much attention is paid to their intellectual development, relatively little is paid to their personal development. From our work in the counseling centers of universities, we have come to realize that many students seek counseling services not because of serious problems but rather because they want to develop aspects of personhood in addition to their thinking abilities. Students are hungry for personal nourishment, and they actively seek group experiences in which they can be nourished and can grow by nourishing others. In a weekly group with fellow students (and a group leader), they can formulate goals, explore areas of themselves that they've kept hidden from themselves—areas that are presently causing them difficulties in interpersonal relating—and identify the internal blocks that have been impeding the full utilization of their capacities. By dealing with their personal problems, students are able to free themselves of certain emotional blocks to learning. Many who have clarified their values and made decisions about what they want from life have become far better students, approaching their studies with a sense of enthusiasm and commitment.

Preparing for and Structuring a Group

After the decision has been made to form a group, one of the first tasks is to announce the group to those who might be interested. We sometimes do this by distributing a flier containing a brief description of the group. It is also a good practice, we feel, to visit several classes and speak about the group. Appearing in person to describe the purposes and structure of the group is a most valuable way to make meaningful contacts.

After the publicity has been taken care of, we arrange for individual sessions with potential group members for selection and screening purposes. In deciding whom to accept, we consider how big the group should be, what age range and sex distribution we would like, and what types of problems we're planning to deal with. In screening applicants, our foremost consideration is the readiness of the individual for the particular group. We try to select people who want to be in a group and who seem willing to look at themselves and to make changes.

After we have completed the selection process and notified the accepted applicants, we hold the first group session, which we present as an opportunity for the members to decide whether they really want to invest themselves in the group. During this session, the members get acquainted and explore their fears and expectations. We tell them that, if they elect to become members of the group, they will be expected to attend regularly, to develop contracts to meet certain of their goals, and to be actively involved in the sessions. Confidentiality, members' rights, putting into practice what is learned in group, and principles of group process can be parts of the agenda of the first session. Before the session ends, we ask members whether they have any questions or concerns and whether they want to continue. We let the members know that, if they decide later in the week that they don't want to return, all they need to do is call us. Of course, members can drop out at any point during the group, but we usually ask members who want to do so to discuss it with the group. If a member does not discuss it with the group, the remaining members don't have the chance to express to the member what they feel. Discussing the departure with the group also allows the departing member to express negative feelings that he or she might otherwise carry around for a long time. For everyone's sake, then, the issues involved in a premature termination should be aired.

A Sample Initial Session

To illustrate the mechanics of an initial session, I (Jerry Corey) will describe the first session of a semester-long weekly group I led on a college campus.

Nine people (three men and six women) arrived and sat in silence, waiting. Even though they had expressed a desire to participate in a counseling group, nobody seemed willing to begin. They waited, as they might have done at the first meeting of a class, to hear what was expected of them. I suggested that the members learn one another's names. A person began, the next person said his own name and the name of a person who had started, and so on. This took only a few minutes, yet when it was done everyone had learned all the names. Then I asked "Why did you come to this group? Could each of you tell the group what you hope to leave with in 15 weeks?" I feel that at this point in a group's evolution it is important to let members express themselves in any way they choose, for this initial presentation gives valuable clues that can be worked with during the remaining weeks. The nine members differed a great deal in their styles of presentation, including their ability to express their expectations clearly. Here are some examples of these opening statements.

Linda (age 19): She spoke softly and briefly, and as she spoke her eyes were on the carpet. She smiled often, and her hands shook. She remarked that she hoped to come to like herself better, for now she felt bad about herself much of the time. She then addressed me and said that she was frightened of authority figures and felt as though she should wait to be told what to do. She said she wanted to do what was appropriate.

Ralph (age 32): He spoke for a long time, but what he said seemed vague. He said that what he wanted to do in the session was work on guilt feelings, work on his hostile feelings toward women, understand his relationship with his mother, examine his "authority-figure hang-up," and work on his resentment. He seemed stiff and unrelaxed, and he stared into space while he talked. He admitted that for him to come to this session was a big step that he felt good about taking.

Elaine (age 35): She identified herself as a failure, a loser—a helpless, weak, and fragile person. She never stated clearly what she hoped for as a result of group participation, but she did talk about her depression. She said she had visited the school psychiatrist a few times and gotten a prescription for Valium but that she felt she had gotten nowhere. As she spoke, she listed many reasons for which she was not to blame for her misery; in other words, she rationalized her failures. She admitted that she was frightened of being confronted and that, because of her fear of criticism, she was thinking of quitting the group.

As I listened to these statements, I thought about what they indicated about the speakers. Most were frightened, and most had only a vague notion of what they expected from group counseling. They had taken the first step toward making themselves known to others, though, and later in the session they began to speak more specifically about behavior they were hoping to change. At the end of the session, they talked about the session as a group, and most of them left feeling more excited than when they had come in, two hours before.

Some Problems Commonly Discussed in College-Student Groups

Some themes seem to arise often in our college-student counseling groups. A list of these common themes, which provide the content of the group encounters, would include the following: the desire to be genuine, college problems, interpersonal difficulties, psychosomatic illnesses, denial of problems, the search for pat answers, sexual conflicts, dealing with hostility, feelings of rejection, the desire for acceptance and approval, wanting to love and be loved, relationships with parents, uneasiness about one's body, trusting self and others, feelings of loneliness, emptiness, and alienation, how to feel alive, value confusion, search for meaning in life, dependency problems, identity confusion, problems associated with drugs and alcohol, religious conflicts, vocational indecision, anxiety, man-woman relationships, insecurity, and lack of self-confidence.

This list could be extended, but our purpose here is just to give a picture of the kinds of problems dealt with in groups for college students. All of these are issues that normal college students have to wrestle with in the course of their development. The emphasis in such groups is thus more on helping relatively well-adjusted people work toward more effective adjustment than on "curing" sick people. These groups, then, can be considered *actualization* groups rather than therapy (in the remedial sense) groups.

As a concluding note, we wish to emphasize the possibilities that a university counseling center holds for those who want training and supervision in group leading. A counselor on the staff might be willing to assume responsibility for training students to lead groups of their peers. This kind of program would be of real benefit to the volunteer, to the many students who would relate well to a peer leader, and to the counseling center, which would be able to serve more students at no additional expense.

PERSONAL-AWARENESS COURSES ON THE COLLEGE LEVEL

A number of college courses are highly suited to a group approach in which students explore their conflicts and interpersonal relationships. This is true of courses in the psychology of personal and social adjustment, humanistic psychology, group therapy, human relations, and other such subjects. These courses might be structured such that a certain topic is explored each week, or they might be structured as free-flowing encounter groups. In what follows, I (Jerry Corey) will describe a self-awareness college course that I teach known as "Character and Conflict." I'll also give suggestions on how my methods can be adapted to suit courses in various subjects taught by various methods.

An Experiential Group Class

At California State University at Fullerton, a course called "Character and Conflict" was initiated during the spring semester of 1970 by Dr. William Lyon, a clinical psychologist. This course developed into one of the most popular (and controversial) courses on campus. It was Dr. Lyon who first combined this class, structured as a therapeutic group, with the group-leadership practicum described in Chapter 9. In other words, leader trainees participating in the practicum were given groups of students in the class to lead. Dr. Lyon found that the trainees not only developed therapeutic skills and the confidence to wield them effectively in groups but also evidenced significant gains in their personal growth. They exhibited a great deal of enthusiasm, and, even though they initially felt both anxious and inadequate as leaders of groups of their peers, they were usually amazed at their progress as they continued. This experiment seemed to demonstrate that people who have the courage to work on themselves can significantly affect their peers. It also demonstrated that undergraduates make good leaders, provided they are carefully selected and given the appropriate training and supervision. This combination of class and practicum was extremely innovative and attracted many highly motivated students. Many faculty members participated too, and they carried what they learned back to their own classrooms and designed their courses along more personal lines.

The ''Character and Conflict'' class is described in the college catalog as follows:

> An exploration—via lectures, discussion, and group encounter—into the problems and techniques of resolving the conflicts created by the individual's struggle to achieve and maintain personal autonomy while living successfully in an automated world. Topics include: autonomy, masculinity-femininity, love, sex, marriage, loneliness, death, meaning, and encountering others.

''Character and Conflict'' is an intensive group experience for personal and interpersonal growth. The course is not an unstructured encounter group, though. Rather, it is a theme-oriented group experience; students hear brief lectures, read selected articles and books, write reaction papers, discuss selected topics, work on their personal concerns, and learn the principles of group process.

Each week there is a different theme and focus. Of course, themes can be developed to suit the needs of a particular class. I use themes because I've found that they generate significant group interaction; they also stimulate students to begin to introspect. Some of the themes, and the questions I ask to provoke thought about them, follow.

1. *Identity*. Who are you? What is important in your world now? What are the main factors that have influenced your life? What kind of person do you wish to become? How do you perceive the world?
2. *Independence*. To what degree have you gained psychological independence from your parents?
3. *Sex roles*. What are the implications for you of the changing concepts of masculinity and femininity? How can you resolve your conflicts about your role?
4. *Love*. How capable are you of loving? What are the barriers in your life that prevent love, and what is it like for you to experience love?
5. *Sex*. What are your views regarding sexuality? What are your main concerns regarding your own sexuality?
6. *Marriage*. What are the dynamics within and between two individuals that determine the success or failure of the relationship? What are your feelings about marriage?
7. *Loneliness*. What are the creative aspects of loneliness? Do you cope with your own loneliness or do you escape from it?

8. *Death*. How do you feel about death? Does this affect the way you live?
9. *Search for meaning and values*. What are the values that give your life meaning, and where did you get them?
10. *Evaluation of the course experience*. What has this course meant to you? What have you learned about your own attitudes, values, beliefs, and behavior? To what extent have you carried this learning into your outside life? What areas do you need to continue working on in your life?

The primary purpose of the course is to help the members increase their awareness of the values and attitudes that underlie their behavior in daily life. I try to get the participants to think seriously about how each of the themes of the course applies to them. I feel that, if I can create an atmosphere that encourages the participants to openly and honestly explore their feelings, thoughts, and actions in these critical areas, I can help them choose the course that their life will take. The intent of this course is *not* to provide group therapy. The course is not a substitute for intensive psychotherapy, which aims at uncovering unconscious material and working toward major personality and behavior change. Rather, the course is essentially an *invitation* to self-exploration. It is my hope that many participants will extend the influence of this group experience by becoming involved in other personal-growth groups or even individual or group therapy.

How the Class Is Organized

How group process can be applied to a class depends on the number of students in the class, the purpose of the class, and the philosophy of the instructor. Lectures by the instructor, by guests, and by students themselves can be valuable as catalysts of group interaction. Generally, I begin a three-hour class with a lecture or demonstration or some other type of presentation. My purpose is to sharpen the focus of the students on the topic of the week and to stimulate interaction among the members.

In most of my courses, there are 40 students. Since the size of this group would prohibit significant interaction, the class divides into four groups. Two advanced students from the practicum in group leadership (Chapter 9) co-lead each group. This gives me the opportunity to circulate among the groups during the class session. Afterward, I meet with the group leaders; they discuss their experiences during the session, and I give them feedback on what I saw.

To illustrate how a college course can be designed as a personal-growth type of experience, I will outline in a little more detail the way my class is structured.

1. Eight students are selected for the practicum in group leadership; these people will function as co-leaders in the "Character and Conflict" course.

2. As supervisor in the practicum and instructor of the class, I meet with these group leaders for a three-day workshop before the semester begins. The workshop is an intensive group experience designed to prepare these leaders for the responsibility of facilitating their own groups.

3. Weekly, the group leaders and I meet during the hour before the group class meets. During this pre-session, the leaders discuss ideas related to the topic for that

week and explore ways of opening their group and keeping the members focused on various aspects of the topic under consideration.

4. Co-leader pairs usually stay together and with the same group for five weeks, at which time the leaders select new partners and new groups are formed. The main functions of the group leaders are: to introduce the topic, to get the members started exploring the topic in a personal and meaningful way, and to help create an accepting (yet challenging) atmosphere in which members are encouraged to relate freely with other members as they develop ways of realizing their goals.

5. Each week, immediately after the class, the leaders meet with me for a post-session evaluation. At this time, the leaders discuss their experiences with their groups, including any problems they had, and I offer a critique of what I observed when I visited the group.

6. During the week, the co-leaders get together and discuss the progress of their group. They prepare to work with the next topic, agreeing on some approaches to use, and resolve any problems that have arisen between them.

7. During the eighth week (midsemester), the group leaders plan a 12-hour marathon for the class. They plan for a range of specialized groups, each to last a couple of hours. These might include assertiveness-training groups, groups for men (or women) only, fantasy groups, and creativity groups. Class members may request other types of groups. Usually the majority of the students in the class attend the marathon, although attendance is voluntary. This extended session allows people enough time to work intensely in personal-conflict areas. It also provides a departure from the usual format of the class. During the marathon, there are a few sessions involving the whole class, but most of the time the students are with their regular groups, or in dyads, or with one of the specialized groups. Usually students report that the marathon was exciting because it gave them an unusual opportunity to get to know other class members and the chance to have a variety of experiences.

Alternate Approaches to Group-Oriented Courses

Not all of the faculty members who combine the group-leadership practicum with the ''Character and Conflict'' course do it as I do. Some of my colleagues do not require that their group leaders have experienced individual and group counseling, and most do not begin with a three-day intensive workshop with their group leaders. Some other instructors do not organize by topics, as I do, but rather use a more loosely structured format. Each instructor brings his or her own ideas to the course and approaches it in a different way.

There are other ways of holding a group-style class, if peer counselors or semi-trained group leaders are not available. Group leaders can be appointed from among the members of the class, and new students can assume leadership every five weeks. Of course, another possibility is to teach the basics of group process and experiential learning to the entire class during the initial sessions and then during the remaining sessions let the participants take turns leading their groups. Leaderless groups are an option, in which case everyone would get together at the end of a class session and tell what their group had done during the session.

The rationale for including a description of my self-awareness course, and its relationship to the group-leadership practicum, is that it illustrates how group work can be a vital part of a college student's program of studies. Many different courses can be adapted to give students experience as group facilitators. In addition, such self-awareness groups do not have to be restricted to the academic world. Many of the same procedures can be used in crisis clinics, in community counseling agencies, in day-treatment centers, and in mental-health agencies. Psychologists can hold training sessions for staff, interns, volunteers, and college students who wish to gain supervised experience leading groups. Many of the procedures I've described can be modified to suit the needs of various types of people and organizations.

Conclusion: Some Personal Remarks

I would like to share some of the feelings I've had while teaching the personal-growth course I've described.

Many students who enroll in "Character and Conflict" have never experienced a group, and surely not as a university course. Some of these students find it difficult to become active and participating group members. Some experience problems in expressing their feelings or thoughts on topics, some complain that the topics are too restricting, some feel threatened by the student group leaders, some resent the role of the group leaders, some are reluctant to disclose personal matters or otherwise take risks, some are willing to talk about problems in an intellectualizing way but refuse to be specific, and some complain of being manipulated. Every semester I sense certain of these resistances. I have come to realize that some resistance is an inevitable part of the process and that open exploration of these resistances is necessary (although sometimes painful). Sometimes, though, when I can't see progress being made, I feel discouraged.

On the other hand, I have continued to teach the course with a good deal of enthusiasm, for, while problems are inherent in the process, overall student reactions indicate that the course has value. When a class accepts the challenge to engage in honest self-searching and open exchanges, I become excited, for I can see genuine positive changes in the students. At times like these, the rewards outweigh the costs.

SUGGESTED READINGS

Alberti, R. E., & Emmons, M. L. *Stand up, speak out, talk back!* New York: Pocket Books, 1975.

Chaikin, A. L., & Derlega, V. J. *Sharing intimacy: What we reveal to others and why.* Englewood Cliffs, N.J.: Prentice-Hall, 1975.

Corey, G. *The struggle toward realness: A manual for therapeutic groups.* Dubuque, Iowa: Kendall/Hunt, 1974.

Corey, G. *Theory and practice of counseling and psychotherapy.* Monterey, Calif.: Brooks/Cole, 1977.

Corey, G. *Manual for theory and practice of counseling and psychotherapy.* Monterey, Calif.: Brooks/Cole, 1977.

Deaux, K. *The behavior of women and men*. Monterey, Calif.: Brooks/Cole, 1976.

Egan, G. *Interpersonal living*. Monterey, Calif.: Brooks/Cole, 1976.

Fensterheim, H., & Baer, J. *Don't say yes when you want to say no*. New York: Dell, 1975.

Frankl, V. *Man's search for meaning* (Rev. ed.). Boston: Beacon, 1963.

Freedman, M. *Homosexuality and psychological functioning*. Monterey, Calif.: Brooks/Cole, 1971.

Gale, R. *Who are you? The psychology of being yourself*. Englewood Cliffs, N.J. Prentice-Hall, 1974.

Goldberg, H. *The hazards of being male: Surviving the myth of masculine privilege*. New York: Nash, 1976.

Harris, T. *I'm O.K.–You're O.K.* New York: Avon, 1976.

Hodge, M. B. *Your fear of love*. New York: Doubleday, 1969.

Koestenbaum, P. *Existential sexuality: Choosing to love*. Englewood Cliffs, N.J.: Prentice-Hall, 1974.

Koestenbaum, P. *Managing anxiety: The power of knowing who you are*. Englewood Cliffs, N.J.: Prentice-Hall, 1974.

Kübler-Ross, E. *On death and dying*. New York: Macmillan, 1969.

Kübler-Ross, E. *Death: The final stages of growth*. Englewood Cliffs, N.J.: Prentice-Hall, 1975.

Levy, R. *I can only touch you now*. Englewood Cliffs, N.J.: Prentice-Hall, 1973.

Lyon, W. *Let me live!* (Rev. ed.). North Quincy, Mass.: Christopher, 1975.

Maslow, A. H. *Toward a psychology of being* (2nd ed.). New York: Van Nostrand Reinhold, 1968.

May, R. *Man's search for himself*. New York: Dell, 1973.

Moustakas, C. E. *Loneliness*. Englewood Cliffs, N.J.: Prentice-Hall, 1961.

Moustakas, C. E. *Loneliness and love*. Englewood Cliffs, N.J.: Prentice-Hall, 1972.

O'Neill, N., & O'Neill, G. *Shifting gears*. New York: Avon, 1975.

Prather, H. *Notes to myself*. Moab, Utah: Real People Press, 1970.

Rubin, T. I. *Compassion and self-hate: An alternative to despair*. New York: Ballantine, 1976.

Smith, M. J. *When I say no, I feel guilty*. New York: Bantam, 1975.

Steiner, C. *Scripts people live: Transactional Analysis of life scripts*. New York: Bantam, 1975.

13. GROUPS FOR
COUPLES

We decided to include a chapter on working with couples not only because some of our readers may want to do this kind of work but also because the techniques we use with couples can be used, with some modification, with many other types of groups—particularly groups that address the problem of interpersonal conflict.

In this chapter, we will describe the structure and process of the three-day weekend workshops for couples that we lead. First, we want to tell how we became interested in couples and decided to design this kind of group.

Marianne was the first of us to design and conduct a couples group; the couples belonged to a Lutheran church. One month later, we attended a couples group ourselves, as members. We liked learning about ourselves; even though the workshop lasted only a weekend, it caused us to take a critical look at our relating style and prompted a few rich insights. A few months later, we decided to offer a couples group together, because (1) we had begun to believe in group work that focused on a couple, since humans are relational beings and since many of the problems people bring to any group have to do with their intimate partner, (2) our interest in working with couples was growing, and (3) many of the participants in our week-long residential personal-growth groups had requested that we lead a group for couples with a focus on relationship problems and ways of renewing relationships. So, two years ago, we began to offer weekend workshops for couples. Each such workshop lasts three days, with the couples—usually five—living at our home in the mountains of Idyllwild.

Our couples workshop is designed primarily to provide an opportunity for people in an intimate relationship to examine the quality of their relationship, to determine what barriers are preventing genuine intimacy, to make decisions concerning how they want to change their life with each other, and to explore their conflicts. The workshop is for any woman and man who define themselves as a couple. Whereas most of the couples who participate are married in the conventional sense, some couples are just living together, and some are attempting to decide whether they want to become an intimate couple. We've had newlyweds, and we've had grandparents; generally, there's an interesting variety of people in each group.

During the workshop, we sometimes ask questions, to provide some focus. For the most part, however, the couples determine what topics will be explored; they are asked to think about what they want to deal with in the group before they arrive for the weekend. The content of the workshop thus varies from group to group. Still, certain themes regularly emerge:

- how to remain separate individuals while benefiting from an intimate relationship,
- the myths about marriage and how they lead to unrealistic expectations,
- sex roles as they affect a marriage,
- alternatives to traditional marriages,
- open versus closed marriage,
- the importance of commitment in a relationship,
- how to reinvent a relationship,
- sex and loving in intimate relationships,
- the sources of conflict in a marriage, and
- how to detect communication pitfalls and learn to express one's thoughts and feelings directly.

A WEEKEND WORKSHOP FOR COUPLES

The Structure of the Workshop

Generally, the couples who attend have been in one of our groups for individuals and so aren't strangers to us. If we don't know a couple who have applied for the workshop, we like to arrange a meeting with them before deciding whether to accept them. At the meeting, we ask what they're seeking from the group and explain its purpose. We deal with any questions or concerns that they have. Thus, by the time the workshop begins, none of the participants is a stranger to us.

As we've mentioned, our home, at which the workshop is held, is in the mountains; hence the workshop has the special feature of being away from the usual city distractions. We firmly believe that this setting enhances the quality of the work done; maybe for the first time in years, a couple can be alone together in nature, and all the couples can reflect without disruption on what they're learning in the group.

The members arrive at 9:00 a.m. on Friday, not to leave until 3:00 p.m. on Sunday. In the interim, they all live with us in our house, and everyone helps with the preparation of the meals. This communal living is another special feature that enhances the experience.

We work as a group for approximately 24 hours, or eight sessions of at least 3 hours. During the afternoon session of the second day, we frequently work near a running creek, among boulders, trees, flies, and mosquitoes. We divide into pairs and talk informally, and by the end of the afternoon most participants have had a chance to spend some time on a one-to-one basis with most of the other participants. This allows for discussion of commonalities or of anything that may have emerged in the preceding workshop sessions.

Approximately two months after the workshop, we hold a four-hour follow-up session. This allows participants to practice new behaviors with their partners and to discuss the work they've done to fulfill the contracts they made during the final stage of the group. In examining the effects that the workshop has had on their behavior in the real world, the members are, in effect, assessing the impact of the three-day experience.

The Initial Stages

To begin the workshop, on the first day, we generally call together the entire group for a short time and ask a few questions:

- What was it like to come here today?
- How have you felt since you decided to join the group? What were you hoping to get from the weekend when you signed up?
- Did you leave anyone behind whose welfare preoccupies you now, so that you're not fully present?

After the members have discussed these questions and any related concerns they have, we have them devote the remainder of the morning session to working in pairs with someone other than their mate. The reason for beginning this way is that it breaks up the exclusive focus on the couple, and we've discovered that more honesty is generated this way. This pairing also helps the members get acquainted and builds up trust. We ask the members to work for approximately 15 minutes with one person of the opposite sex and then change partners, and so on. Before each new set of dyads is formed, we suggest a question to the members, the answer to which they can discuss with their partners. These questions lay the groundwork for later group work by getting the members to begin thinking about themselves and their mates. During later workshop sessions, we will usually delve in depth into the issues raised by these questions, which include:

1. Why did you come to this particular couples group? What are you hoping to leave with?
2. What are you afraid you might find out about yourself, your spouse, or your relationship? Explore your fears about this workshop.
3. How would you describe your marriage?
4. How do you imagine your spouse just described your marriage?
5. Become your spouse, and describe what it is like to be married to you.
6. What changes would you most like to make in your relationship with your partner?
7. If no change took place in your marriage, what do you imagine your future would hold? How do you think your partner answered that question?
8. How would your life be different if you were not married (or living with someone)?

After the pairings, the group usually reconvenes before lunch to share reactions to the work in dyads. We find out a little about what came out in these exchanges, and we begin to see what the goals of the workshop should be. Members may express fears or reservations, and we deal with these concerns at this time so that they won't interfere with the main work of the group.

The Working Stages

After the initial session, the direction of the group is somewhat unpredictable, for we do not tightly control the process with techniques or themes. Our philosophy is that these groups function best if there is some structure to provide a focus but enough flexibility that the members can draw up their own agenda. Our main functions are to see that the discussion stays on a meaningful, not a superficial, level and to encourage members to participate.

We do make use of techniques, though, when we feel that they'll deepen the level of interaction. For most of the remainder of the chapter, we'll describe approaches that we use in the workshops. Remember that what we do varies with each workshop, in accordance with the unique development of the group. Also remember that, although throughout the chapter we will refer to *marriage, spouse, wife,* and *husband,* these terms should be interpreted broadly, as some of the couples who attend are not married.

1. *Inner and outer circles*. The men form a circle, and the women form a circle outside of it. Pretending that their wives aren't present, the men talk about how it is for them to be married. The women listen silently. After the men have said all they want to say, they discuss what they imagine their partners would say about their marriage if *they* were sitting in the inner circle. When the men are finished, the women and men change places. The women begin by sharing their reactions to what they heard their partners say. Then, as though the men weren't present, they tell how they perceive their marriage and to what degree they feel understood by their husbands.

This exercise usually brings meaningful issues out into the open. After the exercise, we focus on the mates who apparently don't understand each other. The exercise is useful in that it allows us to detect distortions, projections, and conflicts.

2. *Variations on the inner-and-outer-circles exercise*. Throughout the workshop, we suggest variations on the preceding exercise when they seem timely and when they will bring about interaction on a more profound level. For instance, we may reintroduce any of the questions we asked the dyads to answer at the opening of the workshop. Or we may have the inner circles answer one of these questions:

- What are some of the best (or worst) features of your marriage?
- In what concrete ways would you like to change your relationship? What are you doing about making these changes? What more could you do?
- How much do you depend on your partner for confirmation of your worth, and what effect does this have on you? On your relationship?
- What was it in your partner that influenced your decision to form the relationship?
- What was it like for you when you first met? What were your expectations?

3. *Exercise in separate identity and mutuality.* A very important part of our philosophy is our belief that, in order for two people to have a productive relationship, they must be separate individuals who can exist without each other. If two people depend on each other completely, we think it will be extremely difficult for them to examine their relationship and that they will be reluctant to challenge each other. If one partner is excessively dependent on the other, his or her freedom to grow as a unique person will be stifled.

A fantasy exercise can get the members to think about how separate they are from their partner and what would become of them if their partner were not in their life. The participants are asked to imagine that they come home and find a note from their spouse that says that he or she has left and may not return. The participants are to fantasize about their immediate reactions and tell what they would do if the partner didn't return. They might tell what they think they would be doing, thinking, and feeling a week, a month, a year, or even longer after their mate's departure.

4. *Brainstorming.* At different points in the workshop, we use brainstorming to provide alternatives for consideration. One theme that comes up in most couples groups is how to enhance a dull relationship. Couples tend to settle into comfortable but boring patterns; many workshop participants are seeking ways of revitalizing a dying marriage. In the brainstorming exercise, members think of as many ways of reinventing a relationship as possible. The entire group throws out suggestions, and the guideline is, the more suggestions, the better. Nobody is to question or comment on any of the ideas during the 10 or 15 minutes of freewheeling brainstorming. After the brainstorming, participants can focus on the suggestions that seemed exciting to them, and a discussion of ways of implementing these suggestions can follow.

5. *Women's group and men's group.* An approach that we have used at some workshops is separating the group into a women's group and a men's group, with each of us leading the appropriate group. The agenda is determined sometimes by the group and sometimes by us. These subgroups can last an hour and a half to two hours, depending on how much time the participants are willing to invest and what topics are introduced. One common focus of the subgroups is sexuality. Some questions we might ask are: How do you feel about your own sexuality? Do you enjoy your body? Are you able to enjoy sensuality as well as sexuality? In what ways do you feel that your sex life could be improved? What do you most enjoy receiving from your partner? What do you most like to give to the other? What are some attitudes or guilts that interfere with your sexual fulfillment? What is it like for you to be a woman (man)?

We separate the sexes in this way because we believe this allows members to discuss openly topics that they might feel shy about discussing with the entire group, at least at first. However, it is our hope that much of what goes on in the subgroups will eventually be discussed in the general group. After the whole group has reassembled, we ask members to share any aspects of their subgroup experience that they're willing to disclose. Considerable time can then be devoted to discussion of these issues or to role-playing. Unless a general discussion of what went on in the subgroups takes place, there is the danger that a division will be introduced into the group.

6. *Opposite-sides exercise*. In this exercise, the women sit on one side of the room, and the men sit on the other side. Each side has five minutes to issue any and all of its complaints about the opposite sex. During these five minutes, the people on the other side are not to respond. After each side has had its five minutes, the floor is open to any couple who wish to explore a comment that was made. The purpose of this exercise is not to set up debates but rather to facilitate open expression of certain resentments that are usually concealed. We try to get partners to express pent-up hostilities without attacking each other.

A variation of this exercise involves using the same structure but having the men and women tell what they appreciate, respect, and like about the opposite sex. This variation is designed to teach the importance of expressing feelings of love, tenderness, gratitude, and respect. Married people often fail to express these positive feelings to each other.

7. *Incomplete-sentence exercise*. In this exercise, each person in the group in turn finishes an incomplete sentence. (Of course, a person may say "I pass" in response to any sentence.) We usually ask the members to finish a number of the following sentences:

- My greatest joy in marriage is . . .
- I feel disappointed in my relationship when . . .
- The thing I'd most like to change in myself is . . .
- The thing I'd most like to change in my spouse is . . .
- I feel the closest to her (him) when . . .
- If I were not married, . . .
- If our relationship continues to be as it has been, in five years, . . .
- When I get angry with my spouse, I . . .
- It is difficult for me to show . . .
- My greatest fear concerning our relationship is . . .

Or sometimes we ask the participants to suggest incomplete sentences.

This exercise can bring out valuable material, which needs to be pursued openly in the group if full advantage is to be taken of it. Thus, after everyone has completed the sentences, the members are invited to tell what the exercise was like for them or how they felt when their spouse completed a particular sentence.

8. *Marital-games exercise*. One function of the workshop is to increase the participants' awareness of the games they play that prevent intimacy. A task of the participants is to examine the benefits they derive from these games and decide whether they're willing to forgo these benefits and deal directly with their partners. These games should be pointed out by either the members or the leaders as they become evident in a couple's relationship. An exercise can also be initiated in which members are asked to tell what games they see themselves playing with their spouse. Some common marital games can be described as follows.

- The husband does not state directly what he needs or wants from his wife; instead, he questions her about her wants.

- The wife punishes her husband by savoring her hostility.
- The husband tries to meet what he imagines are his wife's expectations and, in the process, loses most of his identity.
- The wife does not do certain things that she wants to do and then blames her husband for her situation.
- The husband initiates an argument in order to prevent closeness.
- The wife plays helpless and weak and then explodes when her husband tells her what to do.
- The husband is usually too tired to have sex when the wife initiates it.

9. *Examining one's parents' marriage.* This variation of the marital-games exercise involves examining one's parents' marriage and then comparing it with one's own. To help the participants carry out this examination, we ask such questions as: In what ways is your marriage like your parents'? How do your parents deal with disagreement? How do they treat their children? What do they most want from life? What do they do for fun? What have you learned from them about marriage?

To do this exercise, each member joins another—preferably someone other than the spouse—and answers one question. Then everyone changes partners. After several pairings have taken place, the members all get together again and examine in depth the influence that their parents' marriage has had on their marriage. The rationale for this approach is that it helps couples see what attitudes of their parents they've incorporated and gives them a chance to decide whether they want to continue holding these attitudes. In this exercise, the members engage in a critical examination of the degree of influence that their parents still exert on them and, if they want to, look for ways of lessening this influence.

10. *Examining partners' values.* Couples can be encouraged to examine openly the compatibility of their values. We see this as a most important function of the workshop. Couples can explore the extent to which they agree on

- the value of a sexually exclusive relationship,
- how children should be reared,
- how money should be spent,
- the importance of doing things together as a couple or as a family,
- the importance of self-awareness and personal growth,
- what constitutes success,
- religion and a philosophy of life,
- what constitutes a good sex life, and
- the need to devote time and energy to renewing the relationship.

The purpose of the workshop is not to teach couples what to value; rather, the aim is to have them clarify their values as separate persons and as couples and to help them communicate in an honest way about what they value. We feel that we've done an important service if couples do begin to talk openly about their values.

11. *Critical turning points*. Generally, the participants spend at least one session focusing on the times and occurrences that they judge to have been critical turning points in their married lives. The members are asked to examine the significance of these incidents with respect to some of their current marital struggles. This exercise is designed to facilitate a review by each participant of his or her married life. This review brings submerged issues to the surface, where they can be dealt with.

For instance, a woman may identify her critical turning points as the births of her children, her decision to complete college, and her decision to commit herself to a career as well as to marriage. Her husband may harbor bitter feelings regarding her decision to go to college and her quest for independence. He had encouraged her dependence on him and was threatened by her success in college and in her career. The more successful she became, the more he withdrew from her. The identification by the wife of her critical turning points may bring this dynamic to the surface and thus offer a chance for both persons to develop new perspectives. The husband can work on his insecurity while learning to accept his wife's strengths and can, it is hoped, begin to feel that he is worthwhile even if his wife is not dependent on him—that it is possible for both to be strong at the same time.

12. *How have you changed?* Many individuals change in the course of their relationship with their partner. At some point in the workshop, we usually focus on the nature of these changes and on how each person perceives and reacts to the changes his or her partner has made or is making.

For example, a man married a woman he viewed as strong, because at the time he felt a need for someone who would make decisions for him and even take care of him. As time went by, he painfully came to recognize that he related to his wife as to a mother. He then decided to treat his wife as a wife, not as a mother, and to take the responsibility of deciding things for himself, instead of playing helpless in order to make her take over. A crucial question is: How has she responded to his changes? Does she encourage his redefinition of himself, or does she attempt to thwart these changes? This exercise can give this couple the chance to reflect on and discuss the changes that have taken place in their relationship.

We encourage the participants to recognize that the need that made them choose a certain partner may change or that the partner may change and no longer fill the need. We encourage a dialogue between spouses about the changes they perceive and about the impact these shifts in needs and motivations are having on the relationship at present.

13. *Role-playing exercises*. As much as possible, we use action-oriented approaches—approaches in which people act out their conflicts rather than merely talk about them. When participants say that they would like to understand a specific conflict more fully, we try to design a situation in which the difficulty can be acted out.

For example, Sam becomes extremely jealous when Carole expresses any interest in other men. He immediately interprets her regard for another man as a sign of his deficiency as a man, and he tends to feel that if he were man enough she would not be interested in others. The role-playing can be set up by having Carole talk to Sam about her feelings of attraction for another man in the group. It is presumed that a dialogue like the ones they have at home will ensue. Then the other members can give Sam and Carole feedback. They may find that Carole, in her manner of communicating her feelings, ignites Sam's jealousy with hints, which she claims are unintentional, of a sexual interest in the other man. Hence she sends conflicting messages; she says directly that he has no grounds for his fears and indirectly that she's interested in other men. As a variation on this exercise, Carole and Sam can exchange roles; Carole can play Sam as she sees him, while Sam becomes Carole as he perceives her.

In another case, Betty may complain that all Hector ever talks to her about is his work as an engineer. Betty might play her husband, showing how he talks to her when she would like to discuss something other than engineering. This can give Hector some idea of how Betty feels, and he can discuss how accurate he considers Betty's portrait of him.

In still another case, Elsie may struggle with Jack's insistence on being "logical" and his inability to deal with the realm of feelings. The two can be asked to reenact a typical situation so that the group gets a sample of their interaction. Or Elsie can be asked to exaggerate Jack's logical behavior while Jack exaggerates the emotional behavior of Elsie's that causes him so much difficulty. By reversing roles and exaggerating each other's styles, Elsie and Jack may come to appreciate each other's positions. Again, feedback from group members on how they experience Jack and Elsie can help the couple see themselves more clearly.

Other group members can join the role-playing activities at times by sitting in for someone. For example, in the dialogue between Elsie and Jack, Joan might sit in for Elsie and demonstrate another way that Elsie might respond to Jack when he becomes cold-bloodedly logical. There are also some exciting possibilities in involving several people in a piece of work by having alter egos (that is, by having two members stand behind two partners and say what they imagine the partners are thinking or feeling) or by having several couples work simultaneously on a similar problem.

We find that the manner in which we suggest role-playing determines the willingness of the members to participate. We strive for an informal manner and, in many instances, model the role-playing. This action-oriented approach reduces the boredom and detachment that come from intellectualizing about problems.

The Final Stages

During the final sessions, we emphasize review of what was learned during the workshop, practice of newly adopted styles of behaving, and formulation of contracts to be fulfilled and homework assignments to be carried out before the follow-up session in two months. But we especially emphasize the giving of feedback by participants to one another individually and as couples.

There are several methods of making feedback more interesting and meaningful. One approach involves the members' forming dyads, much as they did in the initial session. This time, the participants tell their partners how they imagine it would be to live with them. At this point, there are plenty of observations to draw on, and the participants are usually willing to be very honest. This exercise can be extremely valuable to the receiver, particularly if he or she hears the same thing over and over. For instance, if most of the people that Sharon pairs up with tell her that they would have a difficult time coping with her sarcasm, or seductiveness, or aggressiveness, then she is likely to reflect seriously on what she has heard and to gain insight into the reactions that certain of her behaviors trigger in others. She can then decide whether she is willing to work at changing some of these behaviors. The advantage of this one-to-one format over a whole-group format in giving and receiving feedback is that it tends to lessen the defensiveness of the receiver and to increase the independence of the giver's observations.

In another exercise, the focus is on each couple for 10 or 15 minutes. During this time, the rest of the group gives the partners feedback based on what they experienced of them in this workshop. This feedback helps the couples see their interactions with increased clarity. As part of the feedback, members can tell each couple the strengths they see in each person and in the relationship, the ways the partners undermine these strengths, the hopes they have for them, and their fears and concerns about them. Again, if this feedback is given with care, directly and honestly, it can be a tremendous resource for partners who are trying to improve the quality of their life together.

In addition to direct feedback, role-playing can be most useful at this time. For example, Gail and Gary sit in the center of the room and play Fred and Rachel for a few minutes. They engage in a dialogue that captures the essence of what they see Rachel and Fred doing. This can be not only therapeutic but also very funny. Then Elsie and Jack jump into the center and present a brief verbal or nonverbal exchange that conveys another aspect of Rachel and Fred's relationship. Other couples do the same. Finally, Rachel and Fred are asked to react briefly to the diverse feedback that was given to them.

Or, assume that Carole and Sam are in the spotlight. One couple might want to mimic, in an exaggerated way, a certain style characteristic of Carole and Sam. For example, the person playing Sam might exaggerate Sam's overly nice manner toward Carole. This can teach Sam and Carole about themselves, and it can also teach them to laugh at themselves. We wish to stress that the humor and lightness do not detract from the message. On the contrary—a humorous presentation can help a couple appreciate the pettiness of their ways and stop taking themselves so seriously.

During the final session, we like to get the participants to think about ways in which they can sustain the growing process that they've begun. We ask the members to tell what significant things they've come to understand about themselves and their manner of relating to their spouse, and we encourage them to state briefly some of their decisions for change. To increase the chances that the couples will indeed change, we ask them to give themselves certain homework assignments to do before the follow-up session in two months. A realistic contract that involves specific actions can be very fruitful in enabling couples to make progress. For example, a couple might say that they learned in the workshop that they have drifted away from each other and buried themselves in outside responsibilities. Their contract might commit them to a variety of new activities. They will go away for a weekend together to a place they've both been wanting to visit. They will keep journals for the next two months concerning their reactions to the workshop and what they learned about themselves as a couple, and they will devote at least 15 minutes a week to talking with each other about the quality of their relationship. They will take square-dancing lessons together—something they've wanted to do but have put off for years because of their busy schedules. She will do something for herself that she has long dreamed of but continued to tell herself that she couldn't do: enroll in an evening class in the community college. And he will do something just for himself: go with his buddies on a long-overdue fishing trip.

It is important that contracts be realistic—that they require activities that the persons are willing to carry out—and that the activities they call for be chosen by the couples themselves rather than by other members or by the workshop leaders. However, at times it may be appropriate for others to suggest assignments that the couple might not have considered. Suggestion of options is also an important part of the feedback process during the closing session.

Before the workshop ends, we usually make a few suggestions concerning how the members can sustain the focus they learned in the workshop in their daily lives. We give them the names of books that offer ideas that they can talk about, and we encourage them to record in an ongoing journal their reflections on the themes that emerged during the workshop. We also suggest resources for individuals or couples who want to join another couples group, or get individual or family counseling, or join a therapeutic group for individuals. Participants are encouraged to think about other kinds of therapeutic experiences that will assist them in making their desired changes. A passive man who has realized in the workshop that he has real difficulty asking for what he wants might consider an assertiveness-training workshop. An overweight woman who has come to the decision that she is tired of her fat and wants to begin to like herself again might think of joining an organization such as Weight Watchers or Overeater's Anonymous or seeking individual counseling.

Finally, we are always interested in some kind of evaluation at the end of a workshop with couples, so we typically ask the members to assess the sessions and to suggest ways of improving the workshop. Not only is this important for us as leaders, but we think that it is also valuable for the members, for it allows them to review their own process as a group. Of course, the post-session two months later is largely an evaluation session, since at that time members assess the impact of the workshop in terms of its effects on their ways of being, both as individuals and as couples.

SOME FINAL COMMENTS

Of course, many variations on the workshop for couples can be designed. For instance, the group can involve a series of six or more three-hour weekly sessions, then a weekend workshop, and then about six more weekly sessions. Another alternative we've considered involves several pre-sessions, followed by two weekend retreats and a series of follow-up meetings. This pattern can be spread out over a period of from three to nine months. We feel that there are some advantages to a combination of ongoing weekly sessions and occasional intensive weekend work-shops. Under this plan, members can learn from a variety of experiences, can practice outside of the group and report on the results, and can benefit from ongoing feedback, challenge, and support. A concern we have about the one-weekend approach is that couples may receive only a booster shot and temporary excitement; we wonder about the degree of permanence of changes that are not intensively and continuously reinforced, as they are in an ongoing group.

Before we conclude this chapter, we want to describe what our experience in working with couples has taught us. One important thing it has taught us is that, if two people are to keep their relationship alive, they must be committed to working hard at it. Both individuals have to consider their relationship to be among their highest priorities. They must be willing to stay with each other during times of crisis and upheaval as well as when everything seems to be going smoothly. We've found that some people file for divorce just when they might have made a breakthrough and begun a new kind of marriage. And we've seen people leave their spouse because they feel that the spouse is stagnating while they are growing. Lately we've begun to encourage the "growing" person to give the other person a chance. Perhaps the spouse will relate vastly differently to the changed partner, or even be inspired to seek the same kind of therapeutic experiences that led to the partner's changes. We are not saying that couples should stay together at any cost; rather, we are observing that a couple working together can make some dramatic, constructive changes, provided the commitment to improving the relationship exists. This is one reason why it is so exciting to work with couples; they can be challenged together and can participate in each other's growth.

SUGGESTED READINGS

Bach, G. R., & Wyden, P. *The intimate enemy: How to fight fair in love and marriage*. New York: Morrow, 1969.

Bernard, J. *The future of marriage*. New York: Bantam, 1973.

Berne, E. *Sex in human loving*. New York: Pocket Books, 1971.

Corey, G. *The struggle toward realness: A manual for therapeutic groups*. Dubuque, Iowa: Kendall/Hunt, 1974.

DeLora, J., & DeLora, J. (Eds.). *Intimate life styles: Marriage and its alternatives*. Pacific Palisades, Calif.: Goodyear, 1975.

Erickson, G. D., & Hogan, T. P. *Family therapy: An introduction to theory and technique*. Monterey, Calif.: Brooks/Cole, 1972.

Fromm, E. *The art of loving*. New York: Harper & Row, 1974.

Hodge, M. B. *Your fear of love*. New York: Doubleday, 1969.

Jourard, S. M. *The transparent self: Self-disclosure and well-being* (2nd ed.). New York: Van Nostrand Reinhold, 1971.

Koestenbaum, P. *Existential sexuality: Choosing to love*. Englewood Cliffs, N. J.: Prentice-Hall, 1974.

Lyon, W. *Let me live!* (Rev. ed.). North Quincy, Mass.: Christopher, 1976.

O'Neill, N., & O'Neill, G. *Open marriage: A new lifestyle for couples*. New York: Avon, 1973.

O'Neill, N., & O'Neill, G. *Shifting gears*. New York: Avon, 1975.

Perls, F. S. *Gestalt therapy verbatim*. Moab, Utah: Real People Press, 1969.

Rogers, C. R. *Becoming partners: Marriage and its alternatives*. New York: Dell, 1973.

Shapiro, S., & Tyrka, H. *Trusting yourself: Psychotherapy as a beginning*. Englewood Cliffs, N.J.: Prentice-Hall, 1975.

14. GROUPS FOR THE
ELDERLY

My (Marianne Corey's) interest in working as a counselor with the elderly is associated with my German background. I have always been involved with old people; when I was growing up, they were always present. In Germany, old and young people live together. More often than not, children grow up in households that include their grandparents. Today, there appears to be an increase in the construction of homes exclusively for the elderly, yet the practice of living with one's children prevails among old people, because Germans continue to believe that the elderly should be taken care of by family members rather than by strangers. The proximity I had to the elderly as I grew up left me with fewer fears about my own aging than most Americans seem to suffer. I have noticed that many Americans are repulsed by the deteriorating bodies of old people, perhaps because they fear their own body's decay. This is truly sad, for I take great pleasure in looking at an old person's face, in which I see a treasure of character, beauty, and wisdom. I remember rumors circulating to the effect that in the United States old people are considered useless and are locked up. Since I've been in the United States, I've learned that the facts are not quite so horrible as I had imagined; however, I do detect many differences between Germany and the United States in the treatment of and attitude toward the aged. A description of these differences is, however, beyond the scope of this chapter.

Until recently, it was considered by many to be unusual for a young person to be seriously interested in pursuing a career working with the aged. People, even old people, asked me ''Why does a young person like you want to work with old people?'' I hear such comments less frequently now, and the number of young people working in the field of geriatrics is increasing with the passing years. Americans are beginning to perceive old people as vital members of society and to treat them with more respect.

While I genuinely like old people and enjoy being with them, I feel that a liking for old people alone does not make a good counselor. This unique population requires a specialist. In order to become such a specialist, I attended the summer institute that is part of the geriatrics program at the University of Southern California and many workshops on the aged. The group work with the institutionalized that forms the basis for this chapter was also part of my education. From these educational experiences, my personal involvement with old people as a child and as an adult, and my professional observations, I have developed a list of the personal qualities that I feel a counselor needs to have in order to work successfully with the elderly:

1. genuine respect for old people,
2. a history of positive experiences with old people,
3. a deep sense of caring for the elderly,
4. an ability and desire to learn from old people,
5. an understanding of the biological aspects of aging,
6. the conviction that the last years of life can be challenging,
7. patience, especially with repetition of stories,
8. knowledge of the special biological, psychological, and social needs of the aged,
9. sensitivity to the burdens and anxieties of old people,
10. the ability to get old people to challenge many of the myths about old age, and
11. a healthy attitude regarding one's own eventual old age.

I feel angry when old people are perceived as near dead, cute, or strange, and I certainly will not care to be regarded as such when I'm older. As I once told a friend, if I am to get old in this country, I want to change a few things before I get there. I decided to include a chapter on groups for the elderly in this book because I strongly believe that group approaches can be developed that would help bring about such changes by helping to meet the needs of this growing segment of our population.

A PROGRAM FOR INSTITUTIONALIZED OLD PEOPLE

My experience of designing a program for the elderly was part of the internship I was required to do for my master's degree in marriage, family, and child counseling. After encountering some difficulties in having this type of field placement accepted by the university as a legitimate part of my training for the M.A., I developed the position that the elderly are a vital part of the family and that a family counselor should have exposure to their unique needs and problems. Once the university had accepted this rationale, and thus my proposal to work with the elderly, I met other difficulties. I had a hard time locating an agency that could give me an opportunity to work in a meaningful way with the aged. The human-service agencies I contacted were not very involved in providing counseling services for the elderly.

I was finally able to arrange to work with geriatric patients in a state mental institution—the only institution I could find that provided counseling for a large number of old people. During a two-hour interview conducted by the program director and a staff member, I was questioned (at first with suspicion) concerning my motives for seeking this kind of experience. The staff member expressed her surprise about my request to work with the elderly, since, as she put it, "Nobody wants this assignment." However, the general tone of the interview was very positive;

how my needs and the needs of the program could be integrated was given serious consideration.

My initial impression of the ward that I was assigned to was that it was very unattractive. The atmosphere seemed depressingly lifeless. Many of the 44 male and female patients were either standing by themselves or sitting in front of a TV; most stared blankly into space. I noticed very little contact among the ward members. They seemed quite isolated from one another, even though they shared a relatively small area. Eight to ten beds occupied a single room, so that there was a complete lack of privacy. The old people were dressed in unattractive state-issued clothing that could have added nothing to their self-esteem. I was convinced that the surroundings were having a strong negative effect on the patients' ability to change. I felt that their environment contributed to their sense of hopelessness and isolation.

One staff member was setting a patient's hair; another was working with patients on art projects. However, most of the staff were in a centrally located glass-walled office from which they could view the activities of the patients on the ward.

I was soon accepted by the ward members; they seemed willing to talk to me if I approached them first. I was to work with a social worker assigned to the ward two days a week, and he and I decided to form two groups. One was to be a pre-placement group for people who were ready to leave the institution and either waiting to be placed in some type of home for the elderly or waiting to return to their own home. The other group would be for patients suffering from organic brain syndromes (OBS), a condition associated with impaired cognitive abilities. People with OBS evidence severe impairments of memory, intellectual functioning, and judgment. They are disoriented, and they show shallow affect.

The Pre-Placement Group

The pre-placement group consisted of three men and four women—a good balance of the sexes and a workable number for two leaders. Before the first meeting, I contacted the members individually and gave them a basic orientation to the group. I told them the purpose of the group, what the activities might be, and where, when, and for how long the group would meet. I let each person know that membership was voluntary. When people seemed hesitant to attend, I suggested that they come to the initial session and then decide whether they wanted to continue.

Before the first session, my co-leader and I decided on a few general goals for the group. Our primary goal would be to provide an atmosphere in which common concerns could be freely discussed and in which members could interact with one another. We wanted to provide an opportunity for members to voice complaints and to be included in a decision-making process. We strongly felt that these people could change their lives and that the group process could stimulate them to do so.

The group met once a week for an hour in the visitors' room. Before each group session, I contacted all the members, reminded them that the group would meet shortly, invited them to attend, and accompanied them to the group room. I learned that it was difficult for them to remember the time of the meetings and that this individual assistance would be important in ensuring regular attendance. Those who were absent were either ill or involved in an activity that couldn't be rescheduled, such as physical therapy. The group was an open one; members would occasionally be discharged, and we encouraged newly admitted patients to join. This didn't seem to bother the members, and it didn't affect the cohesion of the group.

The initial stages. During the initial sessions, the members showed a tendency to direct all of their statements to the two leaders. In the hope that we could break the shell that isolated each person in his or her private and detached world, my co-leader and I began immediately to encourage the members to talk to one another, not to us. When members talked about a member, we asked them to speak directly to that member. When members discussed a particular problem or concern, we encouraged others to share similar difficulties.

In the beginning, the members resisted talking about themselves, voicing complaints, or discussing what they expected after their release from the institution. Their usual comment reflected their hopelessness: "What good will it do? No one will listen to us anyway." Our task was to teach them to listen to one another.

The importance of listening and acting. My co-leader and I felt that one way of teaching the old people to listen would be by modeling—by demonstrating that we were really listening to them. Thus, when our clients spoke of problems related to life on the ward, my co-leader and I became actively involved with them in solving some of these conflicts. For example, one member complained that one of the patients in his room shouted for much of the night. We were able to get the unhappy member placed in another room. When some members shared their fears about the board-and-care homes they were to be released to, we arranged to take them to several such homes so that they could make an informed choice of placement. One woman complained that her husband did not visit her enough and that, when he did take her home, he was uncaring and uninterested in her sexually. On several occasions, my co-leader and I held private sessions with the couple.

Some men complained that there was nothing to do, so we arranged for them to get involved in planting a garden. Another group member shared the fact that she was an artist, so we asked her to lead some people in the group and on the ward in art projects. She reacted enthusiastically and succeeded in involving several other members. One member complained during several sessions that he felt trapped and that he did not belong in the hospital; the staff agreed with this assessment of the situation. He was waiting for something to happen, and with the passing of time he became increasingly depressed. After discussing his case with the director and the social worker, I encouraged this man to take steps to get himself released instead of depending on others to do it. He then obtained a pass that permitted him to leave the ward, and on several occasions he visited his conservator (the legal guardian appointed for him by the state) in an effort to make himself visible to the authorities. Too often patients like him, who are ready to be released, are lost in the paperwork required for hundreds of other cases. Despite our help, it took this man almost a year to get out of the institution.

All of these stories illustrate the importance of a counselor's working with the immediate problems that old people face. Our philosophy was to encourage them to again become active, even in a small way, in making decisions about their lives. There were two things that we learned *not* to do: (1) encourage a patient to participate in an activity that would frustrate him or her and thereby further erode an already poor self-image and (2) make promises we couldn't keep.

Listening to reminiscences. In addition to dealing with the day-to-day problems of the members, we spent much time listening as they reminisced about sadness and guilt they had experienced, their many losses, the places they had lived and visited, the mistakes they had made, and so on. By remembering and actively reconstructing their past, old people can hope to resolve the old conflicts that are still affecting them and decide how to use the time left to them. I believe that this life review is an important and healthy process and that old people need to experience it.

The use of exercises. My role as a leader of this group differed from the roles I had played in other types of groups. I found that I was more directive, that I was much less confrontive and much more supportive, and that I spent a lot of time teaching the members how to express themselves and listen to others. My co-leader and I designed a variety of exercises to catalyze member interaction. The exercises often succeeded in getting meaningful discussions started, and sometimes they were just plain fun. We always began by showing how an exercise could be done. Some of the exercises we assigned the group were as follows.

1. Go on an imaginary trip, and pick a couple of the other group members to accompany you.
2. If you could do anything you wanted to do, what would it be?
3. Pick a new name for yourself and talk about what that name means to you.
4. Bring a favorite photograph and share it with others in the group.
5. Draw a picture of you and your family and talk about your place in the family.
6. Describe some of the memories that are important to you.
7. Tell what your favorite holiday is and what you enjoy doing on that day.

We used these exercises and many others as simple means of getting group interaction going. One of our group sessions fell on the day before Thanksgiving. We asked the participants to remember a special Thanksgiving day from the past—to recall all of the people who were with them and everything that happened. The members received these instructions enthusiastically, and everyone participated. My co-leader and I pointed out to them that the fun and excitement they had experienced during past holidays was due partly to their interaction with people and could certainly be experienced again if they made a special effort this Thanksgiving to reach out to and make contact with one another. The Thanksgiving celebration did, in fact, go well for the group members. Several of them made a point of sitting together, and they reported at the next session the fun they had had.

These exercises, by encouraging the members to express themselves, led to their getting to know one another, which led, in turn, to a lessening of the ''what's the use'' feeling that was universal in the beginning.

Debunking myths. With the old people's group, my co-leader and I explored some myths and attitudes that prevail regarding the aged. Our intention was to challenge the members' acceptance of these myths. The following are some of the beliefs we considered.

- Old people can't change, so it's a waste of time and effort to try to help them with counseling or therapy.
- All people who retire become depressed.
- It is disgraceful for an old person to remarry.
- Young people are never forgetful; old people always are.
- Forgetfulness is a sign of senility.
- Old people cannot contribute to society.
- There are many child molesters among the aged.
- Most young people want to neglect the elderly members of their family.
- Old people are always emotional and financial burdens, whether their children take them into their home or not.
- People should retire at 65.
- Old people are not creative.
- An elderly person will die soon after his or her mate dies.
- Becoming old always means having a host of serious physical problems.
- Old people do not understand the problems of younger people.
- Old people are no longer beautiful.
- Old people are dependent and need to be taken care of.
- Most old people are lonely.
- There is a high degree of alcoholism among the aged—higher than among younger people.
- Old people are no longer interested in sex.
- Old men are impotent.
- Old people are not afraid to die.

Outcomes. To work successfully with the elderly, one must take into account the basic limitations in their resources for change without adopting a fatalistic attitude that will only reinforce their sense of hopelessness. Had my co-leader and I expected to bring about dramatic personality changes, we soon would have been frustrated, because what changes there were were small and came slowly. Instead, we expected to have only a modest impact, and so the subtle changes that took place were enough to give us the incentive and energy to continue. The following are some of the outcomes we observed.

- Members said that they liked coming to the meetings, and they told this to patients who weren't members.
- The group atmosphere became one of trust, caring, and friendliness.
- The members continued the socializing that began in the group outside of the group sessions.
- The members learned one another's names, which contributed to increased interaction on the ward.
- Participants engaged in activities that stimulated them rather than merely waiting for their release.
- The members began to talk more personally about their sorrows, losses, hopes, joys, memories, fears, regrets, and so on, saying that it felt good to be listened to and to talk.
- The enthusiasm of the members and the staff led to the formation of another group for ward members.
- The nurses reported seeing a change in the patients and expressed a desire to learn the skills needed to facilitate such groups.
- Staff members noticed positive changes, such as elevated spirits, in some of the members.
- Staff members became involved in thinking of appropriate activities for different members and helped the members carry them out.

My co-leader and I encountered some frustrating circumstances during the course of the group. Occasionally, for instance, the members seemed very lethargic, but we later discovered that this occurred when the participants had received medication just before the group session. Still, it was difficult to discern whether a member's condition was due to the medication or to psychological factors. It was not uncommon to find a member functioning well one week and feeling good about herself and then to discover, the next week, that she had had a psychotic episode and was unable to respond to anyone. Another heartbreaking reality was the slowness with which patients who were ready for placement in outside agencies had their papers processed for release. People who had to remain in this institution after they no longer needed it could be seen to suffer, both physically and psychologically.

Some small changes that occurred in the group sessions were undone by the routine of ward life. Yet some of the members resisted making their life on the ward more pleasant, for fear of giving the impression that their stay would be a long one. It was as though they were saying "If I communicate that I like it here, you might not let me go."

On the other hand, some members resigned themselves to institutional life and saw the ward as their home, expressing very directly that they did not want to leave. These people had developed such a fear of the outside world that they were willing to give up the chance that it offered of a richer life.

Termination. I was to be co-leader of this group for only three months, and I prepared the members for my departure several weeks in advance. After I left, my co-leader continued the group by himself. On occasion, I visited the group, and I was remembered and felt very welcome. One year later, this group was still in existence, although the membership had changed.

The Group for Patients with Organic Brain Syndrome

Some of the patients on the ward were severely handicapped by organic brain syndrome, and my co-leader and I decided to form a group with these people that would provide them with some sensory stimulation. The group would have the same format as the pre-placement group, but the activities would be somewhat different.

The group consisted of three men and three women, and the sessions lasted from half an hour to an hour. We felt successful after a session if members had not wandered off or fallen asleep. I sat in front of the group and touched the members to make sure they could see and hear me. Each week I told them who I was, where they were, why they were there, and who was present. I moved around a lot, making physical contact with each member; I called them by name. The other leader and I developed a routine of opening the session by providing chocolate candy, or in some cases a cigar, and the members very much enjoyed this ritual. Once I brought in a bottle of perfume, let everyone smell it, and helped the women put it on, which brought many giggles. This allowed for touching, which these people very much needed. The members sat holding hands and sang favorite old tunes while one of them plucked away at a guitar. It was a touching experience to see these people enjoying singing an old and much loved song; they still remembered the words but had to struggle with their physical handicap to sing them. I can still hear the group singing "You Are My Sunshine."

We generated another activity in the OBS group by bringing in a beach ball and encouraging the members to throw it to one another and to go through the struggle of retrieving it. This stimulated the members into activity. We brought in large, colorful pictures and had the members describe what they saw. The members had a tendency to talk very little, so we encouraged them to notice one another's presence and address one another. We brought a tape recorder to some sessions, recorded the songs, and then listened to everyone's voice. We brought in clay one day, but this proved to be a disaster because several members started eating it. This problem could have been prevented, though, had we paid closer attention to what was going on. Bringing my two daughters and introducing them to each member of both my groups delighted my children as well as the group members. This was a natural catalyst; afterward there was much talk among the members about the fun they had had with my children. Weather permitting, we took the members on walks, having them touch and smell flowers, trees, and shrubs. In all of these ways, we encouraged members to employ all of their senses, so that they could be more alive.

Obviously, the goals of this group were much more limited in scope than those of the pre-placement group. Few changes were observed outside of group; members continued not to react to or recognize each other much of the time. However, I felt that it did them good to be aroused from their lethargy, if only for short periods of time. The following are notes I made after the second session.

The OBS group was slow. In the beginning, two people insisted on going to sleep. One member kept wandering off. Later, some talked about a birthday party and shared the fun they had. Everyone sang some songs and held hands. I contacted everyone in group, touching and talking with each one. It is difficult not to get discouraged, and I have to continually keep my goal—to get any of them to converse or react about anything—in mind. As I did last time, I made a point of saying good-bye to each of them individually.

With this particular group, it was rewarding to see even the most minute changes. It was exciting for me to hear one 87-year-old man, who usually showed no responsiveness, giggle when I put some perfume behind my male co-leader's ear. During the initial sessions, he had never uttered a word; now, slowly, he began to talk and sing with the rest. One lady who had not allowed anyone to touch her reached out one day and held another member's hand.

I visited this group three months after I had left it, not expecting to be remembered. I was touched when some members approached me in recognition and reminded me that I had not been to the group meetings! This group was continued after my departure for about a year. As of this writing, it is no longer in existence.

Groups for the Families of the Elderly

I see a pressing need for therapy groups for people who have aged relatives in an institution. Very often a family's feelings of guilt, anger, failure, and hopelessness will keep them away from their hospitalized member, depriving him or her of the joy of visits. Or the family members may visit but transmit their negative feelings to the old person. In either case, everyone suffers from the loss of true contact. Groups, by allowing families to share their concerns with other families, can relieve much of the tension that normally results from the responsibility of caring for a loved one who is old.

My co-leader and I experimented with this idea by holding several sessions with one member and his entire family. The family members talked about the shame they felt over having one of their relatives committed to a mental institution, and the patient expressed the anger he felt over being ignored by his family. After expressing their feelings, the family members made the decision to visit the institutionalized member more often.

Involvement with Other Ward Residents

Due to a lack of staff qualified to lead groups, many patients were not assigned to a group. One way for me to make contact with these unassigned residents was by seeking them out on the ward, so each time I came to the hospital I spent some time walking around the ward. During my first day on the ward, I noticed a woman who was crocheting and told her about my liking for this activity. On my next visit, I brought wool and several crochet hooks. I put a table and several chairs in an area in which I could be seen by a lot of the patients. I invited the woman who had been crocheting to sit with me. Very soon other women approached us and sat down. They took yarn and hooks and began to crochet, much to the amazement of the ward staff. One patient who seldom sat down and who instead usually ran around the ward cursing and uttering obscenities sat with me and crocheted. I crocheted in that spot again and again, and each time she stayed a little longer. It surprised everyone to hear her talk about her life. An informal group of five women and myself was thus spontaneously formed. It proved to be a great catalyst of interaction among ward members. Often several men would stand around and watch the women, who would show off what they had crocheted. I encouraged the women to get together and crochet during my absence, but they didn't do so. As with many other activities, this one only held them as long as a staff member was there to encourage them. I taught two staff members how to crochet, and it became a good means for them to make contact with patients.

I moved around on the ward, meeting as many members as possible. I talked with them, sat by their bedside, put my arms around one or held one's hand, laughed with them, and teased them. It was a good feeling to walk into the ward in the morning and hear many familiar hellos. I danced with many of them, and I encouraged them to dance with each other when the dance band came each week.

SOME GENERAL REACTIONS AND OBSERVATIONS

At times I felt depressed, hopeless, and angry, but these feelings were seldom directly connected with my activities with the patients; the small changes I observed in them were rewarding and gave me the incentive to go on. Rather, I experienced these feelings whenever I saw the system contributing to the physical and psychological deterioration of a person, such as when the staff appeared uncaring and lacking in enthusiasm. I've already mentioned that at times members were forced to stay in the institution because everyone claimed to be too busy to do the paperwork necessary to get them out. I felt angry when I saw student psychiatric technicians or other staff members show disrespect for the patients and when I heard these same individuals call an elderly person by his or her first name yet insist that they themselves be addressed by their surname. I felt discouraged and helpless when, as happened occasionally, an agitated patient would be restrained physically or with medication without ever being asked what had made him so upset in the first place. Another misuse of medication occurred, I felt, when patients were given strong doses of medication to put them to sleep at night. In many cases, a glass of wine would have had the same effect and might have stimulated satisfying socializing among the patients to boot. Another upsetting sight was a patient in a wheelchair being pushed around and not being told where he or she was going.

At times the behavior of a patient was treated as crazy when in reality there was a good reason for it that could have been discovered, had anybody tried. One day a student brought a blind member of my OBS group to the meeting. The blind man proceeded to take off his shoes, and the student shouted at him to put his shoes back on. I approached Mr. W. and kneeled in front of him. I simply said ''Mr. W., you are taking your shoes off in our group session. How come?'' He apologized, saying that he had thought that he was being taken to the physical-therapy room.

In another case, a 75-year-old patient kept taking his shoes off all day long, always gathering up newspaper to put around his feet. Everyone considered this behavior very bizarre. I remembered that during my childhood in Germany I was often told in the winter to put newspaper into my shoes to keep my feet warm. After spending some time with this man, I found that this "strange" behavior was based on the same experience. I learned to be careful not to judge a patient as bizarre or delusional too quickly but rather to take the time to find out whether there was a logical reason for a peculiar behavior.

I felt very helpless when I had to struggle with the heavy diagnostic language used by the staff to record the patients' behavior in their official records. I often found it difficult to understand the notes in the records, and I was concerned that the simple language I was using to describe the group members' behavior in group might be considered inappropriate. A number of staff members apparently had reservations about the use of technical language too, for one day, during an important hospital meeting, it was decided that from then on there would be a minimum of labeling of patients and that, instead, their behavior would be described in a way that anyone could understand. Instead of labeling a patient withdrawn, a staff member would describe the behavior of the patient. This would, of course, be most time-consuming, and several staff members resisted it.

It was sad to see that patients were sometimes discouraged or made to feel shameful when they physically expressed affection for another ward member. Sensuality was perceived by the staff as bad because of "what it could lead to." There is one positive note, however. I had several very good discussions with staff members about our attitudes toward the sexuality of the aged. I felt very encouraged by their willingness to explore their attitudes and their openness to change. By dealing with our own attitudes, misperceptions, and fears, the staff members and I were able to be more understanding and helpful to the patients. Several of us attended seminars on the sexuality of the aging.

It was also sad to see an elderly person describe himself or herself as ugly, having accepted the standard according to which only the young are beautiful. In group, my co-leader and I talked about attitudes toward old people's physical appearance. We were able to work with the members on accepting and liking themselves.

SUGGESTIONS FOR WORKING WITH HEALTHY OLD PEOPLE

The following are a few suggestions for helping healthy, well-functioning elderly people.

1. I find it very exciting to combine a group of persons over 65 with a group of adolescents and have them explore their common struggles—their feelings of uselessness, differentness, and isolation from the rest of society.

2. Old people can be employed or asked to volunteer as teacher aides in elementary and secondary schools.

3. High school or college students who are learning to speak a foreign language can be given the assignment of visiting homes for the aged in which people live who speak the language as their native tongue. This plan, in addition to helping the student, provides some badly needed stimulation for the elderly person.

4. Groups of old people can be formed to explore such themes as love, sex, marriage, meaning in life, death, failing health, and body images. Many of the myths about the meaning of these issues for old people can be examined in depth.

5. It is crucial for the reader to realize that there is a large population of elderly who are not institutionalized but who do have problems coping with the aging process. These people have to deal not only with the many losses associated with old age but also with the pressures and conflicts that the younger generation experiences, and they can profit from personal-growth groups that serve people of all ages.

SUMMARY

The elderly make up a significant part of the population of the United States. By the year 2000, it is estimated, there will be 29 to 33 million older Americans. It should be evident, from this chapter, that this population has special needs and problems and that it should not be ignored by any helping profession. The helping professions must develop special programs for the elderly; they also must find the means to reach this clientele.

My three months on a geriatrics ward in a state institution provided me with a great deal of new understanding. In turn, I believe I provided the staff members with the incentive to carry on where I left off. While the general staff at first considered the interest of my co-leader and me in doing group counseling with these particular patients unusual, they eventually became very supportive and active in our program, for, by showing them a fresh direction in which to work, we renewed their interest in what had often appeared to them to be a hopeless situation. Further, the staff members and I had many lively and productive discussions about the patients in which we gave each other encouragement. With few exceptions, the staff members were devoted to making the patients' stay on the ward as pleasant as possible and were open to any knowledge about the aged that would make them more helpful to the patients they had contact with every day. What I learned in those three months, and what I tried to convey to these staff members, was that the best way to find out what old people need is to listen to them.

SUGGESTED READINGS

Bengtson, V. L. *The social psychology of aging.* Indianapolis: Bobbs-Merrill, 1973.

Birren, J. E. *The psychology of aging.* Englewood Cliffs, N.J.: Prentice-Hall, 1964.

Birren, J. E. (Ed.). *Contemporary gerontology: Concepts and issues.* Los Angeles: Andrus Gerontology Center, 1969.

Britton, J. H., & Britton, J. O. *Personality changes in aging.* New York: Springer, 1972.

Burnside, I. Loss: A constant theme in group work with the aged. *Hospital and Community Psychiatry,* 1970, *21* (6), 173–177.

Burnside, I. (Ed.). *Psychosocial nursing care of the aged.* New York:McGraw-Hill, 1973.

Butler, R. N., & Lewis, M. I. *Aging and mental health: Positive psychosocial approaches.* Saint Louis: Mosby, 1973.

Erikson, E. H. *Childhood and society* (Rev. ed.). New York: Norton, 1964.

Gottesman, L. E., Quarterman, C. E., & Cohn, G. M. Psychosocial treatment of the aged. In C. Eisdorfer & M. P. Lawton (Eds.), *The psychology of adult development and aging.* Washington, D.C.: American Psychological Association, 1973.

Huyck, M. H. *Growing older.* Englewood Cliffs, N.J.: Prentice-Hall, 1974.

Kalish, R. A. *Late adulthood.* Monterey: Brooks/Cole, 1975.

Kaplan, H. S. *The new sex therapy: Active treatment of sexual dysfunctions.* New York: Brunner/Mazel, 1974.

Klein, W., Le Shan, E., & Furman, S. *Promoting mental health of older people through group methods: A practical guide.* New York: Mental Health Materials Center, 1965.

Koestenbaum, P. *Is there an answer to death?* Englewood Cliffs, N.J.: Prentice-Hall, 1976.

Kubie, S. H., & Landau, G. *Group work with the aged.* New York: International Universities Press, 1969.

Kübler-Ross, E. *On death and dying.* New York: Macmillan, 1969.

Kübler-Ross, E. What is it like to be dying? *American Journal of Nursing,* 1971, *71*(1), 54–62.

Kübler-Ross, E. *Death: The final stages of growth.* Englewood Cliffs, N.J.: Prentice-Hall, 1975.

Lehr, U. *Psychologie des Alterns.* Heidelberg: Quelle and Meyer, 1974.

Nouwen, H. J., & Gaffney, W. J. *Aging: The fulfillment of life.* New York: Doubleday, 1976.

Pattison, E. M. *The experience of dying.* Englewood Cliffs, N.J.: Prentice-Hall, 1976.

Rubin, I. *Sexual life after sixty.* New York: Basic Books, 1976.

Troll, L. *Early and middle adulthood.* Monterey: Brooks/Cole, 1975.

Wikler, R., & Grey, P. S. *Sex and the senior citizen.* New York: Fell, 1968.

Yalom, I., & Terrazas, F. Group therapy for psychotic elderly patients. *American Journal of Nursing,* 1968, *68*, 1690–1694.

15. A RESIDENTIAL WORKSHOP FOR PERSONAL GROWTH

In this chapter, we'll describe what we consider to be a unique type of therapeutic group—one with combined educational and therapeutic aims. The week-long ''Residential Workshop for Personal Growth'' is a three-semester-unit course offered by the Summer Session and Continuing-Education Office at California State University at Fullerton. The teachers, or leaders,* of the course combine academic and experiential features by having the students read books about personal awareness and write papers about their reactions to their experiences in the course. As two of the teachers, we believe that this reading and writing helps the students get a clearer idea of what areas of themselves they need to explore. The course is designed for people over 18 who are functioning relatively well in society. In this course, students explore aspects of their life that could stand improvement, break through barriers to self-understanding, explore intimate relationships that are no longer satisfying, revitalize stale aspects of their life, question the meaning of their existence, experiment with new behaviors in a safe setting, and get feedback about themselves from others. In this chapter, we'll describe our screening procedures, the guidelines that govern the activities in the workshop, the ethical issues that are involved, the format, structure, process, and stages of the workshop, the outcomes of the workshop, and the follow-up procedures.

PRELIMINARY PROCEDURES

Screening and selection. Persons applying for the residential workshop are usually required to have had some type of group experience, and applicants who have gone through individual counseling or therapy are favored over those who have not. Most of those who are selected have experienced both individual and group counseling, and many who are selected are actively involved in one of the helping professions.

As part of the screening process, applicants meet with the group leaders for private interviews. At this time, the applicants are asked to state why they want to enroll and what areas they want to explore. They are also asked to give some personal-background data. The applicants are informed of the basic purpose of the group and are invited to ask questions. This interview allows the leaders to assess the

---

*Three instructors—the two of us and Patrick Callanan, J. Michael Russell, or Jean Marie Lyon—lead any one group.

readiness of individuals for the group and allows the applicants to determine whether they want this particular group with these particular leaders. If a participant is found to be receiving therapy, he or she is asked to consult the therapist regarding the wisdom of being involved in an intensive group experience at this time.

At the end of the interview, the applicants are told that they've been accepted, that we have reservations about them (we state the reservations), or that they do not have the prerequisites and cannot be included at this time. Shortly after the interview, we notify the candidates by mail of their final acceptance/nonacceptance. In the letter we send to accepted candidates, we assign a paper that is due at the pre-group session, a month before the workshop. The accepted candidates are not required to commit themselves to enroll until after the pre-group session.

Although we try to assemble a group that is heterogeneous with respect to age, interests, and background, we like the members to have certain characteristics in common: the ability to function relatively well in the world, the motivation to take the risks necessary for personal change, and a commitment to working toward honesty with oneself and others. In our groups, we've had undergraduates and graduates majoring in psychology and human services, high school teachers, college professors, counselors, nurses, members of the clergy, engineers, doctors, members of the various helping professions, and people preparing to work in the helping professions.

The pre-group session. After the candidates have been tentatively selected, and about a month prior to the week-long workshop, we usually schedule a four-hour pre-group session. Generally, there are 15 participants, besides the 3 leaders. This meeting is designed as a get-acquainted session and as a time for clarification of the purposes, procedures, and policies of this group-oriented course. During this initial group meeting, the participants share their expectations and fears about the workshop. Each person tells about any individual and/or group counseling he or she has been involved in, as well as why he or she has come to the workshop. Then the leaders outline: (1) the aims of the workshop, (2) the format and structure of the group, (3) themes typically explored in workshops and techniques often used, (4) their own backgrounds, (5) the nature of the reading program and what, in particular, the members should read, (6) guidelines for the written reports, (7) the basic ground rules and policies, and (8) the importance of setting personal goals prior to the opening of the workshop. The risks of this experience are discussed, as are means of minimizing the risks. This initial group meeting serves yet another function—that of a screening device. Members have a week after the meeting in which to confirm their decision, and the group leaders can, on the basis of information gleaned at the meeting, exclude someone from participation in the workshop. We do this if we feel that a group experience might do the person more harm than good. At the pre-group session, as at the individual interview, self-screening is encouraged; participants are asked to consider carefully whether this is the type of therapeutic group that they really want and need.

The pre-workshop readings and paper. Prior to the week-long workshop, each member is expected to read several books that deal with various aspects of the group process. Our purpose in assigning this reading program is to provide the student with various perspectives on the nature and functioning of therapeutic groups. It is hoped that this reading will help the participants understand and profit from their experience in the workshop.

As we've mentioned, participants are also required to submit a paper at the pre-group session. We ask that this paper be about themselves and that they discuss in it: pertinent historical information, what they want to get from the group experience, the critical turning points in their life, the areas in which they're currently struggling, their personal strengths and weaknesses, and the quality of their relationships with significant others. This paper serves to (1) clarify for the participants their current psychological state of being and sharpen their focus on the areas they want to explore and (2) convey to the group leaders background information on each of the participants that will help us plan an effective group.

GUIDELINES FOR THE WORKSHOP

Rights and responsibilities. The responsibilities of the participants are discussed at the preliminary individual and group sessions. People who wish to have the workshop experience must, first of all, agree to become participating members. In addition, it is the participant's right and responsibility to decide what areas to explore in the group, what to disclose to the group, and when not to participate. We tell the members that the right to privacy and the right to say "I pass" or "I'd like not to discuss this now" or "I'd like not to work at this time" are to be respected.

As group leaders, we accept a certain share of the responsibility for the climate and direction of the group. While we don't burden ourselves with the responsibility for seeing that each person reaches his or her goals, we do accept the fact that we play a crucial role in determining the direction and focus of a particular group, and we accept the responsibility for providing boundaries and safeguards that will minimize the likelihood of destructive outcomes. We are available both during and after the workshop for private conferences should a participant feel a need for extra help.

The purpose of the group. This course is designed to be both educational and therapeutic. It is educational in the sense that the students are taught to reflect on and put into words the nature and meaning of the things they learn about themselves and to understand the dynamics of their group. The experience is therapeutic in the sense that attention is given to people's latent powers and to ways of recognizing and using these powers. The attempt is not to cure deeply neurotic persons or to treat illnesses or to provide cut-and-dried answers to problems. The group is not an instant form of therapy; no claims are made that, in one week, what has been built up over a person's lifetime will be torn down and rebuilt. Rather, the therapy consists of helping people to see how they're living, how decisions made earlier are affecting their life, and what areas they might wish to explore more fully, both during and subsequent to the workshop. Participants have an opportunity to intensively explore current struggles, to examine their values and attitudes, to get feedback on their behavior, to understand the reasons for their behavior, and to decide to change in order to maximize their potential, to increase awareness of their life-style, to experiment with new styles of behavior, and to understand the impact they have on others. The focus is on the development of autonomy and open and honest interpersonal relationships. The experience is designed to enable participants to become more aware of manipulative, game-playing behavior and to develop more authentic modes of being.

The types of techniques employed. Some warm-up techniques are used in the opening group sessions to facilitate member interaction and the building of trust. In later sessions, we rely less on techniques, but when members state that they want to work through certain conflicts we use some of the following techniques: guided fantasies, attention to nonverbal cues, work in small groups and in dyads, role-playing, Gestalt techniques, imitation of other group members' styles, improvisational theater, reexperiencing of traumatic events, confrontation, feedback, support and encouragement, and positive and negative reinforcement.

ETHICAL ISSUES: POLICIES AND PROCEDURES

The issue of confidentiality. The importance of confidentiality is underscored at the beginning of the workshop and at the final session. We try to impress upon members our feeling that breaches of trust that occur without malicious intent are breaches nonetheless. Members are encouraged to keep their own experience private—not to share personal details too quickly, even with intimates. The participants are allowed to explore at the outset any reservations they have concerning revealing private aspects of themselves, and when this happens we emphasize that a productive, trusting atmosphere will not develop unless all of the members feel sure that their confidences will be respected.

The ground rules. The basic ground rule is that each person exercise judgment and accept personal responsibility. At the initial session, several other rules are discussed: (1) no person is allowed to strike another, (2) drugs are not allowed, and (3) sexual intercourse is not allowed. We discuss the ways in which members can use various physical techniques safely, such as by being careful of sharp corners.

We explain to the members the rationale underlying the prohibition of the use of drugs. For one thing, the use of illegal drugs in a course would put the university in an awkward position. For another thing, our aim is to help people to fully experience feelings, and we believe that drugs interfere with our achievement of that aim. To explain the prohibition of sexual intercourse, we tell the members that a great deal of emotional closeness will probably develop and that, although this may be expressed through touching, embracing, massaging, and caressing, as well as through words, the "no sexual intercourse" rule is one of the boundaries we draw in order to provide them with a sense of security while they're learning a variety of ways of expressing closeness. Participants are cautioned against making decisions to form new romantic relationships during the group and told that this can be an escape from working on themselves.

The issue of risks. Participating in a week-long intensive group experience does involve certain physical and psychological risks. Persons who allow themselves to experience themselves as they really are and who critically look at their relationships with others frequently experience pain and struggle. Experiencing depression, despair, fear, panic, and ambivalence, we reassure the members, is just as vital to their growth as experiencing joy, power, creativity, hope, and vitality. Following a group, participants may briefly experience a "high" and then become depressed over the discovery that they're not the new person they had thought they were. Before the members go home, we detail for them the dangers they face and talk about ways of minimizing the risks.

THE PROCESS OF THE WORKSHOP

The setting and the format. The workshop setting is our home in Idyllwild, California. Participants arrive in car pools by 9:00 A.M. and depart one week later in the afternoon. During a typical workshop, the group will work for a total of approximately 60 hours. Each morning, the entire group assembles at 8:00 for a session that lasts until 12:30. After lunch, the group divides into three subgroups of five members each. New subgroups form for each session. The three group leaders meet between sessions to evaluate the progress of the group and to share insights. After dinner, the entire group usually meets for three or four hours, until about 9:00 P.M. Thus, on an average day, the group spends ten hours working. At least two afternoons are free, and participants spend the time reading or thinking about their experience. Participants seem to continually be thinking about the sessions, and they usually spend their free time talking about them with one another. In the evening, the members and leaders socialize informally. People often show a side of themselves during the informal social times that they don't reveal during the official working time, which gives this socializing a value of its own. Each meal is prepared by a team of three, with everyone taking turns. The household chores are also handled communally.

Thus, the group members participate in a great variety of activities and, in so doing, show many sides of themselves—both to themselves and to others.

The initial stages. During the initial stages of a group, we deal with the expectations and fears that the participants have brought with them. Our primary focus is on creating a climate of trust—a climate in which the participants will feel free to reveal all sides of themselves. We encourage the members to be open, disclosing, honest, and direct and to engage in experimental behavior. We especially encourage them to disclose aspects of themselves that they usually keep hidden. At the initial sessions, the participants try to get a clear idea of what they want to have achieved by the end of the week and what they might do to meet their goals. We ask them to tell what events in their past they believe shaped them and what they are like now.

During the first few hours of each workshop, the group members usually feel frightened, uncomfortable, resistant, distant, and disoriented. Each one expects the leaders or some other member to begin. When members do talk, they tend to be vague, to speak in generalities, or to tell stories about other people in their lives. They may freeze up and claim that they don't know what to say or what is expected of them. The group is not yet cohesive; individuals experience anxiety and uncertainty about why they are there and fear both how others will view them if they do open up and how others will view them if they don't. In short, the group is tense, polite, fragmented, and in a state of anticipation.

How do we deal with these initial feelings? We find that what helps group members to recognize and overcome their fears is pairing with another person and talking openly and freely about their feelings. We allow the dyads to exist for about ten minutes, and then we ask everyone to select another partner. We let the partners change five or six times. We leaders join in this pairing process. This series of one-on-one exchanges not only breaks the ice but also gets individuals to focus on the present, gives them a chance to encounter, if briefly, the people they will spend the next week with, and helps them explore the range of anxieties they've brought to the workshop.

After about an hour of these dyads, the entire group reconvenes. Now the quality of the group is much different from the way it was initially. The members are more fully present and more energized, and they tend to speak more freely. At this time, they are able to openly explore their anxieties, for talking openly with each other in dyads has had a bonding effect, and members don't feel so alone. The members can now think more productively about the questions we asked in the initial meeting:

1. What did you leave behind when you came to this group? How was it for you to leave?
2. What are your goals for yourself this week?
3. What do you think might interfere with your working productively in this group? For example, do you think you might distance yourself or keep yourself from asking for what you need?

We find that dealing with these central issues is one of the most productive ways of opening a group. The members bring with them an agenda, and we feel that we can help them the most if we know what it is from the outset.

The working stage. One of the exciting features of the residential workshop is the fact that a group of strangers can drop their social masks and become intimate with one another quickly. People stand a good chance of changing if they commit themselves to a very high level of openness and honesty. Once people begin to trust others and themselves, and once they decide to risk opening up to their inner experiencing, a wide range of feelings and thoughts emerge. During the working stage, group members find themselves:

1. remembering experiences and allowing old hurts to surface,
2. reexperiencing traumatic events that took place in childhood or adolescence and coming to understand how these events are currently affecting their life,
3. ventilating anger, hurt, fear, guilt, shame, and other emotions that have been suppressed,
4. working with feelings provoked by others and with their projections onto others,
5. experiencing the fear that, if they look deep inside themselves, they will find nothing,
6. struggling with the opposing desires for the security of the familiar and the excitement of the unknown,
7. examining the fear that if they reach out they will be rejected,
8. learning that love and fear always go together,
9. recognizing that they are like their parents and working on the unfinished business they have with them,
10. coming to terms with the essential human conditions of aloneness and separateness,
11. learning to recognize and accept inconsistencies in themselves,
12. discovering their sensuality and sexuality and the ways in which they avoid experiencing pleasure,
13. accepting in themselves those aspects that they have tried to deny and to hide,
14. finding and giving expression to the child that lives within them,
15. learning that sadness and joy are related and that if they repress their feelings of pain they will also reduce their capacity to experience joy,
16. experiencing their detachment and isolation fully, without denial,
17. becoming aware that they will never fully work through their feelings about some of their tragedies but that they can avoid being controlled by them,
18. becoming aware that burying their feelings does not lead to a reduction of pain,
19. experiencing power that they have kept hidden not only from others but also from themselves,
20. discovering a spontaneous, inventive, creative dimension of themselves and sharing this facet of their emerging being with others,
21. enjoying humor and learning how to laugh at themselves,
22. facing their fears of going crazy and allowing themselves to lose control, and
23. finding that, once they become conscious of how their past shapes their present, they can decide to be different.

These are but a few of the threads running through the working phase of the workshop. It should be emphasized that we don't expect these issues to be resolved in a week; rather, our intention is to give the members an opportunity to view themselves in a new light and to figure out what they will need to do after the workshop. For this reason, we describe for the members the resources for individual and group counseling that are available to them both on the university campus and in the community.

By examining the list we've just presented, you can see that a great deal of what members do in the workshop has to do with resolving inner conflicts (such as between self-awareness and blissful ignorance) and learning that certain apparently conflicting parts of themselves (such as the experiences of joy and sorrow) are in fact complementary. The members find that much of their energy has been invested in the struggle between their conflicting inner selves. The following are a few of the conflicts that come to light during a workshop.

The struggle between the desire to know oneself and the fear of discovering only emptiness inside. Members often fear that, if they search themselves, they will find that they are merely reflections of what everyone expects them to be, having introjected their parents' and others' standards. They fear finding out that, if the other people in their life are subtracted from them, there will be nothing left.

The struggle between the desire to know oneself and the fear of finding that one is like one's parents. Some people are very upset by their awareness that they have turned out just like their parents. They may want to reject all of the qualities they have in common with their parents, including the positive ones.

The struggle between the desire for security and the desire to break new ground. A young woman in one of our workshops found herself bored with her life—with herself, her husband, and her children. She described how one part of her was saying ''Accept what you have. Settle for security. Don't rock the boat. After all, things could be a lot worse. Don't make waves, or you might lose what you have now—and then what?'' But the part of her that wanted more than security was saying ''Is this all I'm worth? Don't I deserve more? I'm bored and growing stale. If I accept that now, what will my life be like five years from now? I will challenge myself. I will take the risk of revealing to my husband what I'm thinking and feeling. I will demand more, although I realize that I may wind up without security.''

The struggle between the desire to be self-sufficient and the desire to lean on others. A woman in one of our workshops had been on her own for a long time. She had not suffered from this; her life was arranged in such a way that she experienced success in her personal endeavors. Yet she had never fully allowed others into her world. During the workshop, she realized that she feared being hurt by others. She began to see how she distanced herself from others and suppressed her need for them. In short, she began to let herself experience the conflict between her need for others and her desire to go it alone.

The struggle between the desire to drop one's hard exterior shell and the desire to protect oneself. Some persons who come to a workshop have developed a hard exterior shell, behind which they hide. These persons may have acquired their tough exterior in response to a great number of disappointments and hurts. In the workshop, they may let themselves feel their gentleness and compassion and may consider anew whether their suit of armor is necessary.

The struggle between the desire to respect oneself and the desire to feel sorry for oneself. This struggle is exemplified by the group member who was very much overweight and who seemed to make running himself into the ground a way of life. His fat prevented him from liking himself, and it also made him unattractive to others. It was as though he was wearing a sign telling people that he was worth little. And he was treated accordingly. His dependency, self-pity, and helplessness were a drain on others. During the workshop, he realized that, before he could begin to appreciate himself, he would have to allow himself to experience the depths of his self-hatred. When he hit bottom, he decided to climb out of the pit of self-pity that he had wallowed in for so much of his life.

The struggle between the desire to get revenge and the desire to forgive. In every group, we hear the angry cries of those who feel that they were abandoned by their parents. Our cushions are torn, and our battacas are ripped at the seams. The desire to hurt the father (or mother) who was not there when needed is expressed in most groups. Yet, when people have purged themselves of the hatred and rage, they often find that there is room in themselves for acceptance and that they have freed themselves from an obsession. They may realize that they might do better to express to their parents their need for them than to wait indefinitely for the parents to make the first move.

The final stages. During the closing days of the workshop, our primary goal is to help the members integrate and consolidate what they've learned in the workshop. At this point, the emphasis is on conceptualization. The members explore the answers to such questions as: What is the meaning of this week for you? What did you experience during the moments of greatest intensity? What was the nature of the experiences that made you want to flee? In what ways and for what reasons might you distort the meaning of this entire experience? Under what circumstances might you forget most of what you learned about yourself at this workshop? What would make you regress to old ways of being? Will you really be any different when you return home? Can you carry what you've learned here to the outside world? What do you want to say to those you love? How do you want to reinvent yourself and your relationships with your loved ones? What decisions have you made? Will you follow through, or will you soon dismiss this experience as unreal? What would you hope to be able to say to this group if it met again a year from now?

The closing phase of the group is designed to bridge for the participants the gap between the world they've experienced in the mountains for a week and the world they will soon reenter. The workshop is not meant to be an end in itself but rather a means by which people can come to a better understanding of their internal world, in order, ultimately, to be able to reshape their external world. The aim of the workshop is to help the participants see the richness of their capacities, the ways in which they prevent themselves from realizing their potentials, the mechanical ways in which they relate to others, and the advantages of recognizing and utilizing the power they have as persons.

FOLLOW-UP PROCEDURES

The reading program. After the week-long workshop, the members are expected to develop a personalized program of reading to follow until the follow-up meeting. We recommend that they select books that deal with the themes that they found themselves most often dealing with during the workshop. These readings will, it is hoped, provide material that will help the members understand their group experience. The reading program is one concrete way in which the workshop can continue to be an influence in the lives of the participants.

The writing program. Three follow-up progress reports, in the form of reaction papers, are required during the two months following the workshop. We encourage the members to write about how well they are managing to apply what they learned at the workshop to their outside life. We ask them to write about the meaning of the workshop experience and about its highlights. (See pages 116–117 for a list of questions members use as guidelines in writing their reports.) The papers serve the purpose of getting the members to clarify and crystallize their thoughts and feelings about the workshop experience; they also serve to keep the leaders informed about the directions taken by the participants.

Follow-up activities. A list of the names, addresses, and phone numbers of everyone in the workshop is given to each member at the initial workshop meeting. At the last workshop meeting, we encourage the members to contact others in the group when they feel a need to talk to someone. We discuss the fact that they may well revert to old patterns or meet with frustrations upon their return to the outside world, and we invite members to call on us or one another, particularly during the first few weeks after their departure from the mountains. Individual sessions with the group leaders are available to those who want them. We emphasize the fact that one week may not be enough time in which to change long-established patterns, so that, although they may have experienced significant breakthroughs, they are probably not "finished." We tell the members where they can find individual counseling or another group if they feel a need to continue working.

The entire group meets for a follow-up evaluation session two months after the workshop. This session, lasting at least four hours, is designed to add a note of reality to the workshop experience. Too often, strangers meet for a marathon or workshop, depart feeling "high" and intensely close to one another, and never see one another again. By meeting two months after the week-long group, the members are able to acquire some sense of the value of the workshop—that is, its impact on the daily lives of those who participated. From the distance of two months, the participants can make a more realistic assessment of the value of the workshop than they could have made immediately following it. Also, the knowledge of the participants that in two months they must account to the others for their activities can be an incentive to them to actually implement some of the changes they decided on during the workshop.

One-year follow-up evaluation. A year after the workshop, the members are contacted by mail and asked to respond in writing to a questionnaire dealing with the meaning of the workshop for them after a year's time. Sometimes we also tape-record an interview with each participant. Thus, we are continually evaluating this form of therapeutic intervention, in terms of its influence, over time, on the behavior of those who participated in it.

The outcomes of workshop participation. It is difficult to generalize about the outcomes of these personal-growth workshops, simply because each participant's experience of the workshop, as well as each person's mode of applying in-group learning to outside life, is unique. This task is made even more difficult by the fact that each group is unique and so each workshop develops its own character. Still, on the basis of the follow-ups we've done, we feel it's safe to make some generalizations. The following are some of the attributes that participants seem to develop in the workshop and carry out into their personal lives, to some extent, according to their self-reports:

1. a willingness to experience the pain and struggle that inevitably accompany an awareness of one's personal problems and unresolved conflicts,
2. an increased desire to get more out of life,
3. a tendency to confront the significant people in one's life, telling them what one feels, what angers one, and so on,
4. a tendency to demand more of the important people in one's life,
5. a greater willingness to risk—to do daring things, to live with uncertainty, to gamble when it counts—and more faith that one will succeed when one takes risks in a relationship with another,
6. a tolerance for one's own backsliding,
7. a tendency to play games less and to be intolerant of inauthenticity in oneself and others,
8. a willingness to experience hurt and to express hurt directly when it is being experienced,
9. a readiness to dissolve neurotically dependent relationships,
10. greater self-esteem and self-confidence,
11. acceptance of the parts of oneself that one does not like,
12. recognition of the fact that one is to a large extent the product of one's choices and therefore responsible for one's own behavior,
13. a tendency to live in tune with what one feels as opposed to doing what one thinks is expected of one,
14. a willingness to experiment with new behaviors and a greater degree of flexibility, spontaneity, and trust in one's impulses,
15. an ability to fuse the parts of oneself into a whole being,
16. a capacity to withstand, and even invite, challenges from others to become more,
17. an ability to come to terms with the issue of safety and stagnation versus danger and change, and
18. an awareness of how and why one keeps oneself from getting what one says one wants from people, from life, and from oneself.

The week-long experience provides an intensity that is found only rarely. How the members use this experience outside of the sessions is what really counts. At the very least, the participants have experienced alternative ways of living and opened themselves to new possibilities. And this recognition of possibilities may free them—even stimulate them—to grow. Where they go from there depends on how much they value themselves. The choice is theirs. As one of our group members recently put it, ''I never knew I had a choice.''

SUGGESTED READINGS

American Psychological Association. Guidelines for psychologists conducting growth groups. *American Psychologist,* 1973, *28*(10), 933.

American Psychological Association, Ad hoc Committee on Ethical Standards in Psychological Research. *Ethical principles in the conduct of research with human participants.* Washington, D.C.: Author, 1973.

Apfelbaum, B., & Apfelbaum, C. Encountering encounter groups: A reply to Koch and Haigh. *Journal of Humanistic Psychology,* 1973, *13,* 53–67.

Arbuckle, D. Koch's distortions of encounter group theory. *Journal of Humanistic Psychology,* 1973, *13,* 47–51.

Bennett, F. Encounter groups: Growth or addiction? *Journal of Humanistic Psychology,* 1976, *16,* 59–70.

Diamond, M., & Shapiro, J. Method and paradigm in encounter group research. *Journal of Humanistic Psychology,* 1975, *15,* 59–70.

Hartley, D., Roback, H., & Abramowitz, S. Deterioration effects in encounter groups. *American Psychologist,* 1976, *31,* 247–255.

Heider, J. Catharsis in human potential encounter. *Journal of Humanistic Psychology,* 1974, *14,* 24–48.

Howard, J. *Please touch.* New York: Dell, 1971.

Kegan, D. Paperback images of encounter. *Journal of Humanistic Psychology,* 1975, *15,* 31–37.

Lieberman, M., Yalom, I., & Miles, M. *Encounter groups: First facts.* New York: Basic Books, 1973.

Paul, L. Some ethical principles for facilitators. *Journal of Humanistic Psychology,* 1973, *13,* 43–46.

Rowan, J. Encounter group research: No joy? *Journal of Humanistic Psychology,* 1975, *15,* 19–28.

Schutz, W. Not encounter and certainly not facts. *Journal of Humanistic Psychology,* 1975, *15,* 7–18.

Siroka, R., Siroka, E., & Schloss, G. (Eds.). *Sensitivity training and group encounter: An introduction.* New York: Grosset & Dunlap, 1971.

Smith, P. Are there adverse effects of sensitivity training? *Journal of Humanistic Psychology,* 1975, *15,* 29–47.

Solomon, L. N., & Berzon, B. (Eds.). *New perspectives on encounter groups.* San Francisco: Jossey-Bass, 1972.

EPILOG

In this epilog, our aim is to summarize some of the main points we developed in Part 1 of this book and to comment briefly on the material we presented in Part 2.

What follows is a list of basic concepts and guidelines that we hope you will remember.

1. Group approaches to therapy have some distinct advantages over individual approaches, but they also have limitations. It is a mistake to think that groups are for everyone, and we believe that anyone who is designing a group should be able to state clearly why a group approach will be of value. This written rationale should include descriptions of the goals of the group, the means that will be used to accomplish these goals, the role of the members, the leader's function and role, and the means that will be used to assess the outcomes.

2. There are psychological risks associated with participation in a group. We believe that it is the leader's job to mention these risks to the members and to develop means of minimizing the risks.

3. We believe that a therapeutic group is a means to an end. Participants can use the group to learn more about themselves, to explore their conflicts, to learn new social skills, to get feedback on the impact they have on others, and to try out new behaviors. The group becomes a microcosm of society, in which members can learn more effective ways of living with others.

4. Members should clarify their goals at the beginning of a group. Developing contracts will help them to do so, and doing homework assignments will help them to attain these goals.

5. We have discussed general guidelines for behavior in groups, but we think that anyone who leads a group should develop his or her own guidelines. We also think that group leaders should teach these guidelines to the group members. Some of the behaviors we think a leader should stress are: keeping the group's activities

confidential, taking responsibility for oneself, working hard in the group, listening, expressing one's thoughts and feelings, and applying what one learns in the group to daily life.

6. Some of the factors that we believe operate in groups to produce positive changes in the participants are: the hope, commitment to change, and willingness to risk and trust that the members bring to the group; the caring, acceptance, and empathy that the members offer one another; the intimacy that develops; the freedom to experiment; the opportunity to get feedback, to experience catharsis, and to learn interpersonal skills; the laughter that is often generated; and the sense of cohesiveness that develops.

7. We described eight theories of intervention that are applicable to group practice. Our position is that effective group leaders are those who are willing to develop and refine a theory of their own. Since each established group theory stresses a particular dimension of group process, we encourage a selective borrowing of concepts from each of them. The important point is that a group leader devote time to conceptualizing group process.

8. We offered specific guidelines concerning how group members should behave in order to get the most from their group experience. We also discussed member behaviors we consider nonproductive. We encourage you to review this material and assess your behavior as a group member or as a student in your course on group counseling.

9. Although we described various group techniques in this book, we firmly believe that the personality and character of the group leader are the most important variables in the making of an effective group leader. Group techniques cannot compensate for the shortcomings of a leader who lacks self-knowledge, who is not willing to do what he or she urges group members to do, or who is poorly trained. Character traits of the effective leader, in our view, include courage, willingness to model, presence, caring, a belief in group process, openness, nondefensiveness, personal power, endurance, a sense of humor, imagination, and self-awareness. We ask you to think about your personal characteristics and to try to decide which will be assets and which liabilities to you as a group leader.

10. In addition to having certain personal characteristics, a good group leader is knowledgeable about group dynamics and has skills in group leading. We suggest that you make frequent use of the leader inventories we presented as means of thinking about personal areas you might need to improve and competencies you might need to develop.

11. Group leaders are faced with the need to take a stand on a number of basic issues, including: how much responsibility for what goes on in the group is the leader's and how much the group member's; how much and what type of structuring is optimal for a group; what kind of self-disclosure is optimal in a group; the role and function of a group leader; and what the ratio of confrontation to support should be.

12. We offered an outline to use in developing a proposal for a group. We suggested that you discuss in your proposal the selection procedures you plan to use, the composition that you plan for the group, and details such as where and when you

will hold the group. We recommend an individual screening session for all applicants and a group pre-session. The initial stages of a group are crucial, for during this time the trust level is being established. During the first few meetings, issues such as who will wield the power in the group and whether the members will focus on themselves or others are being decided.

13. We have described how a group evolves and what characterizes a group in the working stages. We suggest that you review the contrasts between a productive group and an ineffectual group. You might think about some of your group experiences and decide how effective these groups were. Also, you might think of ways in which the effectiveness of groups you have participated in (either as member or leader) might have been enhanced.

14. Group members need to be prepared for the termination of their group experience. If members are to get the most from a group, they must focus on how they can apply what they've learned in the group to their life. If you want to determine the impact of a group you've led, we strongly suggest that you plan a follow-up session. This session will give the members the chance to share the experiences they've had since the termination of their group. We described the guidelines we follow in our follow-up groups, but we encourage you to devise your own procedures.

15. Ethical and professional issues were treated in this book. A point we wish to stress is that ethical codes have been established by professional organizations such as the American Psychological Association, the American Personnel and Guidance Association, and the American Group Psychotherapy Association. In other words, the ethical standards governing group practice are not decided on by the group leader alone. Group leaders should familiarize themselves with these established codes of ethics and with the laws that may affect group practice. The latter is particularly important for leaders who are working with children or adolescents.

16. A professional issue we dealt with at length was what it takes to make a competent group leader. We outlined a desirable academic background for group leaders, but we also emphasized the importance of an internship experience in which group leaders in training can get supervised experience leading and co-leading groups. Ongoing training groups, as well as personal-growth groups, were described as essential for group leaders in training. We also endorsed the concept that personal psychotherapy (both individual and group) is valuable for those who want to become group leaders.

In the second part of this book, we described types of groups that you may someday find yourself leading. In writing these chapters, we drew on our experiences leading groups for children, adolescents, college students, couples, and the elderly. Our intention was to describe how we set up these groups and to share with you approaches that we have found useful with them. We attempted to present our ideas in a fashion that would encourage you to bring your own ideas and your own style of leadership to whatever type of group you might lead.

In closing, we want to say that writing this book has stimulated us to reevaluate our views and practices as group leaders. We clarified many of our positions in the process. For the most part, writing this book was an exciting project, for we were sharing the philosophy that underlies our group practice.

We hope that, as you used this book, you modified the exercises at the end of the chapters, and any other material, to suit your needs. We also hope that the book helped you think productively about groups. Now that you've finished the book, we would greatly appreciate your feedback concerning what parts of it you found most (and least) meaningful. If you have any suggestions on how this book can be made more useful, we ask you to write to us care of Brooks/Cole Publishing Company. Our hope is that this book has motivated you to read more about and to experience group leadership. To the extent that you have become excited and motivated to learn more about group process, we have been successful in our project.

APPENDIX: PRACTICAL SUGGESTIONS FOR GROUP LEADERS DESIGNING RESIDENTIAL GROUPS AND WORKSHOPS

People who have led residential workshops with us and members of our groups have suggested that we include in our book some practical suggestions for preparing for a residential group or workshop. We agreed with them and developed this appendix.

Finding Accommodations

We have a home in the mountains that we visit on weekends and in the summer, and we frequently use this as a site for workshops and counseling groups. We ask people to bring sleeping bags along with the rest of their gear. You might investigate mountain resorts, which may offer cabins for rent or special facilities for retreat groups.

Buying the Groceries

We have found that the most efficient and economical way for us to handle the grocery shopping is by buying all of the groceries for all of the people ahead of time. We plan menus for the week and purchase all the food accordingly. The cost of the groceries, plus the cost of certain utilities, is divided among the participants. When we have 15 people for a week-long workshop, the living expenses come to about $5.00 per day per participant.

Preparing, Cooking, and Cleaning Up after Meals

We prepare a sign-up list with a schedule of the meals for the week. Teams of three people sign up for one day's duty. Their task is to prepare the breakfast, lunch, and dinner and to clean up afterward. The following are the kinds of meals we plan:

Breakfast: Scrambled eggs, toast, jam, cream cheese, coffee, tea, orange juice, and grapefruit. (For variety, the eggs can be fried, or pancakes or French toast can be substituted for eggs.)

Lunch: Lunch generally includes a sandwich of some kind and cheese, potato chips, fruit, and coffee or tea.

Dinner: Dinner includes a main dish, a hot vegetable, salad, potatoes, bread or rolls, and coffee or tea. Some of the main dishes we often plan are tacos, meat loaf, chicken, stew, spaghetti, and hamburgers.

Other Practical Hints

The following are our solutions to a variety of practical problems.

1. We have bought a lot of coffee mugs, so that each person in a workshop can have one. Each mug is a different color and design, so each person can keep the same one all week. This arrangement prevents excessive use of paper goods.
2. At the end of the workshop, one person is appointed captain of the clean-up crew. He or she assigns the household chores, and usually within less than an hour the house is clean.
3. The day's meal crew prepares the dinner while the others are eating lunch, and one of the crew members puts it into the oven during the afternoon. This permits the group to have an afternoon session and still have dinner on time.
4. We have noticed that people do not bring radios but frequently do bring musical instruments and make their own entertainment after hours. We find it a good idea to tell members before the workshop to bring their guitars with them. Otherwise, they may leave them at home, for fear of acting inappropriately.
5. Before the workshop, we give the members a list of the names, addresses, and phone numbers of all of the people in the group, so that they can form car pools. Car pools provide not only transportation but also a chance to get acquainted before the workshop.

We have included these practical suggestions for leaders of residential groups because we are convinced that taking care of many of these necessary details *before* a group will lead to a smoother-functioning group. If the practical matters such as meals and lodging are not carefully worked out in advance, much valuable time can be lost, and interruptions in the group process can occur. Of course, if you organize a residential group, you will want to work out your own solutions to the practical problems that it presents. These are merely suggestions, and they are presented to give you an idea of the kinds of details that you need to consider in planning a residential group.

INDEX